The Rise of Managerial Bureaucracy

Lorenzo Castellani

The Rise of Managerial Bureaucracy

Reforming the British Civil Service

palgrave
macmillan

Lorenzo Castellani
LUISS Guido Carli
Rome, Italy

ISBN 978-3-319-90031-5   ISBN 978-3-319-90032-2   (eBook)
https://doi.org/10.1007/978-3-319-90032-2

Library of Congress Control Number: 2018939730

Cover credit: decisiveimages/Getty Images

Printed on acid-free paper

This Palgrave Macmillan imprint is published by the registered company Springer International Publishing AG part of Springer Nature
The registered company address is: Gewerbestrasse 11, 6330 Cham, Switzerland

The Civil Service has been neglected by historians. We know a lot about the machinations of politicians in most twentieth-century governments. Yet the role of civil servants, and the Civil Service, is too often neglected.
Peter Riddell, Director of Institute for Government, 2011

PREFACE

In 1969, the historian Henry Parris published his seminal work *Constitutional Bureaucracy*, where he gave account of the changes in British Central Government from the beginning of the nineteenth century to the middle of the twentieth century, identifying the transition from a patronage bureaucracy to a constitutional one. Nearly fifty years later, many other institutional transformations have occurred, marking the transition from Parris's constitutional bureaucracy to a new, managerial bureaucracy that originated from the political, economic, cultural and social changes that had begun by the end of the seventies. This work provides the history of that last transformation, which took place between 1979 and 2007, the period of the Thatcher, Major and Blair Governments, focusing on the Civil Service, the bureaucracy of the central government of the UK.

The period examined is particularly important for this institution because it represents nearly 30 years of waves of reforms inspired by neo-liberalism, monetarism and managerialism with the rise of the New Public Management paradigm (Hood 1991, 1995; Pollitt 1990) and by the need to answer the fiscal crisis of the state in late 1970s and 1980s and to manage the pressure on government imposed by the expansion of global markets, rise of globalisation and 24/7 communication in the nineties and in the new century (Raadschelders and Vigoda-Gadot 2015). These reforms informed a cycle that was completed just in the middle of the first decade of the twenty-first century, and this process crossed different governments, prime ministers and parties without losing momentum.

Sources of the Research

It would be helpful here to make a distinction among different types of sources: legal and constitutional sources, archive sources and other sources. Legal and constitutional sources are available for the entire period considered on the sites of the UK Government (www.legislation. gov.uk) and in the Hansard (Parliament) database (http://www.parliament.uk/business/publications/hansard/). Archive sources are of different kinds: files in the National Archives, Kew and Thatcher Foundation Archives cover the period 1979–1990. Parliamentary archives (http:// parlipapers.chadwyck.co.uk/marketing/index.jsp), which consist of parliamentary debates, White Papers, Command Papers, parliamentary committees' reports and oral evidence, court judgements and Civil Service statistics (www.ons.gov.uk), cover the entire period considered (1979–2007), and they are the pillars of this research. There are other sources no less important, such as civil servants' diaries, Prime Ministers' and civil servants' biographies and autobiographies, political books of the period, academic articles, journals, speeches, *Who's Who* and *Who Was Who*, *Civil Service Yearbook*, interviews quoted by other authors, Institute for Government papers and the UCL Constitution Unit database.

Methodological Framework

In terms of methodology, the book has a very strong historical background (which makes it different from the existing literature), but I will more thoroughly explain in the introduction some concepts of political science that I have used as tools to develop my historical analysis, such as path dependency (Pierson 2004). Furthermore, particular attention is devoted to British administrative traditions (Painter and Peters 2010), looking at them in relation to the reforms of the 1980s, 1990s and 2000s. Indeed, the aim of this research is to explain the dynamic of institutional development of the Civil Service from the Thatcher to the Blair Governments, giving an account of continuity in administrative traditions and managerial changes of central government bureaucracy through the use of legal, public and archive sources. The book can be considered a mixture of history and public administration, a historical research that does not abdicate to trace "Weberian models" and to use a methodology to set up the research and to outline its findings.

As some authors have argued, the British Civil Service can be considered to be "a case study in path dependency" (Richards 2003), and a detailed historical analysis of archives and documents seemed to confirm this theory. From a historical institutionalist perspective, the Civil Service, and more broadly the British state, can be identified as possessing a path dependency whose equilibrium has only rarely been disturbed. We can argue that the British political elite has tended to regard both the constitution and the Civil Service as institutions to be proud of, and thus, any form of changes should only ever be limited and partial (see Thelen et al. 1992; Rose and Karran 1994). The central argument of this research, at methodological level, is that while there have been a number of periods in the last fifty years in which the British Civil Service has undergone a process of reform (most notably the 1968 Fulton Report and from the 1980s onward), the nature of change has been evolutionary rather than revolutionary. Even when the parties have been elected on a radical platform—as was the Thatcher Government in 1979 and Blair in 1997—their period in office has been marked by an unwillingness to provide a new constitutional settlement that would fundamentally transform the foundations on which both the Civil Service and the state are legitimised. It is therefore argued here that although in those 30 years the British Civil Service has undergone structural, cultural and personnel reforms similar to those experienced by other liberal–democratic states, the reform process itself has always been constrained by the continued maintenance of constitutional conventions and administrative traditions that define Britain's institutional arrangements. The Westminister model of government continues to condition the way both ministers and civil servants operate within the British political system (see Marsh et al. 2001). During the period examined, the different governments reformed structure, careers and administrative techniques, but their reforms cannot be regarded as a radical overhaul of the Civil Service they inherited, since the traditional Westminster model remained intact. Moreover, even if the governments had a different political colour, their reforms show continuity on both sides: attempting to introduce a managerial culture and new techniques imported from the private sector and preserving, and reaffirming, the institutional/constitutional traditions of the Civil Service. In parallel, the civil servants reacted to reforms, absorbing and contributing to introduce new organisational frameworks and to develop new administrative techniques and reaffirming through a codification process the traditional beliefs and values of their institution. In conclusion, it is important to recognise the structural context that has constrained the process of reforming the British Civil Service. The theory advanced in the mid-1990s by public administration scholars of the "end of the Whitehall paradigm" may have been overstated. Structurally, much has changed. But other elements of the Whitehall–Westminster model persist. For example, as Kevin Theakston (2000: 58) observes, "Senior civil servants continue to play a vital role at the fulcrum between politics and administration by virtue of their expertise in making the system work. Ministers (Conservative and Labour) do seem to look for and to value the traditional mandarin skills—of managing the political interface, political nous, and a thorough knowledge of the governmental and parliamentary process." The point here is that while some elements of the Westminster model have clearly been eroded, others are still firmly in place, so it may be premature to write about the death of the Whitehall paradigm.

Indeed, analysis of the historical facts shows that many changes occurred in the organisation of the Civil Service, the process of managerialisation was settled and implemented, organisation and structure were reformed, the relationship between ministers and civil servants changed progressively, but the traditional principles of the Civil Service, such as access by open competition, meritocratic career, permanency, neutrality, integrity, impartiality, centralisation and institutional self-government, mostly persist.

As Peters (1999: 65) notes, "There will be change and evolution, but the range of possibilities for that development will have been constrained by the formative period of the institution." Thus, even when reform of Whitehall has occurred, the impact of change has been evolutionary rather than radical. This leads to the conclusion that the reform of bureaucracy in Britain provides a convincing example of institutional path dependency. As a leading constitutional historian, Geoffrey Elton once wrote "True administrative revolutions are rare." They took place, he said, "only when the State itself is being refashioned fundamentally." Otherwise, public administration "usually develops by slow degrees" (Elton 1953). Indeed, as I attempt to demonstrate in this work, the soundness of administrative traditions has turned out to be more resilient than political discourse.

Rome, Italy   Lorenzo Castellani

REFERENCES

Elton, G. (1953). *The Tudor revolution in government: Administrative changes in the reign of Henry VII.* Cambridge: Cambridge University Press.

Hood, C. (1991). A public management for all seasons? *Public Administration,* 69(1), 3–19.

Hood, C. (1995). The "New Public Management" in the 1980s: Variations on a theme. *Accounting, Organizations and Society, 20*(2/3), 93–109.

Marsh, D., Richards, D., & Smith, M. J. (2001). *Changing patterns of governance: Reinventing Whitehall?* Basingstoke: Palgrave.

Painter, M., & Peters, B. G. (Eds.). (2010). *Tradition and public administration.* Basingstoke: Palgrave Macmillan.

Pierson, P. (2004). *Politics in time: History, institutions and social analysis.* Princeton: Princeton University Press.

Pollitt, C. (1990). *Managerialism and the public services: The Anglo-American experience.* Oxford: Blackwell.

Raadschelders, J. C. N., & Vigoda-Gadot, E. (2015). *Global dimensions of public administration and governance.* Hoboken, NJ: Wiley.

Richards, D. (2003). The civil service in Britain: A case study in path dependency. In J. Halligan (Ed.), *The civil service systems in Anglo-American countries.* Cheltenham: Edward Elgar.

Rose, R., & Karran, T. (1994). *Governing by inertia.* Abingdon: Routledge.

Thelen, K. A., Longstreth, F., & Steinmo, S. (Eds.). (1992). *Structuring politics: Historical institutionalism in comparative analysis.* Cambridge: Cambridge University Press.

Contents

CHAPTER 1

The Civil Service: Definition, Organisation and Historical Background

In order to better understand the subject of the book, it would be useful to give a definition of the British Civil Service. The most widely used definition of a civil servant is the one proposed by the Tomlin Commission in 1931: "Servants of the Crown, other than holders of political and judicial offices, who are employed in a civil capacity and whose remuneration is paid wholly and directly out of moneys voted by Parliament" (Cmnd 3909, 1931). The term was first used in the late eighteenth century to distinguish the covenanted civilian employees of the East India Company (through which India was governed until 1858) from military personnel. This use of the adjective "civil" to connote "not military" carried over into the context of the early nineteenth-century British Civil Service, but was gradually adopted to convey the crucial distinction between holders of permanent posts and those whose jobs changed hands when there was a change of government (Parris 1969).

However, it was not until well into the nineteenth century that political and permanent officials clearly emerged as two separate and distinct species of public servant. Departments remained autonomous and differentiated in their structures and practices. In such circumstances, the term "civil servant" and any notion of a coherent entity called a "civil service" had and could have had no useful meaning. Even after the major reforms in central administration that took place in the middle of the nineteenth century, the expression only gradually became common currency. Until 1870, as Chapman and Greenaway point out, "statesmen and leading administrators were reluctant to talk of the 'Civil Service'; they used

© The Author(s) 2018
L. Castellani, *The Rise of Managerial Bureaucracy*,
https://doi.org/10.1007/978-3-319-90032-2_1

instead such terms as the 'public offices' or the 'public establishments'" (Chapman and Greenaway 1980).

Hence, the terminology is of quite recent origin. And, even in the hundred years or so that "civil servant" has been part of the day-to-day vocabulary of public affairs, the precise content of the term has never been defined. This situation was created too by the fact that the civil servant of late Victorian Britain was a very different animal from his modern counterpart; he was the product of a very different social and political order. The state that employed him has changed greatly in size, shape and nature. Similar problems arise when we try to draw international comparisons by using the traditional vocabulary of British civil servants to refer to the central bureaucracies of France, the USA or Germany.

The neutral ideal type of bureaucracy designed by Max Weber gives some guidelines for undertaking basic comparison across time and space. The problem in defining the British Civil Service was that other concepts like "Crown" or "departments of government" were themselves slippery concepts. This was underlined by Mackenzie and Grove in their author-itative account of British Central Government, which pointed out that "we are met at the outset by the fact that there are no precise criteria, either legal or historical, by which to determine the scope of the Civil Service. There is a central core which is unmistakable, but at the margin no sharp line divides those public servants who are within the Civil Service from those who are not" (Mackenzie and Grove 1957). Some 20 years later the Expenditure Committee of the House of Commons reached much the same conclusion.

Defining civil servants became of considerable importance once patronage was reduced in 1870. It is no good preventing politicians from nominating their own candidates if they can still insert their nom-inees under a different traditional guise (Craig 1955). This problem has re-emerged with the continuing debate about the appointment of tem-porary special advisers into the twenty-first century. The absence of firm definition is the expression of the reluctance of British administrative reformers to place central bureaucracies within a coherent framework of public law. The Superannuation Acts, dating from the early nineteenth century, and providing a rare example of statutory intrusion into the operation of the Civil Service, are often taken as a basis for an official defi-nition of the scope of the Civil Service for statistical and other purposes, though in fact the definition they provide is somewhat tautological.

Despite these difficulties, the definition from the Tomlin Report is still the most useful. In the absence of the sort of neat definition that can be found in other countries with Civil Service Acts, the definition stood the test of time, until comparatively recently. We have to consider that the British Civil Service was a peculiar institution for a number of reasons. Officials did not normally have written contracts, presumably because they were servants of the Crown, though they had implied contracts. Defining the Civil Service became a useful example of how the British unwritten constitution worked in practice. Civil servants were known to have modest privileges, or benefits, as a result of being servants of the Crown; for example, they had a non-contributory pension scheme and they held a job "for life." As the texts on bureaucracy put it, following Max Weber's definition of the ideal type bureaucracy, employment in such Civil Service was "based on technical qualification and ... protected against arbitrary dismissal" (Blau 1956: 30). The British Civil Service in the early and middle years of the twentieth century built upon the advantages that resulted from these characteristics. No one contributed more to this process than Sir Warren Fisher, who regarded the Civil Service as a fourth service of the Crown, after the armed services. Fisher did much to encourage a sense of belonging to the service and emphasised the need to maintain the highest possible standards. His approach was continued by Sir Edward Bridges, who, when he was the Head of the Home Civil Service, also tried to develop a sense of belonging and loyalty to a distinctive service.

Following the creation of the Civil Service Department (CSD) in 1968, the publication Civil Service Statistics also at first accepted the Tomlin definition, though from 1972 the wording was modified. In 1972 it read, "A civil servant is a servant of the Crown (not being the holder of political or judicial office) who is paid wholly and directly out of money voted by Parliament and who works in a civil capacity in a department of government" (Civil Service Department 1972: 12). This was further modified in 1976 by adding the sentence: "However, some civil servants work for Crown bodies which are not government departments, such as the Manpower Services Commission and its two agencies or the Health and Safety Executive, and are paid out of grants-in-aid to these bodies" (Civil Service Department 1976: 12). By 1994, the definition as it appeared in Civil Service Statistics had been changed again, this time presumably to adjust to the creation of Next Steps agencies, especially those with trading fund status. This, the 1994 definition, omits all reference to what had previously been regarded as the key financial clause; there is no longer any reference to pay being drawn wholly and directly out of money voted by Parliament. It stated that "a Civil Servant is a servant of the Crown working in a civil capacity who is not: the holder of a political (or judicial) office; the holder of certain other offices in respect of whose tenure of office special provision has been made; a servant of the Crown in a personal capacity paid from the Civil List" (HM Treasury 1994: 18).

This is, on the face of it, comprehensive, though much less specific than earlier definitions. All officials working in the central administration come within its sphere, but recent explanations and changes have tried to clarify what it means in practice. Since the creation of Next Steps agencies, following the publication of the Ibbs Report (Efficiency Unit 1988), there has been discussion about whether a Civil Service as such can still be said to exist as a recognisable and discrete service, distinct from an aggregation of employees of particular government departments and agencies. This process was stimulated by characteristics of work in agencies, which operated on business-like lines, where staff increasingly began to have contracts with pay and conditions of service that vary from agency to agency, and where staff were given targets to achieve, with incentives including pay related to the achievement of their targets. Sir Robin Butler, Head of the Home Civil Service, said he was quite clear that the Civil Service as a distinct entity still existed, though it is a service that was "unified but not uniform" (Butler 1993). The 1994 White Paper, *The Civil Service: Continuity and Change*, was also confident on this point. It argued that "the importance of the Civil Service as a coherent entity, rather than simply the sum of the staff of individual departments performing specific roles, has been recognised for more than 150 years," and it goes on to quote Butler's key principles. These are "integrity, impartiality, objectivity, selection and promotion on merit, and accountability through ministers to Parliament" (Cabinet Office 1994, para. 2.7).

Other recent publications have also focused on this issue. Sir Peter Kemp, known as "the architect of Next Steps," wrote about "moving away from the model of a single service monolith to one where a loose federation of many smaller agencies, units, and cores predominates" (Kemp 1993: 8). However, he believed there was "no such thing as a single public service ethos" (Kemp 1993: 33) and that "there has never been any real unity" (ibidem: 44). Instead, the "unity of the Civil Service rests on its being a body of professionals, like doctors and lawyers, rather than on any harder commonality" (ibidem). Similar sentiments were expressed in the report by Sylvie Trosa, *Next Steps: Moving On*. Recognising that agencies were semi-autonomous bodies, she stated that "financial, management, and personnel rules will become more and more different; the only element of unity which will be left, besides ethical standards, will be the uniform tag of being a civil servant" (Trosa 1994, para. 2.17). One of her conclusions on the agencies was that "typically, the main protagonists either want to maintain a complete uniformity of rules or alternatively argue that unity of the Civil Service is an obsolete preoccupation, contradictory to the requirements of good management practice ... [however] it seems that the solution can neither be uniformity nor complete diversity, but a mixture of both" (para. 4.5.4).

William Waldegrave, the then minister responsible for the Office of Public Service and Science, explained how he saw the future of public service in the context of reforming Britain's bureaucracies. He did not define the Civil Service, nor did he discuss the problems associated with various definitions, but he explained recent changes as he perceived them. Agencification, he said, "involves the separation of the Civil Service into a number of smaller, increasingly specialised units known as Next Steps agencies" (Waldegrave 1993: 18). This, the result of recent reforms, "will leave us with a smaller ... public service ... consist[ing] of a comparatively small core, and a series of devolved delivery organisations" (ibidem: 23). Furthermore, he saw the new ethos of public service as based on the principles to be found in the Citizen's Charter (1991), as being grafted onto "unshaken, unchanging, unchallenged incorruptibility and political impartiality." These principles were: explicit standards of service that were set, published and prominently displayed at the point of delivery; full, accurate and up-to-date information about how public services are run, what they cost and how well they perform; value for money; regular and systematic consultation with service users; accountability; and well-published and readily available complaints procedures (Waldegrave 1993: 19–24). These principles listed by the Citizen's Charter were very similar to Butler's list of key principles, except for the reference about accountability between Parliament and ministers made by the latter, and both hardly differentiated the Civil Service from good management practices. Even on that criterion, however, there must be some doubts if we consider the second period of this research (1990–2007), because ministers were differentiating between policy, for which they saw themselves as responsible, and "operational matters," which were apparently the direct responsibility of officials from parliamentary committees, the media and the public.

Therefore, to summarise and to have a clearer perspective about a definition for "civil servant," we need to find a way to better define who is a civil servant. In the end, the best method is the use of exclusion criteria. This means considering the categories of public servants who, by general consensus, must not be regarded as civil servants: (a) ministers and MPs are public servants who receive remuneration from public funds, but they are political officers and therefore definitely not civil servants; (b) members of the armed forces are Crown servants, but are not serving in a civil capacity, using that adjective in the original sense (Parris 1969). However, civilian support to the Army is provided by civil servants who work in the numerous divisions of the Ministry of Defence, which is by far the largest department in British Government; (c) judges and chairmen of administrative tribunals are public servants whose independence from government is safeguarded by special rules and conventions. In the case of the higher judiciary, these special rules are of great constitutional weight and historical importance. No one in this category is a civil servant, even if the courts are administered by civil servants; (d) employees of Parliament are not servants of the Crown. They may belong to Civil Service unions. The Clerks of the two Houses were recruited through the Civil Service Commission until 1991, when this was abolished, and they enjoy similar conditions in terms of contracts to the Civil Service, but they are not civil servants; (e) local government employees are certainly public servants but they are not civil servants. A high proportion of local authority income comes from central government transfers approved by Parliament. But local authorities are constitutionally autonomous bodies, and those who work in them are not servants of the Crown. This approach excludes from the civil servant definition many categories such as school teachers and policemen, who in other EU countries are considered to be civil servants; (f) public corporations, the bodies that run what remain of the nationalised industries and other services such as broadcasting, though subject to ministerial directives and in some contexts supported by central government funds, are also constitutionally autonomous; those who work in them, or who are appointed to their executive boards, are neither Crown servants nor civil servants; and (g) quangos, meaning non-departmental public bodies. There are many organisations that operate under the central government, performing ancillary administrative tasks, sometimes in association with government departments, but are staffed for the most part by non-civil servants (Drewry and Butcher 1991).

Hence, to further narrow the broader definition of "civil servant," the best method is first to consider and compare all the definitions provided during the history, and second, using the "exclusion criteria," eliminate all the roles that cannot be considered roles within the Civil Service.

THE HISTORY OF THE BRITISH CIVIL SERVICE: FROM ITS ORIGINS TO THE CRISIS OF THE LATE SEVENTIES

Origins and Development of the Westminster–Whitehall Model

The history that we are approaching is intertwined with the long path of British constitutional and institutional development. The Continuity and Change that mark the life of the Civil Service cannot be avoided, and, even concentrating on a circumscribed period, the long perspective is essential to make a credible historical analysis.

The Civil Service is both a component and a product of the UK constitutional system. It has evolved as state systems and structures have changed and grown over the years. Organic growth and gradual change have been the characteristic modes of development, rather than sudden, consistent change. In contrast to most other nations, there is no founding constitutional statute or basic Civil Service law establishing the purpose, function and responsibility of this vital body of the state. Instead, coherently with the broader constitutional trend in the UK which, again, unlike most other nations, is an uncodified collection of Acts of Parliament, court decisions, conventions, customs and practices deemed to be of constitutional significance, the work of the Civil Service is to be understood with reference to a group of statutes, codes, memoranda and time-honoured procedures (Burnham and Pyper 2008). The origins of the British Civil Service lie in the sets of courtiers surrounding the early monarchs of the nations of Britain that themselves had yet to crystallise.

The evolution of the institution was slow and gradual. It took six centuries, from the ninth to the fifteenth, to refine the organisation of the English Crown's records and distinguish between the monarch's "household" finances and national finances and for staff to be appointed by the monarch to administer government affairs. There was no formal distinction between officials and ministers or between administrators and parliamentarians, as illustrated by the case of Thomas Cromwell, variously MP, solicitor, Principal Secretary to the King and Lord Privy Seal. All were servants of the Crown, all subject to the spoils system; indeed, they remained in post for as long as the monarch decided. Into the nineteenth century, ministers had time for administrative issues; officials were often their political supporter and would leave with their minister when having resigned or having been dismissed. The history of the early development of the Civil Service can be seen in terms of financial administration and thus of the supremacy of the Treasury.

In the nineteenth century too, the Treasury often took the lead in improving the administration and building the Civil Service into a unified institution, and its strong role was to persist in the twentieth and twenty-first centuries (Hennessy 1990: 17–30; Drewry and Butcher 1991: 39–41). On the other hand, another and important element to control the Civil Service issues derives from the "Privy Council," comprising a monarch's religious, official, judicial and political advisers. In modern times, Privy Counsellors are appointed by the Queen, but are chosen by the government from among ministers, opposition party leaders, top officials, judges, archbishops and other senior figures, simply as an honour or to enable them to be told in confidence sensitive intelligence on Privy Council terms. From the Privy Council derives a number of constitutional and organisational arrangements. First, the inner circle of the Privy Council eventually became today's Cabinet government. By the early eighteenth century, it had become the Cabinet of government of ministers, whose role was to advise the Crown. They found it safer to reach a private consensus before giving that advice, thereby augmenting the concept of collective, and confidential, Cabinet government. By the end of the eighteenth century, the Cabinet of ministers, led by the Prime Minister, exercised power, provided it had the support of Parliament, but it acted in the name of the Crown.

There was little administrative help to support Cabinet government until the First World War, not even to keep records on what ministers had decided when they met in Cabinet. When Lloyd George became Prime Minister in the middle of the war, the Cabinet Secretariat, which became the Cabinet Office, was created to support his War Cabinet, using the staff and the coordinating techniques of their interdepartmental secretariat already serving the Committee of Imperial Defence. The continuation of the Cabinet Office after the war was opposed by the Treasury and by Conservative politicians, who aimed to abolish what they considered to be Lloyd George's "power building." However, the incoming Conservative Prime Minister (Bonar Law) had seen first hand the usefulness of the Cabinet Office, and the Cabinet Office and its Secretary stayed (Burnham and Pyper 2008).

Traditionally, the Cabinet Office and the Treasury have remained opponents to be the centre of government, and to be in control of the Civil Service, as was particularly the case in the 1980s. Second, decisions by the "Monarch in Council" have remained an appropriate method of law making long after Parliament became the main source of legislation. The Queen still authorises "Orders in Council" at a meeting of four or more ministers who are "Privy Counsellors." Most of the early monarchs' former areas of competence have been transferred to Parliament, but those powers that the Crown still retains, called Royal Prerogative Powers, such as agreeing international treaties, dissolving Parliament before having new elections and being head of the armed forces, are exercised in practice by ministers and usually the Prime Minister.

An Order in Council is one way in which these powers are exercised. Many examples in history have showed how this instrument has been useful to introduce changes in the Civil Service without the need to rely on a majority in Parliament first. Paradoxically, the short Civil Service Management Functions Act of 1992, delegating personnel functions from ministers to top officials, created considerable suspicion within Parliament, if only for the reason that it was so unusual for MPs to be asked to give their consent on Civil Service functions.

Third, managing the Civil Service is a prerogative power of the Crown, exercised by the Prime Minister. The Civil Service Management Code, which is the set of regulations that govern the recruitment, promotion, conduct, transfer, retirement or dismissal of civil servants, reaffirms the historic principle: "Civil servants are servants of the Crown and owe a duty of loyal service to the Crown as their employer" (Cabinet Office 2006, para. 4.1.1). This declaration is followed by a statement of the contemporary practice: "Since constitutionally the Crown acts on the advice of Ministers who are answerable per their departments and agencies in Parliament that duty is ... owed to the duly constituted Government" (para. 4.1.1).

The British Government has substantial interest in reorganising the Civil Service because, in principle, the administrative structure of the monarchy and the vestigial power of the monarch can be used to establish new rules on its reform. Two Orders in Council during the Blair government showed the usefulness of this power. In 2007, the Civil Service Management Code was "issued under the authority of the Civil Service Order in Council 1995." It gives power to the minister for the Civil Service "to make regulations and instructions for the management of the Home Civil Service, including the power to prescribe the condition of the civil service" (para. 1). In contrast to the widening control, an Order in Council of 1997 gave a new power to the Prime Minister for the appointment of three special advisers, which means temporary political appointees to advise the Prime Minister, who could give orders to permanent civil servants. For example, Blair's chief of staff and his press secretary were appointed under this innovative provision.

Fourth, government departments such as Trade and Education originated as committees of the Privy Council, trying to reform its Civil Service. The Board of Trade, which was created in a permanent form in 1786, is particularly significant for the history of the Civil Service because it was organised on the basis of a clear distinction between its government ministers on the one hand and its small staff of officials on the other. It introduced a clearer differentiation between ministers and civil servants on financial grounds (Pyper 1995: 6). These ministers were also starting to act as a single government and resign together, so that it became administratively the best option if those junior officials who were not identified closely with their minister's politics stayed to serve the incoming government. It was the emergence of formal departmental frameworks that led to the development of a permanent Civil Service in the UK (Burnham and Pyper 2008: 12).

Moreover, the wide collection of departments and boards being set up in the early nineteenth century hardly merited the name "civil service," although a form of commons pension scheme for officials was introduced under pressure from the Treasury in 1810. The term civil servant was first used in the eighteenth century by the East India Company, which was a Crown agency, to categorise those employees who were not military personnel. It was not too much used in Britain, however, until the late nineteenth century, when it came into use to denote permanent officials, that is to say, those who remained when the minister changed. It took the first wave of modernisers to fight against nepotism, patronage, inefficiency and corruption by imposing common recruitment and promotion systems, working practices and a collective ethos on the growing bureaucracy. Some individual reformers, such as the early monarchs Alfred the Great and Henry VII, and the Principal Secretaries,

Thomas Cromwell and Lord Burghley, made significant contributions to the initial development of the British Central Government. Cromwell's employer, Henry VIII, made an unwitting contribution to administrative language when he took over the area of London between Parliament and what is now Trafalgar Square, and turned it into a palace that he called "Whitehall," which is now the site of many government buildings. This became the term to indicate bureaucracy, just as Parliament and its associated political institutions around the Palace of Westminster are collectively called Westminster (Burnham and Pyper 2008).

Although these individuals and many others played a part in transforming the Civil Service into a unified entity, a special part was played by two top Treasury officials, Charles Trevelyan in the mid-nineteenth century and Warren Fisher between the two World Wars.

The periodical interest of Parliament in cutting back on expenditure had provoked a special parliamentary inquiry in 1848. Trevelyan, Secretary to the Treasury, advised it that one way to reduce the growth of bureaucracy would be to recruit officials on the basis of competence, eliminating patronage and clientelism, and to use more productively the junior officials with the higher qualifications. Trevelyan already had experience of bureaucracy and a great interest in reforming the British Civil Service, which was less efficient than the East India Company, for which he had previously worked. His project was supported by William Gladstone, then Chancellor of Exchequer, who asked Trevelyan and Stafford Northcote to produce a report advising on how to recruit and then motivate qualified people. The Northcote–Trevelyan Report of 1854 recommended a division of the Civil Service into superior, "intellectual/generalist" work and lower "mechanical/technical" tasks; recruitment through an open, competitive examination, conducted by an independent board; promotion on the basis of merit and moving staff between departments to make use of them where they were most needed and to create a more unified service; pensions to be granted only after a report on the work done by an official; annual pay increments to maximum in class and further increases to depend on promotion. The reformers clearly expected resistance to their proposals from those who benefited from the old system or were aghast at the idea of "being displaced by middle-class, meritocratic clerks" (Drewry and Butcher 1991: 44). Gladstone could not assist because he wasn't in office at the time of publication. Furthermore, educational reformers were pressing the premiership from outlets for students coming from the public schools and the universities of Oxford and Cambridge, which in the same period were reformed and opened to the rising bourgeoisie.

In 1855, the Civil Service Commission was created to examine candidates to evaluate career advancement by departments. In 1870, with Gladstone now Prime Minister and with Robert Lowe, a reforming Chancellor of the Exchequer, open competition was established as a rule, though the Home Office and Foreign Office were still slow to join in. Some other elements of the Northcote–Trevelyan recommendations, such as the functional separation in two divisions, also took place, but other proposed reforms, notably actions to reduce departmental fragmentation, were still not in place by the end of the First World War despite more reports endorsing them. However, implementation was much more difficult than recommendation. It was not until Warren Fisher was appointed Permanent Secretary to the Treasury in 1919 that a genuine corporate identity developed and the unitary nature of the institution became clearly established. Fisher, who wanted the Civil Service to have the same status as the armed services, created the top role of "Permanent Head of the Civil Service." On the one hand, the move could be seen as reinforcing Treasury interests in controlling expenditure on personnel: an Establishments Branch was established in the Treasury and soon organised common pay scales for all but the top tiers of officials. On the other hand, the appointment was thought to be a way into bringing about "Treasury" or general classes of civil servants at the different hierarchical levels who could be deployed across departments, and it gave the holder the authority to issue guidance to the Permanent Secretaries of other departments, thus developing common conventions (Lee et al. 1998: 141). The Cabinet decided in 1920 that the Prime Minister would have the final say in the appointment and dismissal of all senior civil servants. Warren Fisher then used his position as Head of Civil Service and chief adviser to the Prime Minister in the latter's guise as First Lord of Treasury to put forward names in a way that encouraged officials to seek interdepartmental transfers and work in more than one department on their way towards the top.

Fisher implemented the 1854 Report during the interwar period, but the Northcote–Trevelyan prescription for intellectuals to perform the superior tasks was interpreted narrowly as a requirement for generalist administrators recruited through the generalist examination in which Oxford and Cambridge graduates excelled (Burnham and Pyper 2008: 16). During Fisher's long period at the head of the Civil Service, the number of senior officials with specialist experience fell dramatically. It was the triumph of generalist. His personnel policy was to have important consequences as government intervention in social and Economic Affairs became a characteristic of political life in Britain, and the issue of generalist versus specialist expertise was a fundamental theme of the next big inquiry into the British Civil Service by the Fulton Committee. To summarise, the full effect of the Northcote–Trevelyan Report of 1854 was not felt for some decades after its publication, but it was the final step in the building of a modern Civil Service (Greenwood et al. 2002; Hennessy 1990, Chapter 1).

By the early twentieth century, a corporate, unitary Civil Service could be recognised (Drewry and Butcher 1991; Parris 1969). It was characterised by departmental recruitment to the lower-level posts in departmental offices, but also by a standardised system of national recruitment of university graduates for top posts. This central control over higher-level recruitment coupled with interdepartmental staff transfers for officials moving into the senior rank, a centralised pay system, and a unified approach to the administrative problems faced by all government departments led to the emergence of a harmonious organisational entity. The functions of the Civil Service expanded far beyond its nineteenth-century administrative role in central government, especially after the Second World War with the building of the welfare state, as government became involved in managing pensions, national insurance, health and social care systems, employment offices, and, in time, industries and transport systems. Whitehall's structures and processes were exposed to fresh ideas and new personnel during both the First and the Second World Wars as temporary civil servants from a range of business, scientific and academic backgrounds took up posts in government. However, even as Whitehall reverted to its traditions in the 1950s, concerns were already starting to emerge about the Civil Service's efficiency for purpose, as the UK's economic performance declined and the central institutions of the State came under scrutiny.

The twentieth-century equivalent of the Northcote–Trevelyan Report was the Fulton Report of 1968. While the administrative reformers of the mid-nineteenth century had been inspired by elements of Britain's imperial adventure, especially the experience of the Indian Administrative Service, by educational elites of the Oxbridge system and by the municipal improvers, the Fulton Report and its promoters were influenced in large measure by the corporate and strategic management changes that derived from the private business world: the major US corporations believed they would be more efficient and profitable with greater integration of the manufacturing process. "The report was based on collectivist assumptions about big government, emphasising the need for management expertise in an era of rising expenditure, the expansion of government activities, and large departments" (Theakston 1995: 90). The inquiry also fitted into a wider reform programme of the Labour Government of 1964–1969, with other committees examining the case for corporate management in local government, economic planning regions and reforms to the National Health Service. The recommendations of the Fulton Report have, like those of the Northcote–Trevelyan Report, continued to be debated, whether implemented or not. The recommendations of the Report can be summarised as follows: fusion of generalist and specialist classes into a single and unified grading structure, with Civil Service jobs evaluated to determine the grade; recruitment that takes into account relevance of university studies for future work; specialist training of administrators from the beginning of their careers; establishment of a Civil Service College (CSC) to provide training; more flexible recruitment, temporary appointments and secondments; transferable pensions; managerial responsibility and accountability for performance; adaptation of government accounting; hiving off of work to non-departmental bodies; introduction of departmental policy planning units to ensure that decisions are made in the light of possible future developments; and governmental review of the progress made in implementing changes recommended by the Report (Cmnd 3638, 1968).

Successive governments lost interest in the details of the Civil Service reform in the face of serious economic crises, and the top officials successively neutralised the measures they saw as most damaging to the Civil Service they knew, even if younger officials, especially those with technical qualifications, had rather looked forward to the new management opportunities that were proposed. Nevertheless, some significant changes were introduced in the early 70s, including a rationalisation of the staff grading system to give more opportunities for specialist administrators at senior level, the beginnings of managerial training for officials, a few experiments with executive agencies and advent of a new accountable management, planning and budgeting system. The partial introduction of Fulton's recommendations, which were already rather restricted by the Committee's official terms of reference together with a growing concern about the quality and efficiency of the Whitehall machine, left the Civil Service exposed as being "underdeveloped" when the Thatcher Government came to power in 1979 armed with a precise conception about the role of the "mandarins" as the symbol of a discredited system of big government, bureaucratic oppression and state intervention. The impact of the subsequent modernisation, which was developed by Margaret Thatcher's government and its successors, the governments of John Major and Tony Blair, is the object of our analysis.

THE SEEDS OF THE MANAGERIALISATION PROCESS: THE FULTON COMMITTEE AND ITS REPORT (1966–1970)

Following definitions and an overview of the institutional development of the Civil Service, it's time to focus on the history of the Civil Service before 1979. The Fulton Committee and its report (1966–1968) was undoubtedly a major chapter in the historical development of the British Civil Service.

The Fulton Committee was appointed in 1966, and the report was produced in 1968. We can consider three reasons that qualify the importance of the Fulton Report for historians. First, it was the first major report on the Civil Service after the Second World War. As a result of the well-known Northcote–Trevelyan Report of 1854, there had been major inquiries on the service every 20–30 years. The most important were the Playfair Commission (1875), the Ridley Royal Commission (1887–1890), the McDonnell Royal Commission (1912–1915), the Tomlin Royal Commission (1929–1931) and the Priestley Royal Commission (1953–1955). In the decade immediately prior to the Fulton Report the Estimates Committee produced the Treasury control of expenditure (1957–1958) and recruitment (1964–1965). The Plowden Committee (1961) had analysed the role of public expenditure in the Plowden Report, highlighting much about the way Whitehall worked. Fulton continued the periodical line of inquiries into the Civil Service. Partly for these reasons, Fulton reported little that was truly innovative. This was not a surprise because it was the product of a wider contemporary milieu. It expressed a very critical position towards the Civil Service because, during the relatively long economic decline in Britain, top mandarins were very much criticised. They were at the centre of government: it was felt that they should accept their part of the blame for the crisis of the state. A series of consistently hostile comments highlighted their failures (Balogh 1959; Abel-Smith 1964; Nicholson 1967).

Considering this climate, it would have been difficult for the Fulton Committee to have said much in a reformist way that was worth saying and had not already been said. There has long been discussion about the influence exerted by the Fulton ideas, both in the years immediately after the publication and in the longer term (Fry 1995). Such debate is still going on. Without taking position, it would be wrong to claim that the influence of the Fulton Report ended in a few months or, on the other side, argue that everything that happened after 1968 had its roots in this report. Its importance, and what produced such a debate, lay in the fact that, among all the official reports on the Civil Service, it was the most critical.

Then, it became particularly influential because it reflected a prevailing trend among contemporary reformers towards the Civil Service. In the end, Fulton provided a blueprint for those who sought to challenge the bureaucratic status quo. Indeed, it became the point of reference for many years to come for both supporters and dissenters. The Fulton Report opened with this statement: "The Home Civil Service is still fundamentally the product of the nineteenth-century philosophy of the Northcote–Trevelyan Report. The tasks it faces are those of the second half of the twentieth century" (para. 1). The report considered the Civil Service ossified in the previous century: the very successful framework of the Northcote–Trevelyan continued to resist, and, despite over one hundred years of administrative changes, had left the service underdeveloped. It issued a list of complaints: specifically, it claimed that there was too much of the "culture of the generalist," and specialist knowledge was not spread among senior civil servants where it was more necessary; the grading system was too rigid and inconvenient to exploit skills of civil servants; and these formed a too-elitist institution based exclusively on an Oxbridge education.

Furthermore, there was too much mobility within departments and too little career development, and this was partly because the Treasury was not able satisfactorily to manage both the economy and the Civil Service; there was a lack of systematic training, a further reflection of the British philosophy of administration, and this feature was linked with an excessive emphasis upon advising ministers, so that senior officials were giving too little attention to the efficient management of their departments. Finally, there was a lack of clearly defined responsibility and accountability among individual civil servants within the hierarchy.

In order to modernise the Civil Service, Fulton made 158 specific recommendations. The bulk of these were focused on overcoming the generalist culture, with correspondingly greater emphasis upon the role of the specialists; building a classless service; unifying grading; giving more equitable opportunities; recruiting graduates from a broader range, and having regard for the nature and relevance of applicants' qualifications; curbing excessive mobility between departments within Whitehall by employing more coherent career planning, with careers resolving around either the economic/finance or the social service functions, and transfer between these broad areas being allowed only in exceptional circumstances; creating a CSD, taking away from the Treasury all responsibilities for personnel management and staffing and setting up a CSC to give a new emphasis to post-entry training at all levels, partly to direct greater attention to the management of their departments by senior civil servants whose near monopoly on policy advice to ministers would be tempered by the enhanced role for specialists; creating within each department policy units or think tanks; developing "accountable management," with individual civil servants at various levels in the hierarchy being given clearly defined responsibilities for areas of work for which they would be held accountable if not outside Whitehall; and "hiving off" certain functions within each ministry to semi-independent bodies or agencies. The aim of the Fulton Report was to make the Civil Service more efficient and more managerially minded. The Wilson government swiftly endorsed the principles embodied in the report. In November 1968, the CSD was settled and its Permanent Secretary, Sir William Armstrong, was also the Head of the Home Civil Service. The CSD was a disempowerment of the Treasury and assumed most of its responsibilities for staffing and personnel in the Civil Service. It was the Treasury's lower moment in the British Government. Furthermore, the CSC, established in 1970, was the replacement for the Treasury Centre for Administration Studies (CAS). The CAS provided training for the new entries in the higher grades of the service, insufficient training, according to Fulton. The CSC was established to cover a wide range of post-entry training. With this new institutional arrangement, the Treasury retired into a corner, weakened but not defeated. As we will see, it later returned triumphantly to recover failures of the CSD.

The implementation continued in the seventies. In 1971, the Administrative Class, the bureaucratic elite, was merged with the

Executive Class and the Clerical Class to form a new Administration Group. To provide a more broadly based entry training, the Administrative Trainee Scheme was launched. This framework was completed by the creation of an "Open Structure" in January 1972. This meant that posts at and above under-secretary level were a unified category and they would no longer formally belong to any discrete administrative group. The last change was in the departments where there was a slow introduction of new forms of organisation. Pilot schemes created new units of accountable management, but resistance to significant changes soon became evident and there was little political will or bureaucratic commitment to tackle it. William Armstrong told the Expenditure Committee that running a government department was not like running a bank (Expenditure Committee, The Civil Service, HC 535, q. 1510, 1977). Government was different from business management because of its political dimension. The resistance to this change was an example of the "mistake-avoiding culture" described by Sir Derek Rayner, a former top-level manager of the private sector who became the architect of Thatcher's Civil Service reform in the 1980s: "In business one is judged by overall success … the civil servant tends to be judged by failure." The scope for delegation was limited by "the conventions of public accountability, the highly centralised arrangements for the control of the spending by the Treasury and of manpower and pay by the CSD, and the need for equity and consistency in the treatment of cases" (Garrett 1980: 132).

In most areas of governmental departments, it was not possible to measure in quantitative or financial terms performance and objectives. Without a proper accountable management regime, the information and budgeting systems could not operate. Initially, there was some progress in the application of the technique called Management by Objectives (MBO), which was developed by the private sector in the sixties. The CSD had launched 45 projects covering 12,000 managers by 1974, but the process then was stopped. Fulton had considered MBO as a tool for areas of administrative work, but CSD had used it in executive operations, quasi-commercial works and support services. As Theakston wrote: "Some of the schemes had apparently been over-elaborate and costly to install, but it is also clear that top administrators had not been enthusiastic and that the unions were concerned about the pressure put on low-ranking officials by target-setting and performance-monitoring arrangements" (1995: 106). A number of governmental functions were hived off during the seventies following the recommendations of the Fulton Report, but, again, this approach was applied only in a few parts of Whitehall. Another prescription was to adopt planning units in the departments in order to plan costs and activities performed by the department. The dominant view in Whitehall was that planning was a political responsibility and it should involve only the policy division and not the Civil Service as a whole. Dismissive comments by the Permanent Secretary to the Department of Education in 1976 about "the flabby type of futurological day-dreaming" suggested that there were senior officials who did not take planning seriously (Barberis 1996).

In the late seventies, the Fulton Report was considered a failure for the central government. Fultonites complained about "the lost reforms." The position of John Garrett, a former member of the Fulton Committee, was that "in general the Civil Service of 1980 is not much different from the Civil Service of 1968 ... The top management of our large and technically complex departments of state is still dominated by generalist arts graduates from public schools and Oxbridge." Whitehall had not been immobile, but "there has not been any sense of pushing through the great strategy for development that Fulton envisaged. After 1969 no politician with sufficient weight cared sufficiently to understand the strategy or to see the importance of reform." A civil servant told the historian Peter Hennessy in 1975 that "Fulton was a joke" because "they accepted everything he said and then did what they wanted to." Some academic observers argued about the administrative system's "remarkable capacity to absorb and transform reform proposals, adapting them subtly to its perception of what is tolerable" (Garrett 1980: 3; Hennessy 1990: 205). The Fulton programme was detuned for the whole of the seventies, but a decade later the impact of the report was revalued. After 1979, Mrs. Thatcher abolished the CSD but provided the political commitment necessary to implement the Fulton-shaped management reforms (the Financial Management Initiative—FMI—and the Next Steps) as well as extending unified grading.

However, even if the Thatcher Government developed many Fulton recommendations, the ideological perspective of the two initiatives was very different: Fulton focused on the promotion of more efficiency for a big Civil Service and Thatcher's reform aim was to roll back the state. The Whitehall view in the 1980s and the 1990s was that Fulton had been a "milestone" on the way to the "lasting reforms" of the Thatcher years and that it had "laid a trail for many of the key changes in the Civil Service over the next two decades." Also some members of the Fulton

Committee embraced this view. In broader terms, we can argue an indirect influence of Fulton on the Conservative Government's reforms. Its proposals were coming from a process of periodical review every 20 years seen after the Northcote–Trevelyan Report (Theakston 1995: 107). The Secretary of the Fulton Committee, Richard Wilding, commented on Thatcher's Civil Service reforms: "Lots of foundations were laid by the Fulton Committee ... Without accountable management it would not be possible to contemplate the Ibbs changes" (Fry 1985: 257–259). We can argue that the Fulton Report planted the seeds for further reforms rather than set them up. Thatcher and her successor had their own ideas, views and agenda for the Civil Service. Fulton was not the only source of ideas before Thatcher's era, but it was a very important first step towards the administrative reformism of the following years.

1970–1974: Heath's Attempt to Modernise the Central Government

Edward Heath was the Conservative Prime Minister in the period 1970–1974, and he was a former civil servant who was fascinated by reform of the machinery of government. His approach in government was managerial, rational and problem-solving. Political adversaries criticised him as a "civil servants' Prime Minister" because his key advisers were civil servants rather than party or political cronies and undoubtedly he had a high regard for his previous institution, and he was focused on reform to make government more efficient and to achieve better policy-making (Theakston 1995: 111). The plan of the Conservatives in 1970 to overhaul the machinery of government was wide and, at the same time, very detailed. Heath had a very strong and developed vision of the Civil Service: he "hankered after a French-style Civil Service with highly trained officials not afraid to take a strong line." In opposition, Heath had changed the approach of his party to the reform-enforcing think tanks through the creation of a party policy group to formulate solutions for a new pattern of department, the Public Sector Research Unit, which worked on new analytical, budgeting and managerial techniques pioneered in the US government and in the private sector. Former senior civil servants advised the Prime Minister on the creation of a possible Prime Minister's Department and a new central planning staff (Hennessy 1990: 238). As Kevin Theakston wrote: "The Conservatives' aim was for 'less government, but better government' with a more 'rational' departmental structure, executive functions 'hived off,' and clear objectives and systematic control supported by new decision-taking methods and by a stronger and more strategic central direction" (1995: 108). Whitehall was not opposed to these plans, and most senior civil servants had been sharing the same general ideas about the central government's reform. In particular, the idea of large and functional departments had wide support at both a political and bureaucratic level. The Treasury officials prompted practices for evaluating individual spending programmes and their results in the annual Public Expenditure Survey Committee (PESC). The government's plan of reform was set out in October 1970 in the White Paper *The Reorganisation of Central Government* (Cmnd 4506, 1970). In many ways, in the paper there was a socialist–Fabian approach whose aim was to search for a better functioning of government and not its reduction. The main reforms were the creation of two giant departments, the Department for Trade and Industry and the Department of the Environment (DoE), the introduction of Programme Analysis and Review (PAR), the hiving off of functions and carrying out of some activities from departments, and the establishment of the think tank, at the service of the Cabinet Office, called Central Policy Review Staff (CPRS). In broader terms, Heath had built a smaller Cabinet focused on established priorities and a system of larger and "federal" departments. In the Cabinet there were 18 people compared to the 21 of Wilson's previous government, and the departments were merged, passing from nine to four. With this method there was less overlapping of functions and, consequently, less duplication and more strategic capacity. The unified departments eliminated the interdepartmental compromise and divisions in favour of a unified line of management. On the other hand, the wideness of departments created some problems: the DTI, with 18,000 officials, had a huge heterogeneity and an enormous range of very different functions and this framework favoured the wide spread of policy responsibility. There was a team of nine ministers and four Second Permanent Secretaries. These super-departments needed a new breed of ministers, effective and managerial, but only Peter Walker proved capable of managing the new asset, being at DoE (1970–1972) and then DTI (1972–1974) (Theakston 1995). The different "sectors" of the DoE began to drift apart after 1972 (Radcliffe 1991). These facts proved that the super-departments were too difficult to manage, and, after the energy crisis of 1973, a separate Department of Energy was created in January 1974. The successors, prime ministers Wilson and Callaghan, completed the dismemberment with the division of the DTI into two departments and the setting out of the Department of Transport, a function subtracted by the DoE. By the mid-1970s, the idea of the giant departments was only a memory.

The PAR, introduced from 1971, was established to control and to make a systematic critical analysis of objectives, costs, outputs and new options. The aim was to provide information to ministers about what was going on in their department, in order to achieve better policy-making and costs-management. However, as a tool for more rational government, PAR was a failure because it fell prisoner to political and bureaucratic plays (Gray and Jenkins 1982).

The idea of basing PAR in the CSD found opposition from the Treasury, which never considered it a priority from a financial point of view. To deal with the Treasury, an interdepartmental steering Committee called PARC was created that made more bureaucratic and slow the pace of analysis and programme reviews. The Treasury considered PAR as a problem of expenditure reduction; it did not take positively the involvement of the CPRS that argued for more funds to PAR in order to improve the effectiveness of the programme because this meant increasing public expenditure. On their part, the largest departments reacted against this spending review and tried to protect their plans from cuts and budget reduction. Considering these difficulties, PAR did not produce savings on the scale forecasted. Another problem was the diminished political support for the initiative because most ministers considered PAR useless or irrelevant in influencing their political decisions. Finally, the Heath government "U-Turn" at the end of 1972, with its continued expansion of public expenditure, completely wasted the PAR system, which became pointless without the political support of a government that wanted "to roll back the State." It survived, absolutely disempowered, after 1974 and it was formally abolished by Mrs. Thatcher in November 1979 (TNA, CAB 184/384, "Programme Analysis and Review (PAR) : 1976–1979 programme," 2 November 1976).

At the same time, "hiving off" was making very little progress. In 1971, the Civil Aviation Authority was created, a function hived off from Whitehall. In broader terms, the opposition of the Civil Service unions to devolution of functions to other bodies was strong. The result was that no major public sector areas were privatised in the Heath years. As far as Civil Service manpower was concerned, the outcome of reduction was modest: in four years, the overall reduction was only 5000, with the number of non-industrial civil servants actually increasing. An interesting experiment was the establishment of "departmental agencies" that could be considered the ancestors of the Next Steps executive agencies. There were created separate units of accountable management operating within a departmental framework. The Defence Procurement Executive was created in the Ministry of Defence (MoD) in 1971, and Derek Rayner, a crucial figure for Thatcher's Civil Service reform, was its chief executive. The Property Services Agency was set up in the Department of the Environment DoE in 1972, and the Employment Services Agency and the Training Services Agency were created in the Department of Employment. In January 1974, the Manpower Services Agency appeared, a unit contested by officials and established to cut Civil Service staff. Its 18,000 employees were no more considered part of the Civil Service but they regained their civil servant status in 1975 after a wave of protest against the government (Theakston 1995).

The CPRS was, as said, a think tank to serve the Cabinet. Probably it was the most visionary and successful experiment of this set of reforms for central government promoted by Heath's premiership. It was set up in the early months of 1971, and it generated a certain amount of media attention for its autonomy, its team of free thinkers at the centre of government, and the personality of its Chairman, Lord Rothschild, a scientist and former head of research at Shell Company. The think tank was a mix of outsiders and civil servants and its staff numbered around 15–20 people. Its aim was to clarify and monitor the government's overall strategy, the selection of priorities, and the analyses of alternative policy options and long-term problems. Its staff defined its role in more subversive terms as thinking the unthinkable and the grit in the machine, contesting the over-smooth working of Whitehall (Blackstone and Plowden 1988).

As noted, CPRS served the Cabinet as a whole, but the Prime Minister was in practice the think tank's most important interlocutor and it was very dependent on prime ministerial support to live and work effectively in Whitehall. Rothschild built a very close relationship with Heath and became one of the most influential advisers. The CPRS mission was to prepare ministers to the Cabinet meeting, briefing them about policies of other departments and informing them about proposals of ministers and the wider problems of the government.

The think tank organised and distributed around 50 "collective briefs" a year to the whole Cabinet in which short notes or reviewing departments' plans were presented. Departments usually disliked the intervention of the CPRS in their domestic policies and ministers mostly remained departmentally oriented. However, this was an innovation to give a better orientation in the collective ministerial decision-making. The group was also committed on more complex and longer-term projects, including issues that intersected departmental boundaries. For example, it produced reports on energy policy, the Concorde aeroplane, the role of the City of London, roads and transport, and nuclear power, having an indirect influence on Whitehall policies on some key problems. The Treasury excluded the CPRS from fiscal argumentation and it rejected the idea to open up budget policy-making. However, the think tank was involved in the annual public expenditure round and it became a very important "player" on general economic policy issues (Drewry and Butcher 1991).

Another function given directly by the Prime Minister to the CPRS was to preserve the general strategy of the government. Every six months the group organised presentations to the Cabinet, using slides and charts, reporting how the government had performed in relation to the established objectives and looking at big issues that were rising in the public debate. For example, CPRS, in one of these meetings, warned about inflation in May 1972, anticipating this happening and influencing the Heath government's development of a statutory incomes policy (Fry 1995).

After 1974, the CPRS changed its heads in this order: Sir Kenneth Berrill (1974–1980), Sir Robin Ibbs (1980–1982), John Sparrow (1982–1983), and it did not maintain the same influence and wide-ranging role of the early years. The strategy session ended in 1974. The Policy Unit at Number Ten gave Wilson, Callaghan and Thatcher more personalised and party-oriented advice and at the same time the practice of appointing special advisers for Cabinet ministers increased and weakened the role of the think tank (Theakston 1995). The CPRS was progressively bound into the machinery of government and pushed more into producing reports on single issues. As already said, the think tank depended on strong support from the Prime Minister and none of Heath's successors enforced the role of the CPRS: Wilson and Callaghan were not interested in developing it, and Thatcher considered it useless. The CPRS reflected a view of policy-making as a rational, data-analysis and technocratic process. In the mid- to late seventies, politicians like Wilson and Callaghan lost interest in the long-term and overall strategy and were forced into crisis. In 1979, the strong leadership of Mrs. Thatcher came close to abolishing the CPRS, and her style of conviction politics and centralised power further compressed its influence and the scope of its work for the Cabinet. The think tank was already badly damaged in 1977 for its controversial report on diplomatic service and it was further undermined by a leak on health policy in 1982. After the election of 1983, Mrs. Thatcher abolished it.

To conclude, Heath's "new style of government" was not really effective. Central government faced the difficulties of giant departments' reform then break-up after 1972. PAR was disempowered by the Treasury and the other ministries and it was ineffective in reducing public expenditure. Little functions were hived off. The only two successes were the administrative unit, but it was too early to extend their governance to all the public sector as would happen in the late 1980s, and the CPRS, but the innovative think tank worked effectively and at its best only during the four years of the Heath government. Douglas Hurd, Heath's Number 10 political secretary, argued that "because of his justified respect for his senior advisers, Mr. Heath tended to exaggerate what could be achieved by new official machinery ... a little more scepticism about machinery would have been wise" (Hurd 1979: 92–93; Campbell 1993: 222). Like Wilson, Heath seemed to have lost interest in reforming the central government soon after the oil crisis, and his attention moved from reshaping Whitehall to other issues. In some ways, Heath's reformist ideas about the Civil Service prepared the ground for Thatcher's proposal of change. This was, for example, the introduction of businessmen in government, the developing of accountable management and the concept of separating policy and management through setting-up of administrative units which were the ancestors of the executive agencies. These issues came onto the agenda again during the Thatcher years and she didn't lose interest in completing the reform of the Civil Service. As Theakston noted: "She took a much more robust and confrontational attitude than did Heath to the Civil Service as an institutional interest and, crucially, maintained tight control over budgets to keep up the pressure to find more efficient, streamlined, and economical methods" (1995: 114).

Malaise and Crisis in the Public Sector: Towards Thatcher's Era

The mid-seventies represented the height of the Civil Service crisis. Its size, its veto-power, its inefficiency and inflation-proofed pension were perceived as privileges and obstacles to reforming the system. Criticism of the Civil Service from left and right and especially from the public was strong. The long and wide economic crisis made by stagflation, the 1973–1974 oil shock and the recourse to the IMF in 1976 meant for the Civil Service, and for the public sector broadly, that reforms were no more avoidable. The policies strategy was now focused on economy, cost-control, cutbacks and the search for greater efficiency. The Treasury's imposition of the cash limits system created a short-term control on public expenditure that substituted for economic planning in the long term. The CSD planned a cost of central government review and the Civil Service manpower policy was oriented towards cuts: between 1976 and 1979, there were 15,000 jobs cut (Fry 1995).

In the meantime, civil servants felt they were on the cliff of a political and organisational change. As Painter argued: "There had been the disheartening spectacle for civil servants of the habitual volte-face by ministers, as much within the life-span of a single administration as the product of two-party adversary politics. The trauma of frequent policy changes had been exacerbated by continuous administrative upheaval." The malaise of civil servants exploded against Wilson's break-up of the DTI in 1974, because they were "tired of being pushed around from pillar to post." The notion of "overloaded government" became common, and this feeling was shared by some civil servants, who agreed with the idea that central government had too many functions and too many administrative and managerial issues to face (Painter 1975: 434). In order to face discontent of middle and lower grades of the Civil Service, the CSD created the Wider Issues Review Team in July 1973, which produced a report in 1975 called *Civil Servants and Change*. Contesting the stereotype of the mandarin as a middle-aged, London-based, Oxbridge-educated man, the report pointed out that a third of staff was under 30, two-thirds of the clerical class were women and less than a fifth worked in London. Then, the report put forward a programme for improving staff relations and conditions. The idea of the Wider Issues was to move from the traditional Civil Service establishment approach to a modernisation towards a human resources and personnel management approach. However, the context in which the report appeared was not favourable to reform using a managerial approach. Indeed, to promote managerial techniques against a backdrop of public hostility towards the Civil Service, public expenditure crisis, cash limits, staff cuts, and deteriorating industrial relations was almost impossible. At the same time, the old model of government pivoted on the "good employer" was one of the causes of the disease. The Priestley pay system, with its idea of a "fair comparisons" principle in calculating Civil Service pay, came easily under attack by the public. To stem this friction, the Conservative and Labour Governments of the seventies chose to limit, defer or stage Civil Service pay increases.

The easiest way to control pay for the government in the crisis of the late seventies was to make the public sector an example for the other workers. Indeed, in 1976 the Labour Government suspended pay research and the Treasury's cash limits now established criteria for pay bargaining and settlements. This situation transformed the industrial relations in the Civil Service. Until the early seventies, Civil Service relations with trade unions had been relatively calm: consensus and stability in staff relations were the result of fifty years of "Whitleyism," the practice established between government and trade unions to agree certain benefits for civil servants in return for the surrender of the right to strike. But by the end of the seventies, the crisis of Whitleyism had started, and Civil Service industrial relations became very complicated. The Civil Service was intensively unionised. The behaviour of Civil Service unions became very similar to that of the mainstream unions: they began pressing their interests with greater insistence and were willing to use the strike weapon, which returned in the industrial relations of the public sector.

The first Civil Service strike occurred in 1973 as a protest against the Heath government's income policy. In 1979, there was a series of selective strikes that defeated the Labour Government's attempt to reform Civil Service pay policy. A new adversarial moment was created by the unions and this meant that "Whitleyism is dead, in spirit if not in body" (Drewry and Butcher 1991). John Garrett wrote in 1980: "This harsher climate had taken its toll on the Civil Service before the Conservative Party returned to office," and he added, "the innovative and optimistic atmosphere of the late 1960s has given way to a sour hostility between the Civil Service unions and the government and between politicians and the Service" (Garrett 1980: 191).

To conclude, the problems of low morale, discontent with the pay system and deteriorated industrial relations were inherited by Mrs. Thatcher, not created by her. The reforms of the new Conservative Government elected in May 1979 would change the structure, the functioning and the profession of the Civil Service; these reforms became a great organisational shift in the administrative history of the UK because the most profound overhaul since Northcote–Trevelyan was made and the most ambitious attempt to reform the Civil Service of the twentieth century was started.

REFERENCES

Books, Journals, and Articles

Abel-Smith, B. (1964). *Freedom in the welfare state* (No. 353). London: Fabian Society.

Balogh, T. (1959). The apotheosis of the dilettante. In H. Thomas (Ed.), *The establishment* (pp. 83–128). London: New English Library.

Barberis, P. (Ed.). (1996). *The Whitehall reader*. Milton Keynes: Open University Press.

Blackstone, T., & Plowden, W. (1988). *Inside the think tank: Advising the cabinet 1971–83*. London: Heinemann.

Blau, P. (1956). *Bureaucracy in modern society*. New York: Random House.

Burnham, J., & Pyper, R. (2008). *Britain's modernized civil service*. Basingstoke: Palgrave Macmillan.

Butler, Robin. (1993). The evolution of the civil service—A progress report. *Public Administration, 71*(3), 395–406.

Campbell, J. (1993). *Heath: A biography*. London: Jonathan Cape.

Chapman, R. A., & Greenaway, J. R. (1980). *The dynamics of administrative reform*. London: Croom Helm.

Craig, S. J. (1955). *A history of red tape: An account of the origin and development of the civil service*. London: Macdonald & Evans.

Drewry, G., & Butcher, T. (1991). *The civil service today*. Oxford: Blackwell.

Fry, G. K. (1985). *The changing civil service*. London: Allen & Unwin.

Fry, G. K. (1995). *Policy and management in the British civil service*. Hemel Hempstead: Prentice Hall.

Garrett, J. (1980). *Managing the civil service*. London: William Heinemann.

Gray, J., & Jenkins, K. (1982). Policy analysis in British central government: The experience of PAR. *Public Administration, 60*, 429–450.

Greenwood, J., et al. (2002). *New public administration in Britain*. Abingdon: Routledge.

Hennessy, P. (1990). *Whitehall*. London: Fontana Press.

Hurd, D. (1979). *An end to promises: A sketch of government*. London: Collins.

Kemp, P. (1993). *Beyond next steps: A civil service guide for the twenty-first century*. London: Social Market Foundation.

Lee, R., et al. (1998). *At the centre of Whitehall*. London: Macmillan.

Mackenzie, W. J. M., & Grove, J. W. (1957). *Central administration in Britain*. London: Longmans.

Nicholson, M. (1967). *The system: The misgovernment of modern Britain*. New York: McGraw-Hills.

Painter, C. (1975, December). The civil service: Post-Fulton malaise. *Public Administration*.

Parris, H. (1969). *Constitutional bureaucracy: The development of British central administration since the eighteenth century*. London: Allen & Unwin.

Pyper, R. (1995). *The British civil service*. Hemel Hempstead: Prentice Hall.

Radcliffe, J. (1991). *The reorganisation of British central government*. London: Dartmouth Publishing.

Theakston, K. (1995). *The civil service since 1945*. Oxford: Blackwell.

Waldegrave, W. (1993). *Public services and the future: Reforming Britain's bureaucracies*. London: Conservative Political Centre.

Archive Sources, Parliamentary Papers, and Official Publications

Cabinet Office. (1994, May 6). *Press notice*. "Better access to public services information." London: HMSO.

Cabinet Office. (2006). *Civil service management code*. London: Cabinet Office.

Civil Service Department. (1972). *Civil service statistics*. London: CSD.

Civil Service Department. (1976). *Civil service statistics*. London: CSD.

Cmnd 3638. (1968). *Report of the committee of the civil service* (Fulton Report). London: HMSO.

Cmnd 3909. (1931). *Report on the royal commission of the civil service*. London: HMSO.

Cmnd 4506. (1970). *The reorganization of central government*. London: HMSO.

Efficiency Unit. (1988). *Improving management in government: The next steps*. London: HMSO.

Expenditure Committee of the House of Commons. (1977). *The civil service*, HC 535, q. 1510. London: HMSO.

HM Treasury. (1994). *Fundamental review of running costs*. London: HM Treasury.

The National Archives (TNA), Kew, UK

Trosa Report. (1994). *Next steps: Moving on*. London: Office of Public Service and Science.

CHAPTER 2

The Rise of Managerialism in the Civil Service: The Thatcher Years

THE POLITICAL, ECONOMIC, SOCIAL AND ADMINISTRATIVE ENVIRONMENT IN THE EARLY 1980s

The Political Impact of the New Right on the Public Sector

The Conservative Government came to office in 1979 with a clear commitment to reduce the size of the government and eliminate its waste and inefficiency. This aim was linked directly with the administrative reform and to reassert political control over the Civil Service. The determination of the Prime Minister regarding this objective was particularly in evidence. Margaret Thatcher's attitude towards the Civil Service was described by one of her colleagues as "ferocious" (Cosgrave 1985). She considered the public administration an obstacle and a hindrance to government action in reforming the state. She came to office determined to tackle and overhaul it (Thatcher 1993). In developing her vision on the Civil Service, Mrs. Thatcher had been strongly influenced by a number of close advisers. In 1978, Leslie Chapman, a former official of the Property Services Agency, wrote a book entitled *Your Disobedient Servant*, in which he harshly criticised the Civil Service organisation and management. His arguments were considered sympathetically by the Conservative opposition, and he was appointed Thatcher's adviser during the 1979 election campaign.

Chapman was passed over following the election in favour of Sir Derek Rayner. Rayner, who was a member of top management at Marks

© The Author(s) 2018
L. Castellani, *The Rise of Managerial Bureaucracy*,
https://doi.org/10.1007/978-3-319-90032-2_2

& Spencer, arrived at Number 10 Downing Street with the idea of infusing managerial behaviours of the private sector into the public one. Less severe in his attitude to the Civil Service than Chapman, he devised, with the strong support of Mrs. Thatcher, an efficiency strategy which used civil servants themselves to identify areas of waste and duplication and to make recommendations for change (Metcalfe and Richards 1987). Sir John Hoskyns, the head of the Prime Minister's policy unit, was involved in the Civil Service debate. Whitehall, he sustained, lacked strategic direction, a deficit which should be considered particularly severe in the context of Britain's economic decline (Hoskyns 1983). He argued that the civil servants had lost their strategy for national revival. This problem was exacerbated by their political neutrality, which made it necessary for them to withdraw the "last five percent of commitment" to governmental objectives. He believed that neutrality should be abandoned and the Whitehall professional bureaucracy should be overcome in favour of a spoils system, in which the executive power would have chosen top-level civil servants from outside (Hoskyns 1983). From this debate, a number of problems linked to the Civil Service were delivered to the public debate. First, the aim of the new Conservative Government was to reduce the power of civil servants. In pursuit of this objective, the government proceeded with a strong commitment to attack the influence of Civil Service unions, to decrease the rights of civil servants to engage in politically related activity and to introduce measures designed to compress civil servants' privileges (Ponting 1986).

Second, the Civil Service's efficiency in implementing the government programme had to be increased. The Prime Minister soon made it clear that she was willing to "skip a civil service generation" in order to promote those whom she believed would pursue government policy with vigour and effectiveness (Hennessy 1990: 631).

Third, the size of the Civil Service would be reduced, a policy consistent with the aim to reduce the public expenditure, a point set as a priority by the first Thatcher Government. Fourth, private sector solutions would be adopted to deal with public sector inefficiencies. These issues were present in the administrative debate by the mid-1960s; in fact, the Plowden Report of 1961 argued for "management training" for civil servants. Privatisation and managerial methods would be pursued with considerable vigour.

Fifth, non-departmental bodies whose primary rationale was deemed to be survival rather than productivity would be shut down (see Cmnd 7797, 1979).

On this point, Richard Vinen (2009) writes: "Thatcher's government seemed to have acted with a determination and ruthlessness that had not been in major Western democracies since 1945."

The Social Context: The Distrust of Government and Bureaucracy

The decline in Britain's economic fortunes was accompanied by increasing criticism in the community regarding the size and the role of government. As the recession grew worse and Britain's economic standing deteriorated relative to other major industrialised nations, the search for a scapegoat began. Government provided a ready and easily identifiable target (Gamble 1986). Within the Keynesianism paradigm, the role of government had been considered as a positive force for economic and social development. Fiscal policy provided the essential means through which cyclical fluctuations in economic activity could be moderated. The higher the level of public expenditure, the greater the leverage which fiscal policy could exercise. Keynesians believed it proper for the state to intervene in the market to provide public goods and to mitigate the effects of free market power on the poor and the disadvantaged. Given these beliefs, there had been a consistent propensity for state expenditure to grow as a proportion of gross economic growth (Zifcak 1994). However, with the changes in economic fortunes, the critics of government became more numerous and their influence was greater than before. In the intellectual arena, the most powerful were F. A. Hayek and the American Milton Friedman, both of whom were economists, and both of whom had a vision for society. Hayek believed that central planning was both politically dangerous and economically inefficient. It was politically dangerous because it reduced individual liberty in favour of political coercion, increased the power of the state, weakened the role of Parliament and undermined the rule of law by investing government officials with considerable discretion. Planning was economically inefficient because it damaged competition, increased the prevalence of monopolies and compromised entrepreneurialism (Hayek 1944, 1960). Friedman too fought against effects of big government. He argued that slow growth and declining productivity called for a fundamental reassessment of the role of government in economic activity.

Continued governmental intervention at the expense of market competition threatened not only to destroy economic prosperity but also to reduce human freedom of choice (Friedman 1962). These ideas were embraced enthusiastically by think tanks and politicians alike. Through its "Hobart series," the Institute for Economic Affairs introduced Hayek's and Friedman's ideas to a wider audience. It popularised Niskanen's work on the pathology of bureaucracy and held several symposia on the role and size of government (Zifcak 1994). The Centre for Policy Studies took a similar path. It had been founded by Sir Keith Joseph in 1974. Margaret Thatcher later became its president. Both Joseph and Thatcher cited Hayek and Friedman with approval and it was Joseph who later assumed primary responsibility for carrying the arguments of the New Right from the academic into the political arena. The Centre was also the intellectual home of other prominent Thatcher advisers, such as Sir Alan Walters and Sir John Hoskyns. Politicians, advisers and analysts alike believed that responsibility for the decline in British fortunes should be laid at the feet of the government. Only if government strictly limited its interventions in the market, economy and society could Britain's economic decline be reversed. Just as the role of government was attacked, so also was that of the Civil Service. From a theoretical perspective, public choice theorists such as Tullock (1965) and Niskanen (1971) argued that bureaucrats should be regarded as rent-seekers, their principal objective being to maximise their budgets and increase the influence of their bureaus. These theorists proposed that, unlike private entrepreneurs who would not supply goods beyond the point at which their price equalled their cost, the welfare of bureaucrats rose continuously as agency budget increased. Hence, individual bureaucrats had little incentive to restrain their output even where the marginal cost of providing a service exceeded its marginal value. Consequently, bureaucrats themselves were central to explaining why government had grown significantly. These anti-bureaucratic views found a ready audience in the Conservative political leadership (Dunleavy 1986).

Public sector management was also subjected to harsh criticism. Influential business writers compared management in the public sector unfavourably with that in the private sector (Drucker 1977). They believed that the problem with public sector institutions was that they were rewarded not for effective performance but for honouring their promises. Hence, there was a genetic tendency for expenditure to grow and for delivery to take precedence over productivity. In the policy sphere, public sector management relied too much on civil servants' special status and too little on science, planning and rational analysis

(Johnson 1985). The management theorists argued that governmental affairs would be conducted more effectively if the tenets of private sector management were adhered to. As this view became more popular, techniques developed in the private sector, such as zero-based budgeting, programme budgeting and cost-benefit analysis, were tried in government but without notable success (Wildavsky 1979). Politicians, too, picked up the thread, berating the Civil Service for its inefficiency and lauding the productivity of private entrepreneurial initiative. Both the Heath and the Thatcher Governments employed private sector managers as consultants on Civil Service efficiency on the premise that their diagnosis would be both sharper and more relevant than that developed by the Civil Service itself.

The Economic Paradigm: The End of Keynesianism

The economic situation which prevailed in Britain in the 1970s was quite unlike that in the previous decade. The 1960s had been characterised by great affluence: gross domestic product increased continuously, public expenditure and public services expanded, and personal income rose. Inflation was low and under control, there was full employment, and the economy was growing constantly albeit slowly. In the 1970s occurred a reversal of these trends. Inflation increased dramatically, unemployment reached levels unseen since the Great Depression, the balance worsened, and the dollar value of the pound declined significantly. The Keynesian paradigm, which had prevailed for several decades, was confounded by stagflation, paving the way for the ascendancy of the monetarist alternative. This upheaval set the scene for a strong attack against the excesses of public expenditure. Influenced heavily by monetarist economists at home and abroad, the Conservative Party concluded the government should no longer engage actively in demand management. Rather, the market economy was best left to correct itself. The process of market self-correction could only be obstructed by active governmental intervention in the economy, since public sector growth crowded out private sector investments, thereby reducing the capacity of the economy to re-establish its equilibrium.

The government's first expenditure White Paper was a clear demonstration of these beliefs. It argued that inflation would be attacked by controlling the rate of monetary growth and reducing the public sector borrowing requirement. Taxes would be reduced to restore individual and corporate incentives for investment. Public expenditure would be cut to reduce borrowing and taxation. There were no measures proposed to secure full employment, marking the decisive departure from the post-war Keynesian consensus (Gamble 1994). The government's economic policy had substantial implications for the level and composition of public expenditure. Describing public expenditure as being at the core of the country's economic problems, the government announced its intention to progressively reduce public spending in volume terms for the following four years. The reduction in expenditure was necessary to decrease the rate of growth of money supply in the same period.

The government did not reach its expenditure targets in the first term. Nevertheless, its attempts to cut expenditure were serious and they included substantial reductions in education, housing, environment and social security. These cuts were supplemented by more general measures instituted to increase control of the public expenditure. The government imposed cash limits, made cuts in Civil Service personnel and launched a concrete attack on levels of public sector pay. It was these changes, more than deficit spending reductions, that contributed to spread a feeling among civil servants that they were under attack.

The Administrative Context: The Seeds of Managerialisation

Since the Plowden Report (Cmnd 1432, 1961), and moreover with the Fulton Report (Cmnd 3638, 1968), the Civil Service itself had been faced with the problems of managerial modernisation. Lord Fulton, echoing criticisms made by Lord Plowden in 1961, argued that in its structures and methods of operation the Civil Service had placed too great an emphasis on the provision of public policy advice. As a result, it had neglected the task of effectively managing governmental business. This was a serious problem given that the administration's principal activity was not in fact policy development but service delivery. To accomplish this goal, Fulton made a wide-ranging series of recommendations for change. The most relevant of these for present purposes was that "accountable management" should be introduced throughout the Civil Service. Accountable management involved the designation of discrete units in governmental departments whose outputs could be measured against costs and other criteria and whose performance could effectively be controlled (Zifcak 1994). The Fulton Report argued that wherever measures of achievement could be established in quantitative or economic terms and where individuals could be held responsible for output and cost, accountable units should be established (Cmnd 3638, 1968). Once established, these units would be connected into commands, each of which would be responsible for the achievement of specified programme objectives. These programme objectives in turn would be related to corporate and governmental objectives through a process of strategic planning (Garrett 1980). In the following years, not all went well for the managerialist cause. The new Civil Service Department took responsibility for initiating Management by Objectives (MBO). It did it by setting a number of experimental projects that, however, did not satisfy their reformers' expectations. This was because an information system necessary to support managerial decision-making was either absent or inadequate, advice for MBO specialists had not always been available, and lack of commitment from senior staff had sapped morale and enthusiasm among public servants (Hancock 1974; Garrett 1980). MBO finished its formal development in the mid-1970s, but the techniques introduced survived on a random basis in different areas of the administration. The next major attempt to introduce a "managerial reform" was the Heath government's Programme Analysis and Review (PAR). This was a programme which focused on policy evaluation rather than managerial improvement, but it shared much in common with accountable management. PAR's authors sought to make policy formulation more rational (Heclo and Wildavsky 1981: 280). Under the supervision of an interdepartmental committee, each year every department would evaluate specific blocks of policy. The evaluation of the precedent would establish the basis for future policy development. However, PAR too was not really successful. Insufficiently appreciating the differences between "running a company and running the country," the technique never successfully mixed policy review and political decision-making. Consequently, it was marginalised as the government became more preoccupied in managing economic decline (Pliatzky 1982). The demise of PAR did not stop the attempts to improve Civil Service management. Accountable management, for example, continued to emerge in other guises. Pressure was applied by the House of Commons Expenditure Committee to improve the reporting of public expenditure to Parliament by classifying it in terms of the objectives it was to meet and by developing tangible measures of performance. These examined the operation of departmental units, subjecting their performance to critical scrutiny in the light of their stated managerial objectives (Zifcak 1994).

Thus, while the programmes and managerial reform failed and died, each of them left their mark and slowly the managerial ethos began to spread through Whitehall's passages. While this low-key but steady progress received little attention in academic debate and the popular media, it was sufficiently significant enough to later form the foundation for Whitehall's response to the Thatcher Government's demands for a greater improvement of managerial competences. That response was the establishment of the Efficiency Unit in 1979 and the development of Management Information Systems for Ministers (MINIS) and the FMI in 1982.

THE NEW "RIGHT" APPROACH TO THE CIVIL SERVICE AND ADMINISTRATIVE REFORM

Thatcher's Opposition and the Civil Service

The problem-solving approach that characterised Edward Heath's approach to policy-making in opposition in the 1970s was not the one that Margaret Thatcher adopted after the election as Conservative leader in 1975. Mrs. Thatcher, Sir Keith Joseph and Angus Maude, who was made chairman of the Research Department, had been of the view in the years down to 1970 that principles and ideas should be settled in advance of details. So, as the historian of the Research Department observed, between 1975 and 1979 "there was not an imposing array of policy groups as before 1970" and few resulting policy pledges by the standards of modern oppositions, and yet the Conservative Party "succeeded ... in building for itself a clear identity" (Ramsden 1980: 308–309). As the only valuable principles and ideas available were those provided by market philosophy, the Conservative leadership's identity at least was bound to be an economic liberal one, and this time, in contrast with the 1960s, it was not just within the Party that the intellectual tide was running in that direction. Margaret Thatcher ran over this vision, and she moved radical ideas into the mainstream of the Conservative Party. Heath had moved in different directions, for a while at the same time, and, not surprisingly, he lost his seat. That overload at the centre combined with the exercise of trade union power had rendered Britain "ungovernable" was a fashionable belief in the wake of the events of 1974 (King 1976), but the situation was never beyond remedy by a different form of political leadership. The IMF crisis of 1976 and its imposed settlement marked the end of the Keynesian era, but well before that economic neoliberalism had gained centre stage. Nevertheless, on economic policy issues, the writings of Friedrich Hayek and Milton Friedman gained increasing attention, and their ideas on the role of government were encapsulated in the title of a contemporary book, *Democracy in Deficit: The political legacy of Lord Keynes* (Buchanan and Wagner 1977). Though an organisation like the Institute for Economic Affairs would promote the discussion in the form of *Bureaucracy: Servant or master?* (Niskanen et al. 1973), it tended to have little direct interest in the machinery of central government as such or in the organisation of the Civil Service as had the Bow Group in the past or the Centre for Policy Studies from 1975 onwards, and the Adam Smith Institute was formed too late to be influential at that time. However, the opposition to bureaucratic expansion and self-seeking and budget maximisation was as clear as it was in the growing body of public choice literature (Buchanan 1960, 1975; Buchanan and Tullock 1962; Tullock 1965, 1976; Niskanen 1971). Whatever the elaboration of such theorising, its impact on reality seems almost certainly to have been summarised by Leslie Chapman's book *Your Disobedient Servant*, published in 1978, for this was an insider account which revealed gross operational inefficiency and waste of public money in the Ministry of Public Building and Works and its successor, the Property Services Agency, on a scale that inspired demands for cuts in the Civil Service numbers and activities.

The 1979 Conservative Manifesto

In the Conservative Manifesto of 1979, the programme of the first Thatcher Government, there was not a direct reference to the reform of the Civil Service. However, in different parts of the text could be found indirect clues of the reform that the Conservative Government was preparing for the bureaucratic machine of the UK. In the second chapter, entitled "Restoring the Balance," the Manifesto announced: "Any future government which sets out honestly to reduce inflation and taxation will have to make substantial economies, and there should be no doubt about our intention to do so. We do not pretend that every saving can be made without change or complaint; but if the Government does not economise, the sacrifices required of ordinary people will be all the greater." In another passage, the programme of the Conservative Party maintained that "the reduction of waste, bureaucracy, and over-government will also yield a substantial savings" (Conservative Manifesto 1979). And again in the paragraph dedicated to trade union reform: "In bringing about economic recovery, we should all be on the same side. Government and public, management and unions, employers and employees, all have a common interest in raising productivity and profits, thus increasing investment and employment, and improving real living standards for everyone in a high-productivity, high-wage, low-tax economy" (Conservative Manifesto 1979). The manifesto was expressed in broad political terms. It underlined the principles of the Conservative political offer, concentrating on different issues: the labour market, trade unions, stopping inflation, tax reductions, schools, immigration, privatisation and international relations. Anyway, these measures imposed implicitly a change for central government administration. The need for this reform would be expressed immediately in the first weeks after the establishment of Margaret Thatcher at Number 10 Downing Street.

The 1979 Reform of the Select Committees

The year 1979 could be considered a crucial year in the history of the Civil Service, not only for the arrival of the Conservative Government headed by Margaret Thatcher, but even for the parliamentary reform of the Select Committees.

A system for scrutinising the executive through a series of departmental select committees was established in June 1979. The incoming Conservative Government implemented proposals from the 1976–1978 Procedure Committee for a permanent system of committees to "examine the expenditure, administration, and policy of the principal government departments" (Standing Order No. 152, 1979). The departmental committees are designed to mirror each government department and are re-organised following machinery of government changes. Other Select Committees deal with Internal House matters, or regional areas, or cover cross-cutting issues, such as environmental audits.

The establishment of a system of departmental select committees in 1979 followed the recommendation of a special Procedure Select Committee, first established in 1976, which reported in 1978. The proposal was agreed to by the House in June 1979, following the support of the new leader of the Commons, Norman St. John-Stevas. Implementation of the report had become a manifesto commitment in an atmosphere of political demand for a more assertive Commons. However, there had been a debate since at least the time of Richard Crossman as Leader of the House 1966–1968 as to the desirability of establishing a system of departmental committees.

In the nineteenth century, select committees had been an influential part of parliamentary work, often leading to significant legislation. However, the growing use of independent inquiries and Royal Commissions in the early twentieth century reduced the scope of select committees (Parris 1969). There were committees such as those for Nationalised Industries and Estimates that had been eliminated with economic changes. Under Crossman, six subject committees were established, followed in the 1970s by sub-committees under a new Expenditure Committee. Dissatisfaction with the unplanned nature of that system, combined with concern that the balance between the Executive and Parliament was weighted too heavily towards the former, was an impetus to reform. The incoming Conservative Government had given its support for a departmental select committee system in their election manifesto. The proposals were implemented on 25 June 1979.

The new committees were established by the Committee of Selection on 26 November 1979, but none began work until early 1980. The Procedure Select Committee argued for a departmental, rather than subject-based, committee system, in order to focus on individual ministerial responsibilities. It was an accepted principle that the departmental committees should replicate the machinery of government, so that when departments were formed or merged, the select committee system could be modified. The Procedure Committee reported positively in 1990 on the operation of the departmental select committee system, with some recommendations for incremental reform.

The committees provided a near legislative symmetry to the Whitehall departmental landscape. From their advent, the departmental select committees were seen as one of the main arenas for the scrutiny and influence of executive actions, which would go some way to redressing the power imbalance between executive and legislative functions. In fact, civil servants soon lost their anonymity: over 18 months after the introduction of the reform in 1979, 652 officials gave evidence to the Committee (Drewry and Butcher 1991). The work of Committees has become increasingly important in orientating departmental activities and bringing officials as individuals onto the stage of public accountability, even if, officially, they answer on behalf of their minister, who is able to determine the scope of questioning.

The Higher Civil Service and the Thatcher Factor: An Outlook on the Appointments

"The Conservative victory in May 1979 was more than just another change of Government; in terms of political and economic philosophy, it was a revolution," according to Sir Leo Pliatzky, a former Permanent Secretary (Pliatzky 1982: 176).

By 1979, to the extent that ideas determine the party political contest, the restoration of "neo-classical" vision, in its modern guise of monetarism, to the position of economic orthodoxy enabled the Thatcher Government to lead the domestic policy debate against their adversaries, who possessed only tried and failed political solutions with which to reply. Whether this Conservative ascendancy would remain reflected in terms of political predominance necessarily depended on what voters defined as results, and positive results at least required the emergence of an entrepreneurial class in Britain capable of more than holding its own in international competition (Fry 1995). The free marketers in and connected with the new government saw themselves as contending with what Mrs. Thatcher herself called the "Welfare State mentality" embedded in the Keynesian ideas, represented in Britain by what she termed special interest groups that made the country into an entitlement society (Thatcher 1993).

As G. K. Fry wrote, "Such neo-liberal remedies as were deemed politically feasible were applied to the economy; the Thatcher Government, as part of its ambition to put private enterprise back on the throne, treated the public sector as usurper" (Fry 1995: 37). Of the various "special interest groups" to be overcome and contested, the career Civil Service was one of the priorities to reform because it was heavily unionised from top to bottom and it was seen as a group of privileged bureaucrats by the Conservatives' propaganda. "The sheer professionalism of the British Civil Service, which allows governments to come and go with a minimum of dislocation and a maximum of efficiency, is something other countries with different systems have every cause to envy," Margaret Thatcher wrote in her memoirs (Thatcher 1993: 18). Similar sentiments had been expressed by Lord Hewart many years before, when, before accusing civil servants of wishing to impose through "bureaucratic encroachments" what he called "the new despotism" (Hewart 1929: 21), he had written of Britain having the "best Civil Service in the world" (ibidem: 13).

Although Mrs. Thatcher recognised the qualities of the Civil Service, and especially of those members who worked closely with her in Downing Street, her administration did not temper their feelings of distrust and dislike until the late 1980s. To judge from her own account of the Civil Service, Mrs. Thatcher closely associated the "gentlemen in Whitehall" with the "prolonged experiment" in "democratic socialism" conducted in the UK between 1945 and 1979, which had been a "miserable failure in every respect," because, "far from reversing the slow relative decline of Britain vis-a-vis its main industrial competitors, it accelerated it" (Thatcher 1993: 6–7). The Thatcher Government's approach to the Civil Service's work was in such open contrast with the attitudes of extreme dependence that characterised the governments of the Wilson–Heath–Callaghan era that the radical nature of its attitude was in danger of being exaggerated (Fry 1995). This did not mean that the status of the Civil Service was unaffected by the Thatcher Government. That government declined to treat the Service as an interest in its own right. The politically aggressive Civil Service unions were defeated in the Civil Service strike of 1981, when the Conservative Government unilaterally broke the Priestley pay system. The Thatcher Government struck at the hierarchy of the career Civil Service in other ways too, initiating a programme of cuts in numbers which amounted to 15% overall between 1979 and 1984, and 16.2% at Senior Open Structure levels near the top of the Service over the same period (HM Treasury 1984: 5).

The Wardale inquiry formulated recommendations about whether or not the Under Secretary grade should be abolished. Though the grade was to survive, one effect of such inquiries, and of the various confrontations and "de-privileging activity," was to push the Civil Service on the defensive. Not satisfied with that, the Rayner efficiency studies and the introduction of MINIS and then of the Financial Management Initiative (FMI) of 1982 were aimed at changing the Civil Service's culture, and this was enforced too by a more direct intervention of the Prime Minister in high-level appointments and promotions (Richards 1997). "I took a close interest in senior appointments in the Civil Service from the first, because they could affect the morale and efficiency of whole departments," Mrs. Thatcher was later to confess (Thatcher 1993: 46). There were those who felt that the scale of the then Prime Minister's involvement in such appointments was politically unfair in two ways. One was that she was instrumental in promoting personal favourites and in blocking the advancement of others who had crossed her. The other objection was that she used to give preference to the officials who shared her political outlook. Clive Ponting was not alone in believing that there was a "politicisation of the Civil Service in the back door" (Ponting 1986: 7–8; for a divergent opinion, see Richards 1997). Early on in her premiership, Mrs. Thatcher actually took to visiting government departments by the front door. These tours were later seen as an unhealthy practice because they led to assessments of senior civil servants being made on the basis of face-to-face impressions. Furthermore, some higher civil servants' careers may well have benefited from working in proximity to Mrs. Thatcher, constituting what one observer called "the Cabinet Office effect" (Richards 1993: 24–25). Mrs. Thatcher wrote: "I was enormously impressed by the ability and energy of the members of my Private Office at No. 10. I usually held personal interviews with the candidates for Private Secretary for my own office. Those who came were some of the very brightest men and women in the Civil Service, ambitious and excited to be at the heart of decision-making in government. I wanted to see people of the same calibre, with lively minds and commitment to good administration, promoted to hold the senior posts in the departments. Indeed, during my time in government, many of my former Private Secretaries went on to head departments. In all these decisions, however, ability, drive, and enthusiasm were what mattered; political allegiance was not something I took into account" (Thatcher 1993: 46).

Of course, the Cabinet Office and the Prime Minister's Office were not the same thing, and, concerning one of the controversial appointments made, the translation of Sir Clive Whitmore, the Prime Minister's Principal Private Secretary, to become the Permanent Secretary to the Ministry of Defence in 1982, it could be observed that Whitmore had spent almost the whole of his career in that Ministry (RIPA Working Group 1987: 44).

As for the promotion of Sir Peter Middleton from Deputy Secretary to Permanent Secretary to the Treasury in 1983, made openly against official recommendations favouring Sir Anthony Rawlinson, some thought that Middleton's preference for monetarism explained his early advancement. However, Clive Ponting and the other civil servants, who denounced Mrs. Thatcher's critical use of appointments within the exercise of prime ministerial powers as back-door politicisation, never demonstrated that the promotions to top-level posts made were illegitimate. Indeed, all the civil servants appointed were qualified for the posts concerned and there was not a civil servant promoted above his level of skills.

Competence may well have been given preference over shared political outlooks with the Prime Minister. After all, at a lower level Ponting himself, who seems to have made no secret of his social democratic beliefs, initially gained career terms from the Prime Minister's recognition of his energetic part in the Rayner project (Ponting 1986: 11). The First Division Association (FDA), representing higher civil servants, observed about senior Civil Service appointments in the Thatcher era: "Anecdotal evidence suggests it is style rather than belief which tends to be considered important. The style which appears to appeal to the Prime Minister is the 'Can Do' approach, best characterised by decisiveness and an ability to get things done, rather than the more traditional approach which lays greater emphasis on analysis of options with recommendations for action based on that analysis." The RIPA Working Group (1987: 43–44), which was informed of this, concluded that there was no evidence of politicisation, and this was also the assessment made in another scholarly study (Richards 1993: 23).

Efficiency and Managerial Culture: Rayner's Public Management Reforms

1979–1983: The Rayner Project for Public Management

When the Thatcher government took office in 1979, there were three objectives for the management of the Civil Service: the rationalisation of quangos, emergency reduction of manpower and a project for monitoring the public expenditure and reduction of waste conducted by Derek Rayner, known as scrutinies. These actions were coordinated with monetary policy, indeed as Richard Vinen (2009) pointed out: "Ever since the 1960s, government departments had calculated their future spending in terms of 'volume' or 'funny money,' as it came to be known. [...] Automatic adjustment to inflation meant that civil servants and contractors had little incentive to cut costs. The government now began to move towards the calculation of future spending."

The latter objective was the most complex, with greater impact on the Civil Service and many political implications. Derek Rayner was a manager of the leading retail company Marks & Spencer, and he was appointed five days after the election victory of Margaret Thatcher. Immediately afterwards, the Efficiency Unit was created, composed of just Rayner, Priestley and Allen.

The presentation of the Rayner project was attacked by Leslie Chapman, the previous adviser of Margaret Thatcher on the Civil Service reform, who criticised the excessive moderation of the reformist ideas espoused by Rayner, in particular as concerned the rejection of the introduction of external auditing for monitoring Civil Service expenditure and performance (TNA, PREM 19/60, record of the meetings, especially D. Rayner to M. Thatcher, 24 May). On 31 May 1979, the programme proposed by the Efficiency Unit was agreed by the Prime Minister. Rayner's basic idea was to start a process of spending monitoring through the "scrutinies" in ministries in order to eliminate waste, to save public money and to reduce public expenditure. On 6 July, the members of the Efficiency Unit and the Prime Minister established an initial plan of three months (30 August–30 November 1979) for scrutinising the ministries and finding savings. Another campaign agreed by the Cabinet and Rayner's Unit was to analyse the main efficiency problems of the British public administration in six months. The first report produced by the Efficiency Unit identified £80 million worth of savings, with a one-off of £32 million. There was, however, a delay in implementing the scrutinies. The programme established that they should be finished for the end of November, but in April 1980 they were still not finished. This was because of the resistance of some ministers, which compelled Rayner to request access to check the spending of ministries. The possibility of big savings was inextricably linked to political strategy. Meanwhile, Rayner also focused on the mechanisms of the administration through the introduction of new technologies such as computers and monitoring of business (TNA, PREM 19/243, P. Channon to M. Thatcher, 25 March 1980).

However, the start-up plan by Rayner was to establish a long-term management culture in the Civil Service, considering that the impact of the policies that he and his team suggested depended to a large extent on politics and balances in the Cabinet. He considered his mission linked more to the development of managerial culture because this was more easily accomplished and had greater impact in the long run than the cost savings that were tied to the political opportunities. Thirty-nine scrutinies were commissioned by the Efficiency Unit in 1980 and forty in 1981, with two multidepartment scrutinies. Rayner knew that the success or failure of his strategy was based on the commitment of Cabinet ministers, so he established three objectives in order to achieve the result: to find and to eliminate waste and inefficiency, bypassing senior officials and supervisor committees that were considered to be an obstacle in the reduction of the expenditure, working directly with ministers to give them a managerial attitude (TNA, CAB 128/76, Cabinet Meeting, 21 July 1983).

In parallel with these measures, the Efficiency Unit concentrated on the simplification and elimination of forms and activities, a process that would be concluded in 1982 (TNA, PREM 19/62, "Promotion of efficiency and elimination of waste," part. 8, November 1979–February 1981), and it produced savings of £5 million per year. The ministers decided the subjects for scrutinies, which means the area where they believed there was waste and inefficiency, they appointed the scrutinisers, and they decided the actions that had to be taken in order to accomplish the Efficiency Unit objectives. They could also choose external agents, such as consultants, to achieve the results. This led, however, to unsatisfactory outcomes: only 12,000 posts were cut by December 1982, of the 21,000 that had originally been selected for culling, and just £180 million had been effectively saved of the £400 million targeted (TNA, PREM 19/244, D. Rayner progress report to M. Thatcher, 30 January 1981). In 1980, there were three significant events that influenced the outcome of the scrutinies: the merger of the offices provided by the Efficiency Unit for the Department of Health and Social Security (DHSS) was blocked by the conflicting interests of the senior executives of the Public Ministry; the statistical services of the Department of Trade and Industry instead accepted 90% of the recommendations of the scrutinisers and reduced staff by 20%; while the pilot scrutiny given to the CSD led to a cost increase of 25%. Once again, Rayner obtained mixed results. On the one hand, he realised the managerial objectives but he failed to achieve broader political results (Lowe 2011).

In 1981, it was necessary to establish cash limits for general budget needs and to introduce best practices in order to save money and improve efficiency.

For the year 1981, the scrutiny formula was improved: all ministries were required to have an interview with the Prime Minister to identify the cuts in each ministry; full publication of all returns was required for use by departmental committees; ministers were allowed to use management consultants to achieve better performance and bigger savings;

and MINIS (Management Information Systems), developed by Michael Heseltine in the Department of the Environment, were implemented in other ministries (TNA, CAB 128/66, Cabinet conclusions, 20 December 1979). These measures brought to light the resistance to the process of spending review encountered by the Efficiency Unit owing mainly to the reluctance of some ministers and of many Senior Officials.

The second stage of the reform was presented on 31 March 1980, and it was based on a draft proposed by Clive Priestley. The draft was approved by the Cabinet on 1 May. At the time, Margaret Thatcher was expressing impatience with the Civil Service for the difficulties she was finding in reducing the number of public employees and fighting against waste and inefficiency. She blamed this situation on lack of commitment by senior civil servants owing to their desire to defend their privileges (Lowe 2011). The aim of the second Efficiency Unit programme was, at first, to implement managerial training for the permanent secretaries in order to enable them to extend managerial practices to the rest of the Civil Service top grades. Three steps were established (TNA, PREM 19/242, D. Rayner progress report to M. Thatcher, 19 December 1980): reduction of waste and public expenditure; management of resources collectively and within departments; and cultural change in civil servants' approach.

These measures were well known to the members of the Efficiency Unit, as they resembled those set out in a 1970 paper produced by the Heath government and entitled *The Reorganisation of the Central Government*. In April 1981, the Wardale Report was published, suggesting management of the grades of the open structure to obtain savings in Civil Service pay, merging the different grades in which the civil servants' pay was constituted.

The Rayner project, to reduce salary expenditure, planned to abolish three administrative grades and reduce the Open Structure, a term used to define the higher grades of the Civil Service to its size in 1965 (equivalent to a 35-percent cut), but the head of the Efficiency Unit considered the Civil Service Department incapable of meeting this target. The Efficiency Unit plan was also challenged, on a political level, by Soames and other senior ministers, such as Whitelaw and Hailsham, who regarded a 35-percent cut arbitrary and exaggerated (Lowe 2011). Anyway, in November 1981, when the "stringent reviews" was launched by Rayner and his team, the 35-percent cut was downgraded to a mere aspiration by Thatcher herself (TNA, PREM 19/62, D. Rayner to M. Thatcher, 23 January 1981).

The second aim of the lasting reform programme, the strengthening of the collective management of resources at both political and administrative levels, was the most sensitive and so was responsible for the majority of the amendments between its first and final draft. The aims were the more efficient calculation and overall allocation of public expenditure, a better balance between central government and departments in relation to the monitoring of performance, and the existence in each department of an effective management system. To achieve the aim of better management, Rayner suggested merging the Civil Service Department and the Treasury and establishing an inspector general in the Civil Service.

The function of the inspector would be to monitor the application of the best practices and refer to the Prime Minister about the implementation of them. This proposal by Rayner was not accepted by the Cabinet, which would have preferred to directly abolish the Civil Service Department led by Sir Ian Bancroft. The problem the ministers had with the institution of inspector general was the concentration of power in the Civil Service. In order to improve control over public expenditure and the accountability to Parliament of the Civil Service, the Conservative backbenchers proposed putting into place comptrollers and Auditor General departments (TNA, PREM 19/Government Machinery, Rayner Programme, part. 10, "Report on the efficiency of central government," 29 November 1981). The answer of Margaret Thatcher to this request was to move accountancy, finance and the audit division from the CSD to the Treasury. The second initiative was prompted by a Treasury scrutiny of its supply divisions and ultimately resulted in the FMI of May 1982. On 2 June 1981, the control of public expenditure White Paper was drafted: its essential objective was to reinforce Treasury control (TNA, PREM 19/Civil Service, Annual Scrutiny of Departmental Running Costs, part. 1, C. Whitmore to M. Thatcher, 22 May 1981). As initially planned in 1920, Principal Financial Officers (PFOs) and Principal Executive Officers (PEOs) were accordingly to act as Treasury agents within departments, assuring compliance with directives and preventing any untoward developments. Despite the Permanent Secretaries criticising the lack of skills and training on the part of the central officials, the initiative continued, although the CSD had been further disparaged.

The issue of the third objective of the lasting reforms programme was the enforcement of the resources management within departments, and it clearly depended on the success of the central initiatives. Here remained the problem of how to make the management systems work once they had been started. Technically, Rayner had sought since his appointment to encourage greater cost-consciousness through direct departmental payments for common services. This meant that payment would strengthen the consumer–supplier relationship and thereby ensure a more responsive and flexible service (TNA, PREM 19/62, ibidem). As an outcome of these policies, HMSO and the Central Office of Information had placed their services on a full repayment basis by 1981. Departments, working within stricter cash limits, weighted their budget not only for transaction costs but also for the principle of paying for the training of officials from which other departments might ultimately benefit. A compromise was finally reached whereby they were required to pay for job-specific training while the CSD paid for the rest. It thus became another point with which to beat the CSD. This was another step to get a clear definition of the managerial authority of ministers, the role of Permanent Secretaries as departmental accounting officers, and the "authority, responsibility, and requisite qualifications" of PEOs and PFOs. The requirement that all PFOs should be professionally qualified was also ignored, an example of the programme's short-termism. PFOs, it was argued, required vision and political sensibility as much as formal accountancy training.

By November 1981, the Civil Service College was primed to offer new courses in financial management for existing officials, although Rayner was still demanding a more rigorous programme and the appointment of outside experts. The fourth and final objective of the lasting reforms programme was the transformation of the generalist Whitehall culture in order to "drive home the fact that managing activities efficiently is of equal merit to thinking through policies and analysing issues" (TNA, PREM 19/147, D. Rayner to M. Thatcher, "The efficiency of central government: lasting reforms," para. 22–23). Rayner was determined to transform ministerial culture, but, given forecasted Cabinet resistances, specific recommendations were excised from the draft initially submitted to the Prime Minister. The focus was, once again, on civil servants. Rayner had two interrelated targets: the promotion to senior positions of officials with proven managerial skills and the improvements of these skills through the Service.

The first issue was addressed by the introduction in February 1982 of a formal succession policy. Each department was required to indicate annually who would succeed to senior positions in the "normal course of the event," who could succeed if the positions "were unexpectedly vacated," and who should be "in the field for the next but one succession" (TNA, PREM 19/Civil Service, Long-term management and manpower policy, part. 7, 26 February 1981). All potential candidates had to be evaluated on the basis of training and experience. The empowerment of managerial skills was created with the removal of disincentives and the provision of rewards. These disincentives had included a too-rigid hierarchy and the disproportionate promotion of generalists to senior posts at the cost of democracy, individual responsibility and development of managerial (rather than political) skills; Parliament had tended to justify faults and inefficiency as the inescapable cost of democracy rather than valorise the success of skilled civil servants (Lowe 2011: 251–254).

The Wardale inquiry and succession policy aimed to increase individual accountability and encourage managerial skills. There was also an attempt to limit the supply of information to Parliament: CSD officials were worried about the transmission of information to Westminster because answering MPs' enquiries fully was "a fundamental piece of our constitution and ought not to be considered in the same light as" other lasting reforms. Nevertheless, Rayner, supported by successive Cabinet Secretaries, continued to argue for "less perfectionism" and succeeded in persuading Cabinet in May 1980 to begin an inquiry (TNA, PREM 19/148, "Civil Service Numbers and Costs," note by Matt Pattinson, 25 April 1980). The provisions of rewards included honours and pay. Honours involved Prime Ministerial prerogative and so their reform was never referred to Cabinet (TNA, PREM 19/147, Cabinet Meeting, 1 May 1980).

However, a proposal for performance-related pay was advanced. Arguing that this was a common practice in the private sector and would improve morale of the officials, Soames sought to introduce it successively for Under Secretaries in 1981 and Assistant Secretaries in 1982. Officials were divided as witnessed by a minute of the Cabinet Secretary Robert Armstrong (TNA, PREM 19/152, R. Armstrong to C. Whitmore, 3 November 1980). Ministers against these measures led by Whitelaw and Hailsham rejected them on the grounds that it could politicise the Service and undermine the natural collegiality of public service. Many practical objections were also advanced, such as the additional bureaucracy required to monitor and determine payments. On 15 January 1981, Cabinet replaced this proposal with a compromise that established a programme of accelerated promotion and early retirement, but not performance evaluation (TNA, CAB 128/70, Cabinet Conclusions, 15 January 1981).

In the end, scrutiny produced mixed results, depending on ministers' commitment in each department. Up until 1982, 155 scrutinies were made with £300 million saved. The scrutinies continued until 1990 and they were carried on by the Efficiency Unit and Rayner's successors, Sir Robin Ibbs (1983–1988) and Sir Angus Fraser (1988–1990). When Margaret Thatcher left government, 300 scrutinies had been completed with a final saving of £1.3 billion from 1979. In 1993, £1.5 billion had been saved with the institutionalisation of scrutinies (Theakston 1995; Fry 1995).

After the commencement of the scrutiny process, the lasting reforms begun in 1982 were for Rayner his core contribution to administrative reform. Rayner, after all, was considered to be broadly sympathetic to the Civil Service and most of his proposed reforms had been adopted by the CSD, if not in their details, surely in their aims (TNA, PREM 19/148, R. Armstrong to M. Thatcher, 21 April 1980). However, the CSD was also weakened by the lack of strong Prime Ministerial commitment. In fact, it's true that the Civil Service Department remained too anchored to the generalist culture, but Margaret Thatcher, who never showed interest in its organisation, never showed the desire to manage her own department. By November 1981, the programme had enjoyed some important successes. It had prevented a "u-turn" on administrative reform by the Cabinet in 1980, and it had infused into officials a greater attention for management (Theakston 1995).

The Reduction of Quangos: A Spending Review Attempt

The review of Quangos (quasi-non-governmental bodies) was another key policy for public administration reform in order to reduce the public expenditure and to achieve the cash balance. It was self-contained but nevertheless epitomised the nature of administrative reform before 1982. For this job, it was not a minister appointed or a member of the CSD, but a valued individual. In fact, the individual responsible for this procedure was Sir Leo Pliatzky, a senior civil servant of the Treasury, who, in a final Paper (Cmnd 7797, 1979), had forecast the opportunity to abolish

247 quangos of the existing 2115, to produce £11.6 million in savings. However, instead of making a major contribution to a £200 million reduction in public expenditure, the Report merely recommended the abolition of a large number of Quangos with limitative cutting of waste. The Report also made some detailed procedural notes for the introduction of a code of best practices whose circulation was typically delayed so that they might be made more robust by the Efficiency Unit.

The review of Quangos was also damaged by a fundamental confusion of purpose. Before 1979, the attack on NDPBs (non-departmental public bodies) had had three objectives: to reduce public expenditure, to restrict patronage and to reverse the expansion of government (Lowe 2011: 239). It was argued that public expenditure was increasing not just by the bodies' own cost but also by the spending programmes they managed and the subsequent cost of departmental monitoring. Patronage was similarly protected as a source of back-door entrance, especially for trade unionists. Finally, Mrs. Thatcher sought to reduce NDPBs, and particularly new high-spending bodies such as the Manpower Services Commission, in order to reverse the corporatism of the Heath government. On 7 December 1979 (TNA, PREM 19/245, *Report on NDPBs*, 7 December 1979), the Cabinet established an inquiry for different department bodies, but it was not settled for Quangos; in fact, NDPBs were excluded by the inquiry for the spending review. One could find friction between the Conservative electoral manifesto and this policy on Quangos. Before the occupancy of Downing Street, the purpose was to reduce public expenditure, to restrict patronage and to reverse expenditure of government, but in 1979 it became just a "body count." On 28 August, to manage the situation, Pliatzky met the Prime Minister (TNA, PREM 19/245, record of a meeting), and some criteria were established in order to evaluate the opportunity to close non-departmental public bodies. The criteria were judged by permanent secretaries who were given "death–life" power over Quangos even if the final decision was always ratified by ministers. Pliatzky was allowed to interview permanent secretaries on Quangos, and they had to answer on the alleged waste of non-departmental bodies. This inquiry discovered that 20 bodies were responsible for 87% of the total public expenditure of Quangos (TNA, PREM 19/Government Machinery, 22 April 1981, *The future of Quangos*). Anyway, until 1982 there was just a monitoring of the Quangos' spending without any concrete action to reduce these institutions.

Pliatzky's action was a failure in reducing public expenditure and patronage for several reasons. First, the Conservative Party was now making the appointments and the issue of patronage became less important. Rather, the Report paid tribute to the many "worthy people who gave their service for free" and who had been humiliated by the polemical attack on Quangos. Second, a new approach towards government intervention was required, not least because, in response to demands for manpower cuts, ministers were surreptitiously transferring departmental responsibilities. That situation made impossible completion of the "hiving off" of functions from the public sector to the private sector (Lowe 2011: 240).

Furthermore, the Report's inability to identify any major candidate for abolition was significant, especially among the 20 bodies that were responsible for the most of the expenditure. As far as concerned the guidelines on NDPBs, the Report established that: new bodies should be established only as a last resort and, whenever possible, with a finite remit; the value of existing ones should be kept constantly under review; and to maximise parliamentary and public scrutiny, all financial records should be accessible to the Comptroller and Auditor General and a detailed annual report published. Moreover, the review demonstrated the real impossibility of a radical reform for the influence of Party and public rhetoric. The number of NDPBs may have halved by December 1981, but this was largely the result of expedients and so illusory. And new initiatives were launched in 1983, 1984 and 1985. By then, the critique was more soundly based and the objectives more ambitious. Indeed, in the further years until 1990, 872 non-departmental bodies were suppressed, even if 372 were created. Part of the NDPBs were privatised, but Thatcher's governments never showed the willingness to abolish the Quangos as governance bodies (Burnham and Pyper 2008). For obvious political reasons, particularly at local government level, she preferred to appoint people who were politically close to her rather than leave the Quangos field to neutral and professional civil servants.

A Priority for the Prime Minister: Reducing Departmental Manpower

The third expedient of the first Thatcher Government was the emergency reduction of manpower in the Civil Service. The first Cabinet commanded the CSD to freeze recruitment in order to reduce immediate manpower costs by three percent. On 31 May 1979, the CSD promoted an option exercise to cut the Service by up to 20%. In June 1979, the Efficiency Unit established a series of departmental projects to identify specific areas of waste. At the same time, the Treasury exercised pressure and then, in February 1980, more firmly imposed a cash limit on manpower costs (TNA, PREM 19/5, J. Hunt to M. Thatcher, 14 June 1979).

However, it was not clear what the strategy was and whether the prime aim was to reduce numbers or public expenditure. The two options were not synonymous because, for example, a reduction in tax collectors could respectively increase expenditure or decrease revenue. And it was not declared if the objective was to cut waste or reduce the role of government. However, it seemed that the objective could simply be the pure meeting of monetarist target. Indeed, the Conservatives, as was widely acknowledged, had received a "dreadful inheritance," with Labour having unrealistically budgeted for a mere two percent increase in public expenditure (TNA, PREM 19/5, J. Hunt Memorandum, 16 May 1979).

Consequently, without major manpower cuts, the government could not achieve one of its fundamental political aims: a reduction in the Public Sector Borrowing Requirement. Like with the NDPB review, however, ministers collectively were either unwilling or unable to resolve such a problem. Furthermore, the tension originated by these difficulties in managing public sector reform exposed the friction between the CSD and the Treasury, with their respective responsibilities for manpower control and public expenditure, as well as condemning the CSD in Mrs. Thatcher's mind. The initial freeze on recruitment, which lasted from 9 May to 27 July 1979, foreshadowed many of the later political tensions (Lowe 2011: 241). In order to manage the issue and to oblige both ministers and civil servants to confront stark choices, Mrs. Thatcher imposed a radical policy: six months of recruitment freeze and a manpower cut of five percent. This provoked a Cabinet revolt as early as 17 May 1979 on the grounds that such an indiscriminate freeze could be counterproductive. It could, some ministers argued, reduce the efficiency of the operations held in regions and in specialist areas where turnover was high.

Above all, the Cabinet rejected the premise that no policy changes were needed because waste was so excessive (TNA, CAB 128/66, J. Hunt brief to M. Thatcher, 17 July 1979). The Prime Minister was defeated by the Cabinet on this field. As desired by the CSD, the target for reduced manpower costs remained 3% instead of 5%, and the freeze was to be quitted after only three months. The exercise with which the CSD sought to replace the ban for recruitment was the options programme, which required each department to specify how it would reduce manpower by 10, 15 and 20%. This policy was a failure. Three progress reports were considered in Cabinet (September–November), but when the programme's final results were announced in Parliament on 6 December savings of only five percent had been found. It consisted of a reduction of 39,000 posts, of which 11,000 were the result of contracting out, rather than real cuts. In this case, one obstacle was the strong opposition of departments. The three largest departments, which employed 64% of officials (the Ministry of Defence, the Treasury and the DHSS), justified a proposal for respective cuts of only 3, 4.2, and 1.8% (TNA, PREM 19/6, R. Armstrong brief to M. Thatcher, 31 October 1979).

However, there were other reasons for failure related to administrative organisation. As Francis Pym, the Secretary of State for Defence, argued, a better strategy for him was to "build upwards from the facts rather than downwards from arbitrary targets" (TNA, PREM 19/6, ibidem). Before proceeding to any cuts, he aimed to complete the internal policy of investigation he had already ordered. Indeed, many planned cuts were dependent on controversial, and so more difficult to achieve, policy changes such as pay system, for which parliamentary approval was required. Moreover, the objective of a 20% manpower cut alarmed the unions and it provoked a flood of unofficial strikes, such that an emergency Cabinet subcommittee had to be formed to draft contingency plans (Lowe 2011: 242). Finally, the principal problem was the conflict caused by the reduction in numbers through the contracting out of services to the private sector.

This policy was particularly supported by Mrs. Thatcher and Mr. Heseltine, Minister of the Department of the Environment, even if it increased public expenditure in the short term. By the Cabinet meeting on 1 November, Mrs. Thatcher was clearly upset by the CSD's unreliability, and she decided to bet on the Rayner projects which had recently been completed and the MINIS programme settled by Heseltine, demonstrating that manpower could be cut without any policy changes (TNA, CAB 128/66, 1 November 1979). Finally, a cut in manpower costs of 2.5% was agreed, which led to a further saving of 15,000 posts (TNA, PREM 19/6, P. Channon to W. Whitelaw, 24 January 1980;

P. Channon, "Civil Service cash limits," 26 February 1980, para. 10). Derek Rayner was involved to settle the agreement on manpower cuts but simultaneously expressed criticism that, rather than a coherent manpower policy, there were only "sporadic squeezes when other factors required them." This dismay was directed as much at the Prime Minister as the CSD, as was later demonstrated by Rayner's explicit refusal of her preferred policy of "nil recruitment, nil redundancy" (TNA, PREM 19/6, M. A. Pattinson to M. Thatcher, 29 February 1980). However, he managed to preserve her confidence in order to realise his programme of lasting reforms. Furthermore, Rayner maintained a profitable cooperation with Channon, chief official of the CSD, in order to manage a longer-term manpower policy and to achieve the target of reduction to 630,000 civil servants.

The Abolition of the Civil Service Department

The abolition of the Civil Service Department was a critical moment in the contemporary history of the Civil Service because it signalled a transition from an old concerted method with unions and civil servants to a new style imposed by Thatcherism to achieve the targets of reforms.

There were several factors that determined the abolition of the Civil Service Department: the lack of agreement on Civil Service reform between the Prime Minister and the Minister of Civil Service Christopher Soames; the idea of Mrs. Thatcher and Sir Rayner that the department was an obstacle to the achievement of the economic target established by the Cabinet for the Civil Service; the necessity to centralise the control on pay of the public bodies; and the pressure created by the 21-week Civil Service strike in 1981.

Indeed, shortly after the end of the strike on 7 September 1981, the Prime Minister announced her decision to abolish the CSD in a meeting with Rayner and the Head of Civil Service, Robert Armstrong. Then Soames' dismissal followed on 14 September and there was, by mutual agreement, an audience with Sir Ian Bancroft, then Permanent Secretary at the Civil Service Department, on 24 September before the reorganisation was announced to Parliament on 12 November and became operational and fully legal on 7 December (Lowe 2011: 269). The Civil Service Department's abolition was a mixture of institutional contradictions. The role of the Department was widely discussed by the middle of the 1970s, but it was included as core in the "lasting reform" of Rayner's project. Despite this involvement in such an important project of reform, both the Prime Minister and the Efficiency Unit had criticised it relentlessly. Definitely, the idea of abolishing the CSD was effective from the summer of 1980 and Mrs. Thatcher was waiting for the best political occasion to declare it. The problems with the CSD were related to the slowness in implementing government policies or planning them effectively to achieve the objectives established by the Cabinet. Bancroft, the Permanent Secretary of the CSD, and Soames justified their resistance with the low morale of the Service resulting from the reduction in numbers and economic resources.

The CSD echelon accused the government of being "hostile to its own employees" and treating it like a veto player. The Prime Minister denied this statement, replying that "Ministers were not hostile to the Civil Service, though she did feel disgust at the resistance which she had encountered to her efforts to bring about greater efficiency. This she did regard as disloyalty" (PREM 19/Government Machinery, "The future of the CSD," part. 4, September 1981). However, abolition was justified on both institutional and personal grounds. Institutionally, the House of Commons Expenditure Committee had concluded that, with the effective abandonment of Fulton Report style, it had lost its reason for existence. Rayner was equally in favour of discussion, albeit on the very different grounds that the separation of the CSD from the Treasury was "neither justified in principle or by experience." Using a managerial approach, he argued that the optimal use of money and manpower efficiency required united control over both (TNA, PREM 19/147, D. Rayner to M. Thatcher, 26 March 1980). Furthermore, experience had shown that a divided centre was a weaker one. The experience of spending departments had showed how the lack of coordination among them in the management of public expenditure was inefficient (HC 54, 1980–1).

Personally, Rayner expressed his doubts about CSD personnel. He considered that civil servants of the CSD were not interventionist enough in the reform processes. Consequently, they were signally ineffective in prescribing and monitoring reform. In part, this was a result of their jealousy of the constitutional independence of other departments but, in the main, it was because senior staff were insufficiently "seized by the importance of management" and lacked the skills of "background and success in management." In this regard, they were "cautious, introspective, and self-conscious" and "ladylike." Some CSD officials were considered very good, but it was made clear in the summer of 1980 that there wasn't any senior figure judged to be capable enough to be appointed "Inspector General," as projected by Rayner's team in the lasting reforms programme (TNA, PREM 19/250, D. Rayner to M. Thatcher, 22 July 1980).

These perceived weaknesses could have been resolved in one of four ways, each of which was summarised by the Cabinet Secretary Robert Armstrong in his evidence to the Treasury and Civil Service Select Committee when it proposed in 1980 a formal parliamentary inquiry into the future of the CSD. It was for such complexity that the Prime Minister succeeded in the abolition of the CSD only at the third attempt. The first opportunity, selected by Armstrong, was the renovation of the CSD. This was the solution eventually to be recommended by the Select Committee and temporarily adopted by the Prime Minister in January 1981 (TNA, PREM 19/Government Machinery, minutes by M. Thatcher and D. Rayner, 18 and 22 January 1981). The second possibility, Rayner's preferred solution for his managerial approach, was a total merger of the CSD with the Treasury. This was immediately rejected by everyone else on the grounds that it would overload the functions of the Treasury, resulting in decreasing attention towards the management of the Civil Service. The third solution was the creation of an independent Office of Management and Budget. One of its attractions had been the consequent opening up for Cabinet discussion of economic issues traditionally internalised within the Treasury. However, in the cultural realm of monetarism, this was not an option favoured by Mrs. Thatcher, especially as it was the one supported by the unions. The fourth and finally chosen solution in 1981 was the transfer to the Treasury of responsibility for management, manpower and pay, and the remaining CSD divisions, principally those dealing with human resources such as appointments and training, formed a separate personnel office.

In 1980, however, this option was rejected because of the fear of dividing the management of the Service and the argument that the CSD would be too small to justify a separate minister or a Permanent Secretary. The two key facts that led to the decision for the abolition were the inability of the CSD to undertake monitoring and to lead the scrutiny programme in other departments and the combined attack by Rayner, unsatisfied with the contribution of the CSD on the implementation of the lasting reform programme, and the Treasury and Civil Service Committee (TCSC), in response to parliamentary criticism of the CSD. After these two episodes, the Prime Minister decided to abolish the CSD. Like the Select Committee, she convinced herself when she received the first draft of the White Paper responding to the Committee's report. She immediately memoed Rayner: "We have come to the heart of the matter. In spite of all our efforts and admonitions, CSD is not doing the job it was set up to do ... and intends to carry on as now" (TNA, PREM 19/Government Machinery, ibidem). The Civil Service Department was condemned. There was a connection between the weaknesses of the CSD and the actions taken after the end of the strike on the grounds of internal auditing, the Wardale Report on the pay system and departmental running costs, which confirmed her conviction that it was "never going to be the Mckinsey of the Civil Service" (TNA, PREM 19/Government Machinery, Future of the Civil Service Department Report, part. 4, 20 May 1981).

The plan of reform was established in May 1981 by the tandem Rayner–Armstrong, and they reported three options to choose from: an independent Office of Management and Budget within the Treasury; the transfer to the Treasury of the CSD's core responsibilities except for the promotion of the efficiency (to be embedded in the Cabinet Office); and the rejuvenation of the CSD under a dynamic and younger manager (TNA, PREM 19/Government Machinery, C. Whitmore to R. Armstrong, record of a meeting with Armstrong and Rayner, 7 September 1981). Mrs. Thatcher chose the second option, deciding on the abolition of the Civil Service Department. This decision was criticised for several reasons. It continued the division of responsibility for managing the Service; gave the Treasury the responsibility of managing a difficult issue like pay negotiations; was potentially a first step towards a Prime Minister's Department, which Mrs. Thatcher favoured but which both Armstrong and Rayner strongly opposed; and, technically, through the transfer to it of executive powers, opened up all Cabinet Office business to scrutiny by the Public Accounts Committee and the Ombudsman (TNA, PREM 19/Government Machinery, R. Armstrong to C. Whitmore, 21 September 1981).

The technical difficulty was soon resolved by establishing the functions of the CSD, the new Management and Personnel Office (MPO), as an independent unit, related to the Cabinet Office just by its common Permanent Secretary (the Cabinet Secretary, Robert Armstrong, who became Head of the Home Civil Service jointly with the Treasury's Permanent Secretary, Sir Douglas Wass). The MPO thus became an independent enclave in the Cabinet Office. The more fundamental objections were also resolved, at least in Robert Armstrong's outlook, by an examination of similar arrangements in Canada (ibidem).

With the MPO, the management of manpower and pay "would be brigaded with the management of resources" in the Treasury, while the management of people and organisation would be brigaded with the "management of policy-making in the Cabinet Office." In January 1982, the MPO was presented as having a "clear, coherent, and vitally important responsibility" in the promotion of efficiency through the consideration of human factors and not just cost cutting (TNA, CAB 164/1587, W. L. Kendall to M. Thatcher, 1 December 1981). To conclude, after two years of opposition against the CSD, the first Thatcher Government achieved the goal of the abolition. However, the ultimate choice of the Treasury to drive through lasting reforms was taken, therefore, not on administrative grounds but on the political grounds that the Chancellor, together with the Prime Minister, was the guardian of government strategy. The reason for the Treasury's prominent role derived from the aim to eliminate opposition to vigorous manpower cuts and to achieve monetarist goals that meant intensifying the process of managerialisation within departments, avoiding any veto by the Civil Service Department.

1983–1987: The Rise of Managerialism and Central Government Reform. MINIS and FMI, Lasting Reforms and the Open Structure Restructuring

The Embryo of Public Management Reforms: 1982–1984

This three-year period was very intensive for the reform of British public administration, as the results of archive research suggest. In 1982, there was the launch of the FMI, which was fundamental to securing a better spending review and developing managerial skills among civil servants. The year 1982 was also the year of the pension scheme reform after the publication of the Megaw Report. As far as concerned the administrative organisation, there was the abolishing of the Central Policy Review Staff (CPRS) and the merging of the Ministries of Commerce and Industry in a single department. In 1983, there was the appointment of eight new Permanent Secretaries and the appointment of Sir Robert Armstrong as the Head of the Home Civil Service. At the head of the Efficiency

Unit, Sir Robin Ibbs substituted Sir Derek Rayner, who retired from public life. In 1984 there was a restructuring of the Open Structure and it established the basis for the introduction of performance evaluation for civil servants. In broader terms, this was a transition period in which were created the embryo for the further general reform of the British Civil Service such as Next Steps Agencies and the completion of the managerialisation of civil servants' practices.

Lasting Reforms in Broader Terms

Despite their "quick and dirty" image (Metcalfe 1993), efficiency scrutinies prepared the ground for the next phase of reform. The revelations of specific instances of governmental waste and inefficiency confirmed popular prejudices and gave the political oxygen to the reform process as well as strength to reduce sources of internal opposition. Scrutinies made it possible to build a more general case for public management modernisation. The number and variety of actual cases of waste and inefficiency showed that bad management was prevalent and action could be taken to deal with it.

It was a short step from this to the proposition that a general process of management modernisation should be instituted. This second phase of change, Lasting Reforms, was a broadly based effort to improve general management in departments. Lasting Reforms was a theme formulated in parallel with scrutinies, but not developed in practice until after the scrutiny programme had been in place for two years. Rayner invented the formula to summarise the main elements of a general management reform strategy for government departments (TNA, CAB 164/1588, the reorganisation of central departments brief, January 1982). The objective, to shift from procedures-based administration to results-based management with an orientation towards year-on-year improvement in performance, required a knowledge of results and costs along with better methods of using human and financial resources (ibidem). Lasting Reforms relied on the concept of MBO, a philosophy strongly coloured by private sector experience. They assumed that a common stock of management principles could be applied throughout government (Allen 1981). The initiatives of Lasting Reforms showed marked differences from Scrutinies and can be summarised as parallel reforms of management in all departments, strengthening accountable line management, decentralising budget and cost control, and introducing a structure suitable for performance management.

Whereas scrutinies focused on individual instances of bad or inadequate management and proposed specific case-by-case improvements, Lasting Reforms, as the term suggests, were intended to establish the foundations for better management in the future, to be permanent. The main vehicle for doing so was the FMI. The FMI was a major attempt to reform the whole process of financial management in government with the aim of establishing better control of public expenditure. Reducing government spending was central to Mrs. Thatcher's political mission. Early attempts to get this reform process under way were frustrated, not least by the Treasury, which feared that decentralised budgets would weaken central control. Equally important, the FMI represented a challenge to the established practices of management in departments. It entailed changes in the whole methods and culture of public management. Because financial management reform had more far-reaching implications than scrutinies, the dynamic conservatism of the system had to be overcome by a more determined approach than the one that had established the scrutiny programme (Metcalfe 1993).

The FMI was launched in March 1982 after an extended period of bureaucratic fighting, described by one of its advocates as "the wasted year of the FMI." The subsequent White Paper (Cmnd 8616) of September 1982 specified three basic principles, to promote in each department an organisation and a system in which managers at all levels have: "(a) a clear view of their objectives and means to assess and, whenever possible, measure outputs or performance in relation to those objectives; (b) well-defined responsibility for making the best use of their resources, including a critical scrutiny of output and value for money; and (c) the information (particularly about costs), the training, and the access to expert advice that they need to exercise their responsibility effectively." The launch of the FMI was used as an occasion to emphasise that government was subject to permanent budgetary constraints. Departmental management structures and systems had to be redesigned to ensure tight control of resources and achieve better value for money. Great importance was attached to bringing together the previously dispersed functional responsibilities for policy, implementation, personnel and finance, so that a clear line of accountable management was established within departments. As with the scrutiny programme, some mechanisms were needed to drive the FMI forward. One was simply establishing a deadline of the end of January 1983 for all departments to assess existing arrangements and decide how to bring them into line with the FMI principles. The personal back office of the Prime Minister ensured that the deadline was taken seriously. The second mechanism was the creation of a central unit similar to the Efficiency Unit to oversee the development of the FMI across departments. The Financial Management Unit (FMU) was set up as a joint venture between the Treasury and the MPO to advise and assist departments in elaborating their plans and implementing them. It was a means of setting a common management agenda (Metcalfe 1993).

The unit focused its attention in three key areas: (1) the creation of MINIS-type (see next paragraph) top management information systems; (2) procedures and practices for delegated budgeting within departments; and (3) clarification of arrangements for managing programme expenditure, including the inter-organisational dimension of linkages between departments and non-departmental bodies through which public services are delivered. The pressures towards delegated budgeting and the redefinition of the financial relationships between departments and non-departmental bodies anticipated a move towards divisionalisation within departments which was to underlie the fourth, "Next Steps," phase of reform.

Lasting Reforms sought to be broader than just financial management reform. Concern with improving information about results originated the environment to create performance indicators. It also addressed the implications of new management practices for personnel policy, but there was little doubt that the FMI was the spearhead to start up a longer phase of administrative reform. They even included the review of the administrative forms, in order to simplify regulation and enable a better framework between individuals and the Civil Service, that took place between 1981 and 1982 and led to the abolition of 26,193 administrative forms and the reshaping of others (41,000) (TNA, CAB 164/1629, Review of Administrative Forms, Report to Prime Minister, January 1982) in order to streamline the relationship between citizens and the Civil Service. The review of administrative forms cost £250,000, and it produced savings of more than £5 million (TNA, CAB 164/1629, ibidem).

Subsequent developments of the Lasting Reforms can be seen as both an outgrowth of what it achieved and a response to its failure to bring public spending under control. The economic and political factors affecting the growth of public spending and public borrowing proved that the FMI was not sufficient. To overcome the status quo of the system, new initiatives were required, which, again, strengthened Mrs. Thatcher's strategy that macro problems could be solved by breaking them down into micro components as suggested by the strategic *Stepping Stones* document drafted by John Hoskyns and his team in November 1977 when Thatcher was the leader of the opposition.

MINIS and the Financial Management Initiative

The FMI was born officially on 8 March 1982 when the TCSC published its report on efficiency and effectiveness in the Civil Service (HC 236, 1981–2). It made a number of significant recommendations. In the committee's view, it was important that ministers should assume greater responsibility for the management of their departments. The effective management of departmental programmes, it believed, was at least as crucial to the country as the performance of ministers on the floor of the House.

To assist ministers in the performance of their new managerial role, the committee recommended that top management information systems known as MINIS, a system invented by Derek Rayner in 1980 and developed by the Secretary of Environment Michael Heseltine in 1981–1982 to improve circulation of information at departmental level, should be introduced in all departments (TNA, PREM 19/680, C. Priestley brief to M. Thatcher, 30 July 1982). In the world of Heseltine, MINIS decided "who did what, why, and at what cost" (1987: 16–20). MINIS was strengthened in 1983 with the Joubert programme, an organisational structure that fragmented the Department of the Environment into 120 "cost centres," each with an annual budget to cover running and staff costs. The two initiatives compared actual expenditure with planned expenditure, enabling the minister to conduct a systematic budget review. Heseltine considered MINIS as a driver to improve efficiency and effectiveness and he exported it to the Ministry of Defence when he moved there as a minister. The initiative was exported to other departments during the 1980s as well.

MINIS was designed to provide ministers and senior officials with systematically presented information which would enable them to review priorities, set objectives and allocate resources (Likierman 1982: 30).

Each year, departmental activities, performance and future plans would be assessed in particular to determine whether value for money was being achieved, and specific areas of work would be selected for detailed scrutiny in order to select new departmental priorities and resources allocation (Financial Management Unit 1984: Chapter 5). In Whitehall, the advent of MINIS was not welcomed with universal support. Senior officials giving evidence before the TCSC (see, for example, HC 236-II, 1981–2) argued that they were already doing much the same thing, that the system was not exportable to other departments, and that its applicability was heavily dependent on the personality of its sponsoring minister (Likierman 1982: 130). Others contested whether the return from introducing comprehensive reporting in some areas would justify its expense. In their view, principles of financial management should be applied only in areas of expenditure where they were directly relevant, such as in operational areas (TNA, PREM 19/680, Minutes, Meeting of Permanent Secretaries, 7 April 1982). However, Mrs. Thatcher strongly supported it and the Prime Minister's endorsement ensured that other members of the Cabinet applied it.

Next, the TCSC argued that line managers in the Civil Service should have more freedom in managing their resources. Therefore, it recommended that managerial authority should, as far as possible, be delegated from the centre of departments to operational managers. Then, it focused on policy and programme expenditure. In this field, it recommended that there should be an annual cycle of departmental programme reviews. The performance of each programme should regularly be evaluated and the results of the evaluations should be reported to the MPO and Parliament. The committee argued that all these operations should be harmonised through changes to personnel policy designed to encourage the promotion of better managers and the enhancement of their managerial skills. The FMI was the Thatcher Government's answer to these recommendations that were received in September 1982 with Command Paper 8616. The aim of the initiative was to "promote in each Department an organisation and system in which managers at all levels have: (a) a clear view of their objectives, and assess and wherever possible measure outputs or performance in relation to those objectives; (b) well-defined responsibility for making the best use of their resources, including a critical scrutiny of output and value for money; and (c) the information (including particularly about costs), training, and access to expert advice which they need to exercise their responsibilities effectively" (Cmnd 8616, 1982). The approach embedded in the principles of the reform differed markedly from the traditional pattern of management in the Civil Service. This had been forged by methods of organisation in which managers were motivated to concentrate exclusively on the quality of service they were providing; to be relatively indifferent to the costs of the service; and to spend little time confronting costs and results (Wilding 1983). In summary, the FMI prescribed a system of management in which: (a) objectives are set and ranked at the apex of a department and framed in terms sufficiently specific to provide concrete guidance for action; (b) the department is divided into coherent managerial blocks or business, each of which is responsible for the achievement of specific objectives; (c) each manager's objectives are settled as are the expense and borders of his or her responsibilities; (d) a chain of accountability is defined in which each manager is made responsible to the one person for his or her use of resources and programmatic performances; (e) the manager's authority to take decisions is related to her or his responsibility for action; (f) information systems are established to allow ministers, senior and junior managers alike, to monitor their performance against targets and adjust their activities and resources accordingly; and (g) cost and programme information is brought together at the top of the department to enable consistent decision-making about future priorities and resource allocation (Hunt 1986).

The new system could not be introduced entirely, but an incremental approach was necessary. Therefore, the FMU, which had been created as a guidance for the initiative and was composed of a dozen civil servants from the Treasury and the MPO, concentrated its attention on three specific areas of development (Cmnd 9058, 1983). First, following the government's acceptance of the committee's recommendation with respect to MINIS, the unit began work to introduce a top management system in each Whitehall department (Cmnd 8616, 1982; Cmnd 9058, 1983). Then, the FMU focused on the delegation of managerial responsibility. In cooperation with departments, it established a number of experimental projects in delegated budgetary control and worked intensively on the design for a decentralised management accounting system (Chipperfield 1983: 26–29). Then, the evaluation of programmes occurred. The government had not accepted the TCSC's recommendation for a structured cycle of review. Instead, the FMU was charged with responsibility for introducing effective methods to assess whether programmes were meeting targets and providing value for money. Early governmental reports were clear about the political, institutional and methodological obstacles which stood in the path of managerial change. The early reports drew attention to a host of difficulties which management reformers would have to face. In summary, these were as follows: (a) the Conservative Government had imposed tight controls on numbers of Civil Service personnel, yet these controls went against the grain of, according to departmental managers, the flexibility to vary the mix of resources at their disposal (Cmnd 9058, 1983); (b) a balance needed to be struck between flexibility within budgets, which increased the responsibility of each manager for the use of resources, and flexibility between budgets, preserving for senior management the ability to adjust the allocation of resources during the budget year (Cmnd 9058, 1983). Similarly, a balance needed to be struck between departmental flexibility and the Treasury's desire to exercise strict control of the expenditure; (c) if delegation were to be successful, the performance of the programme needed to be tested accurately. Developing adequate measures of performance, particularly the ones based on quantitative methods, posed formidable methodological problems (Financial Management Unit 1983: 10); (d) one important although long-term objective of the reforms was to combine management and budgetary planning. To do this, the timetables for the two needed to be combined, but this posed considerable logistical difficulties (Financial Management Unit 1983: 37); and (e) ultimately, the success of the reforms would depend upon the ability of the reformers to change behaviours and practices embedded in the British Civil Service. Whether the changes proposed would, of themselves, be sufficient to shift these attitudes was an issue at the forefront of the FMU's thinking as it embarked on what everyone recognised would be a thoroughly daunting task (Financial Management Unit 1983: 43).

In 1982, the process to introduce managerial practices in central government was definitely marching forward.

The FMI Further Development (1982–1987)

Between 1982 and 1987, there was published a series of reports which summarised, implemented and assessed the FMI's progress from the government's perspective. One of the first assessments to appear was the FMI's report on the development and operation of top management systems (Financial Management Unit 1984a). The unit reported that most departments had established systems which covered both administrative and programme expenditure and which collected information covering both past performance and plans for the future. However, further development was required to draw clear intradepartmental objectives and to test the assignment of managerial responsibility for programmes as well as administration. Considerable work also needed to be done to create effective linkages between the top management system, PESC and Estimates. The 1984 White Paper (Cmnd 9297, July 1984) revealed that effective progress had been achieved with MINIS. Each department, it argued, had to introduce a top management system. The system had established a useful framework within which ministers and senior civil servants could take decisions on the basis of resource allocation and they could manage appropriate changes in departmental organisation, setting up a vast amount of information. During 1984, the FMU provided a detailed survey of top management systems in five departments. It argued that the systems were generally well established (Financial Management Unit 1985a). This method needed to be implemented to allow top management to set plans for improved performance and value for money, to allocate personnel and other resources, and to review consequent progress as suggested by the officials of the Cabinet Office and the Efficiency Unit (TNA, PREM 19/1175, D. Barclay Report to M. Thatcher, 29 January 1984). By the time of the National Audit Office (NAO) report on the FMI (HC 588, 1986–7), the Joint Management Unit, the successor of the FMU, was doing not so much work in connection with the top management systems. The NAO Report showed the considerable level of progress which had been made by departments in adopting and operating systems which had already proven to be of benefit for both ministers and senior civil servants (HC 588, 1986–7).

In Budgetary Control Systems (Financial Management Unit 1984b), the FMU produced guidelines to instruct departments on how they should proceed with the delegation of financial responsibility. The unit proposed that departments develop a strategy, compatible with the framework set by the top management systems, for decentralising budgetary responsibilities from the centre to senior line management and their subsequent delegation even farther down the line. It was another step towards the separation between policy-making and policy implementation. Only when such a strategy was agreed could the function of cost centres and the assignment of managerial responsibility be implemented effectively (Zifcak 1994: 31).

In 1985, the FMU examined the issue of delegation from a different perspective, that of the PFO. In the report Resource Allocation in Departments: the Role of the PFO (Financial Management Unit 1985b), the unit, considering the experience of a number of departments, drafted a plan for the role that the PFO should play in an environment of delegated managerial control. It suggested that PFOs should relinquish their detailed controls in favour of playing an active role in establishing and monitoring the achievement of value for money targets for programme and administrative expenditure. The recommendation for the general framework was that the Treasury set a similar approach in relation to departments. The Treasury, it said, should exercise aggregate control through cash limits and personnel numbers. Beyond this, the departments should be given a block budget for administrative expenditure, leaving them maximum scope for the internal allocation of their running costs (Financial Management Unit 1983: 37).

In *Policy Work and the FMI*, the FMU identified a number of problems which arose when programmes had not been systematically evaluated (Financial Management Unit 1985c). Programmes had been misconducted or outdated, insufficient information had been produced to assess their value, and, without appropriate information, officials had not been able completely to advise the minister about criticisms of existing policy. Moreover, it recommended that new policy initiatives brought before Cabinet should specify their aims in terms of "what will be achieved, by when, and at what cost." Subsequently, each initiative should be evaluated in the terms proposed (HC 588, 1986–87: 19).

The early White Papers and official reports presented a picture of steady and real progress. Even where difficulties occurred, they were minor and would be overcome in the future, the publications insisted. These conclusions could hardly be different, considering that the reports were written by the reformers themselves.

However, in 1986 the initiative was evaluated from a more independent perspective. The evaluation demonstrated that the results were more mixed, asymmetrical and less successful compared with the early reports. The government accountant, Anthony Wilson, was the first to report (HM Treasury 1986). He led a team which examined the operation of a delegated budgetary control system in six central departments. He concluded that there were encouraging signs of progress in the delegation of running cost controls, operational managers had become more cost-conscious, savings had been made, and budgetary discipline had stimulated local managers to reorganise their work and implement the services. Nevertheless, progress between departments had been asymmetric and the "laggards do much to accelerate their progress by using the developmental work and experience already gained elsewhere" (HM Treasury 1986: 2).

The report concluded that to be effective, budgeting must secure the firm commitment and better involvement of senior management, strong relations must be built between budgets, outputs and results, and the environment created by central agencies must be continuously supportive (Zifcak 1994: 32). However, despite these recommendations, the report illustrated a fundamental criticism of the FMI's progress. Wilson found that top officials had not been sufficiently involved in the budgetary reforms: they hadn't shown enthusiasm for becoming managers (Richards 1987: 34). They had not exercised budgetary responsibilities themselves and they had not used top management systems to set objectives, match resources and allocate responsibilities. Finally, they had not been involved properly in the evaluation of budgetary performance. Although expressed in technical language, these criticisms were consistent. Wilson argued that greater emphasis should be placed upon the development of output and performance measures as the New Public Management paradigm recommended. He recognised that these presented a methodological problem when they were applied to policy implementation and he argued that these problems were matters of organisation and willingness rather than principles. The final part of the report considered the difficulties at the budgetary level. It declared that the manpower limits and centrally imposed pay levels had "represented the most serious detraction from credibility and realism of the whole budgetary process" (HM Treasury 1986: 17). As departmental planning systems became more complicated, Wilson proposed that the government agencies should be considerably more committed than they had been to devolved control. The Wilson Report was attacked by strong criticism in Whitehall. The Treasury didn't appreciate its conclusions, not least because the report suggested that central control must be relaxed (Richards 1987: 35).

The report by the NAO found greater favour in government because it was more positive. The NAO's paper was based on the evaluation of the FMI's progress in 12 government departments. The report concluded that substantial progresses had been made in the development of the management systems and no serious problems had emerged in the departments examined. The NAO found that all departments had developed top management systems which supported the setting of objectives, decisions on priorities, the allocation of resources and the review of the activities. Nevertheless, departments' targets should be formulated more clearly; objectives needed harmonisation at further departmental levels; and in many departments, integration had not yet been achieved between top management and the budgetary system. The NAO found that all departments had introduced budgetary control systems for their administration costs, but the range of costs covered by budgetary systems varied considerably within and between the departments analysed. Considering the remarks of the Wilson Report, the NAO also recommended that considerably greater emphasis be placed on the development of effective indicators of performance. It concluded that programmes should be reviewed periodically and review should concentrate on programmes whose objectives could clearly be defined and which offered good solutions to improve value for money.

These two reports seemed very different to each other. In part, the difference can be explained by the fact that, in its reports, the NAO was unable to contest the pillars of existing Treasury policy. It could just analyse whether or not a policy was operating effectively. Since the Treasury had already accepted departmental plans of work, the NAO was hardly likely to contest them (Flynn et al. 1988: 184). The moderate tone of the NAO's Report may also have been related to the close relationship that existed between the Comptroller and Auditor General, Gordon Downey, and the Head of the Efficiency Unit, Sir Robin Ibbs, for whom he had worked (Hennessy 1990: 614). Departmental officials are traditionally defensive in the face of the inquiry from the Auditor. Defences may have been down when the Wilson team proposed its less informal inquiries. On the contrary, the Wilson team were insiders examining what was happening inside. The NAO's officers were outsiders relying heavily on second-hand information. The two reports were, in effect, refereed by the Committee of Public Accounts (HC 61, 1986/87). It conducted its own examination of the FMI based on the NAO's findings. It was less cautious than the NAO had been in underlining dysfunction. The committee observed that departments had been developing their new management systems for nearly five years but not all had progressed as quickly as they should have. For many departments, full implementation was still many years away. Similarly, it concluded that delegated budgetary control systems had taken so long to develop that support for delegation in departments had been significantly delayed. Then, the committee turned its attention to policy evaluation and programme expenditure. It supported strongly the government's requirement that for new policy initiatives and reviews of existing policy, targets should be set in terms of what would be achieved, by when, and at what costs. The committee concluded by expressing its view that the FMI should be concerned as much with obtaining improved value for money by providing better-quality services as with the achievement of savings through greater efficiency. The FMI that emerged from these external reports, which expressed a different point of view with respect to the designers of the reform, underlined how this was far less radical than it seemed at first sight and that it was weakened by the departmental implementation (Zifcak 1994: 32). Obviously, some progress had been made, but it wasn't enough to achieve a substantial change. Indeed, many fundamental problems remained unresolved even five years after the initiative had been announced.

The Cassels Report: Improving Career Management and Training for a "New Breed" of Skilled Public Managers

These macro reforms, new management information centres, a decentralised style of budgetary delegation and increased accountability were all targets of the FMI. However, the FMI alone was not sufficient "without a new breed of skilled manager." Consequently, the FMI was being complemented by a set of improvements in financial management, like the ones suggested by the Cassels Report of 1983, including improved career management and training for those with potential to rise to senior positions. Taking advantage of the experiences of both the Fulton Report and Rayner Scrutinies, Mrs. Thatcher promoted a review to improve managerial training and techniques for the Civil Service personnel. Alongside the introduction of the FMI, a review by the MPO was established in order to examine personnel work within the Civil Service.

The review was coordinated by John Cassels, the department's Second Permanent Secretary, and the report he published was regarded as a blueprint for the future conduct of personnel management in Whitehall (Richards 1997: 33). The review's brief was to examine all areas of personnel work, ranging from recruitment, redundancy and staff movements to career management, in order to identify new methods with which to improve individual performance targets.

The Report had analysed nine departments and its conclusions were radical: staff to be appointed to jobs and not grades; increased job transfers with industrial and commercial managers; merit pay awards to reward individual effort and initiative; line managers to be allocated more responsibility and authority over personnel matters; and inefficient staff to be dealt with more swiftly (Cassels 1983). There were some criticisms. Civil Service unions argued that this represented a further shift towards the widespread privatisation of duties in Whitehall. The Levene appointment in 1984, soon after the report was published, certainly inflamed the situation: Michael Heseltine appointed Peter Levene, the Chairman of United Scientific Holdings, as a Chairman of Defence Procurement in the MoD. The paper proclaimed that "this was the most significant and controversial of growing numbers of secondments to the top levels of the Civil Service, which challenged the traditional appointment procedures overseen by the Civil Service Commission ... Levene had been appointed with a salary of £95,000, twice the normal rate for this post, without reference to the Commission" (Pyper and Robins 2000: 115). Although individuals were occasionally seconded to Whitehall from outside, a number of the appointments made following the Report prompted some interested parties to suggest that a form of "surreptitial politicisation" was occurring (Richards 1997).

However, these appointments, supervised by the Senior Appointments Selection Committee, were supported by the House of Commons Select Committee on the Treasury and Civil Service and the Royal Institute of Public Administration (1987: 61). They did not find irregularity in the functioning of the appointment procedure: "Only about 2 percent of the members of the Senior Open Structure are 'outsiders' temporarily brought into fill particular vacancies. Whitehall is too cautious in this respect. More could be done centrally to liaise with business, universities, and the rest of the public sector to seek out talent. More Civil Service posts should be publicly advertised, and applications for them encouraged from the existing Civil Service and from outside Whitehall." Interviewed by David Richards (1997: 34) in December 1994, Cassels argued that his paper was written "to produce a more professional Civil Service." He maintained that for a long time the Civil Service had been too professional in the handling of parliamentary affairs, which had enforced the effectiveness of ministers. In the same interview, Cassels expressed his position about the Civil Service in the early 1980s: "I am one of those who feel the Civil Service wasn't as good as it thought it was. It was really alarming how poor they were and quite a lot of things they should have been better at. Above all, they were professional at the politics of it but unprofessional at the realities of it and especially uninterested in implementation. The Civil Service is bad at implementation and always has been, because clever chaps can think up policies all the time, but find it dreary to apply them. We have never been good at doing that. We are always making mistakes."

Cassels then went on to argue that the Civil Service was top-heavy with policy-makers and was lacking at implementation level. He also pointed out that there had been an earlier, failed, attempt at reform that had occurred under the control of the Civil Service Department. He argued that "setting up the Civil Service Department had been a formalised attempt at that, but it turned out to be a complete fiasco. Rather surprisingly as well. [...] the CSD had come to look as though it were a vested interest, looking after the material welfare and privileges of civil servants and not being about an efficient, well-trained, professional Civil Service. That is how it seemed and that is how I guess it looked to Mrs. Thatcher" (Richards 1997: 35).

The Cassels Report was responsible for legitimising a new era in Civil Service appointments through the introduction of a new breed of official; it insinuated that the traditional path of promotions in a Civil Service career was not necessarily any longer "the ground norm." Indeed, a serving official in the Senior Civil Service group observed that: "In the 1980s, the Civil Service placed much more emphasis on personnel development, actively seeking individuals with the ability to manage change. There had been a shift away from what in the early 1960s would have been termed policy-makers, high intellectual types, to those with good interpersonal skills, competent runners of organisations, able to manage staff. People still needed high intellectual qualities but they do also need managerial and interpersonal skills. Therefore, the individual sought after is one capable of managing change and running a staff" (Richards 1997: 36, interview). A first step, which would be completed in 1987–1988 with the Mueller Report and the Next Steps, to study a private sector-style career organisation and flexibility had been made.

The Central Policy Review Staff Abolition: The End of the Government's Think Tank

One significant decision made by Mrs. Thatcher was her announcement, on 16 June 1983, that the CPRS was to be abolished (CAB 128/76, Conclusions of a meeting of the Cabinet. 16/06/1983). The origins of this unit, created to improve government strategy and coordination among departments, can be found in Mr. Heath's 1970 White Paper (Cmnd 4506, 1970). Having considered the importance of interdepartmental committees, the White Paper admitted that there was need to enforce them "by a clear and comprehensive definition of government strategy which can be systematically developed to take account of changing circumstances and can provide a framework within which the government's policies as a whole may be more effectively formulated" (para. 45). In February 1971, it announced the creation of "a small multidisciplinary central policy and review staff in the Cabinet Office" which will "form an integral element of the Cabinet Office and, like the Secretariat and other staffs in the Cabinet Office, will be at the disposal of the government as a whole. Under the supervision of the Prime Minister, it will work for ministers collectively; and its task will be to enable them to take policy decisions by assisting them to work out the implications of their basic strategy in terms of policies in specific areas, to establish the relative priorities to be given to the different sectors of their programme as a whole, to identify those areas of policy in which new choices can be exercised, and to ensure that the underlying implications of alternative courses of action are fully analysed and considered" (ibidem, para. 47). As the first director of the CPRS said, its first aim was "sabotaging the over-smooth functioning of the machine of government" or, as he argued another time, "thinking the unthinkable" (Lord Rothschild 1977). The CPRS was an experiment for the importation of "outside" ideas into a traditionally closed system of government: half its membership, which fluctuated at around 18, consisted of bright young civil servants from different departments, and the other half was made up of outsiders from university, industry and commerce who became temporary civil servants. The studies of the CPRS produced the Programme of Analysis and Review (PAR), which was, in turn, intended to reinforce the interdepartmental expenditure planning reforms (PESC) developed in the 1970s: PAR required departments to justify and defend their various policy programmes in interdepartmental discussion, albeit on a highly selective basis. Both CPRS and PAR were deliberate attempts to break down the isolation of departments by strengthening the collective basis of Cabinet decision-making (Fry 1995).

The government's overall strategy was to enforce the centre to prevail over vested interests of single departments. These experiments were too weak to break a very strong tradition of departmentalism and became difficult to implement after Mr. Heath left office. The PAR was abolished soon after Mrs. Thatcher became Prime Minister and substituted with the small Efficiency Unit led by Derek Rayner and settled under the Prime Minister's office in order to achieve better results with administrative reforms. The CPRS lasted longer and focused on principal Conservative policy issues such as privatisation and the curbing of trade union influence. Some political problems emerged a few weeks before the 1983 election from the leaking of a CPRS Report that advocated a sharp reduction in the role of the welfare state. It was, in the end, too small and too alien to survive without active prime ministerial support. It was abolished mainly because it served the Cabinet, and Mrs. Thatcher preferred a direct and personalised advisory service to the Prime Minister rather than a broader one to all ministers. Mrs. Thatcher's strong leadership, her preference for like-minded ministers and personal advisers and for "can-doer" civil servants in order to reduce the size of the public sector and improve its efficiency were powerful elements in reducing the resistance of departments in policy implementation.

From FMI to the Next Steps Executive Agencies

The FMI was a watershed for the reform of the British Civil Service in the early 1980s. After the spending review led by Derek Rayner and the manpower reduction, the FMI was a breakthrough in the reform and for the process of managerialisation in the public sector. Outside commentators also praised the FMI and the earlier scrutinies as a success, as underlined by Hennessy: "The first eight years of Raynerism represented … a formidable achievement in absolute terms as well as in comparison to anything that had gone before" (Hennessy 1990: 619). Permanent Secretaries showed enthusiasm for this reform. Hennessy (1990: 619) reported the opinion of one of the most influential mandarins of the era: "I never realised what an effort it would be turning this tanker around. But over the past year it has become clear that it (the FMI) will endure. If there was a change of government, we would still want to do it for our own purpose."

Despite this, not all the opinions expressed satisfaction with the FMI. Metcalfe and Richards (1987: 131), who studied this period of reform, argued the long-term, effective management reform was not just a matter of introducing new operational techniques and systems. Reform of Whitehall also had to consider the embedded culture of the administration, "the, often unspoken, set of assumptions about their role within which senior civil servants think and act. [A culture] ... where writing a well-constructed ministerial brief on a topical subject or steering a bill through Parliament has a higher value ... than implementing a new policy or improving the administration of an existing policy." The Civil Service unions argued it was contradictory to ask managers to be fully accountable for their spending, while allowing them little or no control over determining what the size of the budgets should be. They argued that the FMI's downfall, in relation to the demands of government, was "the allocation of real money to managers ... but giving them real money would, of course, mean giving them a real power down the line, the last thing that the central departments, or, for that matter, department-level managements, would contemplate. So we are left with the usual half-baked Civil Service compromise. Civil Service managers have all the rigours and disadvantages of 'developed power, without being allowed to exercise the power'" (CCSU Bulletin 1985: 17).

Whether or not it can be argued that the FMI stood on its own as a step forward in Civil Service reform, it certainly created a new ground. It encouraged a greater cost-consciousness by individual departments and, with it, the greater economies and value for money that the government sought. It also provided officials with a clearer view of policy objectives. The Cassels Report attempted to create a path towards the personnel changes in relation to these reforms. The FMI constituted the first moves towards a programme of decentralisation for Whitehall, which were later better defined by the Next Steps Agencies reforms. As Barney Hayhoe, the then Minister for the Civil Service, concluded, the FMI meant "a push to a greater decentralisation and delegation down the line ... will represent a highly significant change in the culture of the Civil Service ... Recruitment, training, promotion, prospects, and practice will be affected" (HC 38, 1982). The efficiency scrutinies, MINIS, Joubert and the FMI can be regarded as the legacy and evolution of the Fulton Report, based on the principle of the economy and efficiency. The FMI was not a period of revolution for Whitehall, but of continuous change, a step forward from the previous emphasis on effectiveness. The culmination of these changes provided the foundations for the government's largest scheme of reform: the Next Steps.

The Last Effort to Reform: Trade Unionism Transformation in the Public Sector, Civil Service Regulation, Pay and Performances, Recruitment and Training

Transformation of Trade Unionism in the Public Sector: The Government Communication Headquarters Case (1984)

The constitutional relationship between ministers and civil servants has altered in many important respects, and the changing character of trade unionism in the Civil Service is in parallel the cause and the consequence of the constitutional change that has occurred. The extent of that shift is well illustrated by the GCHQ case, which exploded in 1984. The Government Communication Headquarters (GCHQ) is an important part of the UK security system, whose main function is to provide information for government's intelligence. From its inception in 1947, the civil servants who staffed it had been allowed to join national Civil Service unions, and there were long-established practices of consultation between management and staff. However, between 1979 and 1981 there were seven instances of industrial action at GCHQ; most of these were minor incidents, but during the major dispute of 1981 the Civil Service unions decided to hurt the Thatcher Government by directing action at security and defence installations, and GCHQ was closed down for a short period.

The Government was angry and embarrassed by what it saw as an irresponsible menace to national security and took steps to negotiate an agreement that would prevent any recurrence. However, in December 1983, with meetings between unions and management imminent, Mrs. Thatcher privately issued an oral instruction in her capacity as Minister for the Civil Service, banning trade union membership among GCHQ staff. The ban, together with a decision to deprive GCHQ staff of the statutory right of recourse to industrial tribunals, was announced to the House of Commons a month later. It was announced that staff would be offered £1000 taxable compensation for the loss of their statutory rights (Drewry and Butcher 1991).

There was a storm of protest from many quarters, and the unions tried to persuade the government to accept a draft agreement to limit, but not ban, future industrial action at GCHQ. These representations didn't produce a compromise, and the Council of Civil Service Unions (CCSU) decided to seek a legal remedy against the government in the courts. In July 1984, Mr. Justice Glidewell gave a judgement which, although it rejected several of the points advanced on behalf of the unions, ruled that the staff at GCHQ had a "legitimate expectation" that they or their unions would be consulted before withdrawal of their rights and that the applicants were entitled to a legal declaration that the Prime Minister's instruction was invalid. The unions' enthusiasm was short lived. Three weeks later, the Court of Appeal upheld the government's appeal, accepting its contention that the decision to ban the unions and the procedures by which this had been achieved were governed by overriding consideration of national security, which the courts were not competent to question.

In November, this ruling was finally upheld in the House of Lords, though there were crumbs of comfort for the unions, particularly insofar as the law lords repudiated the government's contention that action taken under the royal prerogative cannot in principle be reviewed by the courts. The door was opened to litigation by civil servants and their unions to resolve many kinds of disputes about matters to do with employment and terms of service, so long as "national security" was not invoked by ministers to prevent judicial intervention. The government got its way, but at considerable cost. Whether right or wrong in principle, it was widely regarded as having handled the matter with harshness and inflexibility. Industrial relations in the Civil Service, already in a fragile state, were further damaged, and perhaps changed permanently (Fry 1995).

The case served to unite unions whose interests, in other contexts, were often divided. In seeking to defend national security, the government gave enormous publicity to the hitherto low-profile activities of GCHQ. The case went to the European Commission of Human Rights in Strasbourg early in 1987, and the unions failed to win a hearing before the Court. Despite this outcome, and whatever the legal implications of the GCHQ case, the crucial point is that the affair occurred, changing the balances between the Civil Service as institution and the unions. This event changed the relationship among politicians, civil servants and unions, making it more unstable and weaker.

The Armstrong Memorandum and the Renewed Constitutional Debate on the Civil Service

One of the most debated issues in the constitutional debates of the Conservative era involved the position of civil servants and the relationships among them and ministries. The rise of managerial issues in the public sector, the agencification process at the end of the 1980s and some episodes related to ministerial responsibility opened the discussion on the position of civil servants and the responsibility of ministries. The constitutional lawyer Geoffrey Marshall observed that "a clear and succinct account of the principle or convention of ministerial responsibility is not easy to give. One reason might be that the convention is, like most British conventions, somewhat vague and slippery—resembling the pro-creation of eels." Nevertheless, Marshall added, politicians carry on as if the convention does exist (Marshall 1984: 84–85).

The problem was that with the growth of government, which was affecting the span of control, and the consequences of the Crichel Down case and the appointment of the Ombudsman as regards the perception of the constitutional position ministers still remained responsible in the sense that they were in charge to report upon the activities of the government department of which they were political head to the Crown, to the Prime Minister, and Cabinet, and to Parliament. Civil servants remained non-political in the sense that they generally received their appointments independently of ministers, that they were not allowed to build political partnerships, and that they were not required to perform politically on the floor of either House of Parliament. Civil servants were required to appear before parliamentary Committees, but they were publicly responsible neither for the advice that they had given to ministers, nor for the efficiency with which they carried out their work. Allegations such as the ones pointed out by Clive Ponting that the Thatcher Government was "politicising" the Civil Service in one sense ignored the reality that politics has never been absent from the career Civil Service, which operates in the midst of it. As Sir Gwilym Gibbon once observed, nobody ever said that the higher civil servant should be a "political eunuch." What the career civil servant must abstain from being, he said, is a "political gospeller" (Gibbon 1943: 86).

By the time that the Thatcher Government had reached office, the Civil Service unions had made themselves much more consciously part of the wider trade union movement, and thus much more politically prominent, than, generally, the old staff association had tended to do; and especially, once they had established the centralised council of Civil Service Unions, these bodies represented a challenge to elected government of a kind that the Thatcher Government was disinclined to side-step. The Civil Service strike of 1981 could hardly be said to have been without political intent, because a defeat for government would have menaced its economic plans and its political survival. As it was, the government won, and in 1984 one of the ways it followed up its victory was, as we have seen, to ban union membership for civil servants working at the Government Communications Headquarters and its outstations. The excitement which this action provoked tended to distract from the wider question. Whether a career Civil Service could be heavily unionised when it was supposed to be a politically neutral body was a question that was easier to pose than to answer in a way compatible with an open society (Fry 1985: 122–145).

The disharmony that characterised relations between the Thatcher Government and the career Civil Service was characterised by a form of political loyalty. When the Thatcher Government engaged in "deprivileging" the Civil Service, in some cases disloyalty resulted. Of the "leakers" of the confidential information in the Civil Service who were uncovered, Clive Ponting expressed disgruntlement at the Thatcher Government's behaviour towards the Service material interests (Ponting 1986: 7), and related resentment was expressed by Sarah Tisdall and Ian Willmore (Pyper 1985: 72–81). Clive Ponting's behaviour in leaking material about the Belgrano was a "mistake," natural enough in the confusion invited by the behaviour of so many of the recent governments, was to act as a "political gospeller" and, thus, to fail to appreciate the essentially subordinate position of the official.

In February 1985, during the facts of the Ponting Case, Sir Robert Armstrong, as Head of the Home Civil Service, in consultation with other Permanent Secretaries, thought it appropriate to issue a note of guidance on the duties and responsibilities of civil servants in relation to ministers; it emphasised that the "British Civil Service is a non-political and disciplined career Civil Service, and those civil servants who could not accept the consequences of these arrangements should resign, while continuing to respect the confidences obtained during their work in the Civil Service" (HC 92-II, 1985–86: 7–9). The Armstrong Memorandum was unique. Never before had the head of civil servants publicly written and diffused in such detail what he believed to be the constitutional position regarding the relationship between ministers and civil servants. That the Head of the Home Civil Service felt the need to issue a document of this kind was evidence of the controversy which had come to surround the subject. And to confirm this, the Memorandum was given a generally unfavourable reception not only by outside commentators, who as a breed seem afflicted by compulsive reformism, but also by the FDA, representing many leading officials in the Service.

The embarrassment which the FDA had felt about the implications of the Ponting case for the relationship between ministers and officials had led it earlier to promote the idea of a code of ethics for civil servants. The first general statement of principle in the FDA's draft code stated that: "Civil Servants in the United Kingdom are servants of the Queen in Parliament. Executive government as a function of the Crown is carried out by Ministers who are accountable to Parliament. Civil Servants therefore owe to Ministers the duty to serve them loyally and to the best of their ability" (FDA News, December 1984: 3). This seemed to be much the same position as that taken in the Armstrong Memorandum's second paragraph, where it said that "civil servants are servants of the Crown" and that "for all practical purposes the Crown in this context means and is represented by the Government of the day."

It was, though, the independent status of the career Civil Service which was at the heart of the debate about the Armstrong Memorandum. The Memorandum was organised around the constitutional convention of ministerial responsibility and, hence, effectively denied that the Service could or should have an independent status in relation to the activity of governing. Those observers who considered the doctrine of ministerial responsibility to be a myth were naturally unfavourable towards the Memorandum, tending to prefer arrangements to be established which reflected what they saw as the reality of extensive Civil Service influence over ministers, even control of them.

The FDA also wanted these arrangements to be compatible with open government, and for civil servants to serve ministers subject to the explicit conditions, and informed the House of Commons TCSC of this (HC 92-II, 1985–86: 59–67). That Committee's Report on Civil Servants and Ministers: Duties and Responsibilities, published in May 1986, failed to address fully the core issues it was charged with reviewing, preferring to adhere uncritically to the reforming agenda of the time. At one point, the Committee declared that "the evidence that we have received does not suggest that the Government has made a convincing case against some form of Freedom of Information Act" (HC, 92-I, 1985–86, para. 6.5).

These considerations stimulated the Thatcher Government to manage the issues proposed by the Committee's Report (Cmnd 9841, 1986). The Westland affair "dramatically exposed the difficult nature of the relationship between Ministers, civil servants, and Parliament," the TCSC believed (HC 92-I, 1985–86: vii), though the affair primarily involved personal rivalry between two members of the Thatcher Government, namely Michael Heseltine, the Secretary of State for Defence, and Leon Brittan, the Secretary of State for Trade and Industry. These two Cabinet Ministers differed over what would be the best arrangements for safeguarding the future of the Westland helicopter company, which was in financial difficulties; Heseltine wanted Westland to be taken over by a European consortium and Brittan favoured the company being taken over by American-controlled interests. The matter came to be discussed in early January 1986, when Brittan authorised the disclosure of confidential material from the Solicitor General, which cast doubt upon the accuracy of a statement made by the Secretary of State for Defence. Heseltine resigned from government because his preferred solution to Westland's difficulties was ignored. Brittan was then forced to resign shortly afterwards, having seemed to mislead the House of Commons about events relating to the publication of the Solicitor General's letter. Whether or not the Prime Minister knew of and, hence, condoned the leaking of the letter became the centre of the dispute. That six civil servants were involved became another controversy. The six civil servants were Bernard Ingham, the Prime Minister's Chief Press Secretary; Charles Powell, Private Secretary in the Prime Minister's Office; Collette Bowe, Head of Information; John Mogg, the Private Secretary to the Secretary of State; and John Michell, Under Secretary in charge of Air Division, all of the Department for Trade and Industry; and the familiar figure of Sir Robert Armstrong, Cabinet Secretary and Head of the Home Civil Service. The Defence Committee of the House of Commons investigated the Westland affair, and in July 1986 it produced two Reports on the subject, together with a substantial volume of evidence. That Report, called Westland Plc: the government's decision-making (1986) examined the affair in detail, and it discovered nothing that was either novel or exciting. The Defence Committee sought to explain the uninteresting nature of its Report by pointing to the fact that, while it was able to summon Sir Robert Armstrong and another Permanent Secretary, Sir Brian Hayes of the Department for Trade and Industry, to appear before it, the Committee had been denied the opportunity to cross-examine Mr. Ingram, Powell, Mogg, Michell and Miss Bowe. The Committee recommended that the situation in which such exclusions were possible should be changed (HC 519, 1985–6, lxv–lxviii).

The government's initial response to this proposal was one of reception (Cmnd 9916, 1986, para. 44), and its attitude came under attack from some of its own supporters when the relevant Reports were debated in the House of Commons in October 1986. Two months later, the House of Commons Liaison Committee reinforced the calls for a relaxation of restrictions (HC 100, 1987–8, para. 19) and the government had earlier hinted at concessions. It was difficult to see what form such concession could take which would not be undermining of the type of career Higher Civil Service that was essential to running of British Central Government as currently organised. The most that the Conservative Government was likely to do was to make minor modifications to the Osmotherly Rules of 1980, the guidelines which state that civil servants who appeared before or who submitted papers to parliamentary committees did so "on behalf of the Minister," and a White Paper, published in February 1987, did no more than that (Cmnd 78, 1987: 4).

If the Armstrong Memorandum raised major constitutional questions, the answers were determined by structure. Civil servants were responsible to ministers. Their relationship with the Crown was an indirect one, unlike that of the armed forces, which were organisations of a different kind, not least in disciplinary arrangements and ordinary roles. More generally, civil servants did not seem to have a direct responsibility as servants of the Crown in addition to their role as servants of the Government of the day (Woodhouse 1994).

As the Memorandum highlighted, higher civil servants could not aspire to act as guardians of the Constitution in the same manner as some saw the Crown as doing in a political crisis or national emergency. They did not have any comparable responsibility for the continuity of the state, and besides the massive gulf in status, the Civil Service never enjoyed anything remotely like the popular authority of Monarchy. Civil servants did not have a prior responsibility to Parliament. Except in the case of Accounting Officers, they had no direct relationship with Parliament at all. Thus, there was no useful purpose served by suggestions that civil servants appearing before Parliamentary Select Committees should have more freedom to answer questions on policy matters.

To conclude, the Armstrong Memorandum only stated the traditional constitutional interpretation, given the structure of British Central Government at the time. The Memorandum was the first sign of reaction against a more unstable relationship between politics and the Civil Service. It aimed to enforce constitutional traditions in order to self-protect the

Civil Service from a more reactive politics which aimed to reshape it into a more flexible, less monolithic and less powerful institution.

The Changing Structure of the Civil Service: Pay and Promotion System

As in all developed bureaucratic structures, the pay and promotion system represents one of the pillars on which the administrative hierarchy is built and careers are organised. Civil Service wages seem to have been quite modest in the interwar period, when, of course, economic liberalism ruled, and they remained so until the "Priestley formula" for Civil Service pay, a creature of Keynesianism's influence, promised civil servants relatively high rewards. The promise of Priestley was often denied by income policies, but the main practical objection to the implementation of the fair competition principle, and the "relativities" that went with it, was the substantial overall cost of the resulting salary settlements (Fry 1995: 72). In much the same spirit, it attempted to reform the career hierarchy and to remove the index-linking provisions to the Civil Service pensions. Then in 1980, the Thatcher Government tried to cut the knot of Civil Service pay.

The government explicitly declined to implement the latest finding of the Civil Service Pay Research Unit as regards the broad mass of civil servants and then abolished the machinery concerned. The Megaw Committee of 1981–2 was appointed to review Civil Service pay, with the implication that it ought to try to turn the clock back to before Priestley (Fry 1985: 96–121). The expectations and the claims that the Priestley era had fostered were not easy to manage. The Thatcher Government did not help its own cause when it failed to abolish the Review Body on Top Salaries (TNA, CAB 164/1587, D. Rayner to M. Thatcher, 2 December 1981). Established in 1971 by the Heath Government, then supposed to be in economic free marketer mode, the Review Body had since then periodically made recommendations about the salary levels of the highest grades of the Civil Service and those of other public sector groups, based on outside comparisons with the private sector.

The formal objective of the team led by Sir Geoffrey Wardale, appointed in January 1981, was "to examine the contribution of different management levels to work involving staff of the Open Structure (excluding those in purely specialist hierarchies); to consider in the light of that examination the case for shortening the chain of command both by abolishing grades and by restricting the number of management levels in particular areas of work; and to make recommendations" (Wardale Report 1981, para. 1.1). In 1981, the Under Secretary grade accounted for 591 of the 784 posts in the post-Fulton Open Structure (Wardale Report 1981, para. 21), and with this number, its survival was possible. The Wardale inquiry concluded that "there are ... a number of Open Structure posts [that] can be removed and should be" (ibidem, para. 6.2) but that "there are chains of command in which all existing levels, using all available Open Structure grades, are needed, and where there would be a risk of serious damage if a level was removed. Therefore, no Open Structure grade should be abolished" (ibidem, para. 6.1). The extensions of unified grading, in the form of expanding the Open Structure, would take place under the Thatcher Government. The most prominent of recommendations of the Fulton Committee that had not been implemented had been its proposal that unified grading should be introduced from the top of the bottom of the Home Civil Service. As Fry (1995: 74) pointed out, "obstruction on the part of then Head of the Service, Sir William Armstrong, was blamed by some, and there was certainly opposition from the representative of the former Executive Class whose members' prospects would be disproportionately and adversely affected by a change to unified grading, which would primarily benefit members of specialist groups."

When the Open Structure was established in 1972, unified grading was only extended to Under Secretary level. Sir Robert Armstrong later observed that the further extension of unified grading had not been managed by his predecessor. It was an objective to be achieved by stages, and plans had been made to take such grading down to principal level (Fry 1995: 272–275). The reform of the Open Structure was discussed in the Cabinet by 1981 (TNA, PREM 19/679, L. Brittan to W. Whitelaw, 23 November 1981), when a preliminary draft was written in November 1981 soon after the abolition of the CSD. A first step was made in early 1982, when the Cabinet agreed in reducing the "administrative size" of the Open Structure, and in the review was included a new path for recruiting by 1983. With the amendment of the 1978 Order in Council on the Civil Service, it was established that the function of manpower management passed from the Civil Service Commission to the MPO (PREM 19/680, HM Treasury, *Review of the Open Structure Posts*, 2 July 1982).

The extension of the Open Structure down to Senior Principal and equivalent grades in 1984 encompassed some of the 5600 staff previously organised into approximately 100 grades (HM Treasury 1984: 6), and its further extension to Principal and equivalent levels in 1986 involved 5500 staff previously organised in approximately 60 grades (HM Treasury 1986: 6). Numbered grades, having been introduced at the top of the Service in 1984 and the Open Structure from 1 January 1986 onwards, had the following arrangement: Grade 1 Permanent Secretary, Grade 1A Second Permanent Secretary, Grade 2 Deputy Secretary, Grade 3 Under Secretary, Grade 4 Executive Directing Bands and corresponding Professional and Scientific grades, and Grade 5 Assistant Secretary and corresponding Professional and Scientific grades, Grade 6 Senior Principal and corresponding Professional and Scientific grades, Grade 7 Principal and corresponding Professional and Scientific grades. The rationalisation of salary scales seemed to be more in the spirit of the Fulton Committee than that of the FMI, although a more radical approach was indicated, as will be seen, by experiments with performance-related pay, which the Prime Minister made clear in April 1987 were being made permanent (HC 114 Deb. 6s. Written Answers, c.656) after they had been discussed in the Cabinet by 1982 (TNA, CAB 164/1709, *Policy on Civil Service Numbers*, report by T. Flesher, Downing Street, 2 December 1982; TNA, CAB 164/1740, *Civil Service Management Development*, report by MPO, January 1983).

There was little sign of reformism even in the restructuring of the lower grades of the Administration Group. This followed from the government's plan to introduce new technology into departments and its recognition of the need for the cooperation of the staff concerned, who in some instances would need to be redeployed. The main elements of the deal were as follows. The Clerical Assistant and the Clerical Officer incremental pay scales were shortened with effect from 1 January 1986. The staff in Clerical Assistant and related Data Processing grade were absorbed into a new grade of Administrative Assistant with effect from 1 January 1987. With effect from the same date, the existing grades of Clerical Officer and Senior Data Processor were combined to form the new grade of Administrative Officer, involving a general additional increase in the salary minimum six months later. Data Processing Staff retained their existing allowance. While the Local Officer II Grade in the DHSS remained a separate departmental grade, its members also received the same pay increases as the New Administrative Officer grade, with the result that its relative position was enhanced (Fry 1995: 275).

The most important point about the deal, and while it was worth exploring in detail, was that it was very much across-the-board settlement of the traditional kind. As a similar sort of settlement was obtained for what could still be described as the Executive part of the Administration Group, little seemed to have changed, but, also in the first part of 1987, a deal was concluded between the Institution of Professional Civil Servants and the Treasury which that department considered the first serious effort in its bid to establish a "new pay regime in the Civil Service" (Treasury 1987: 1). "The difficulties of introducing pay rates" in the Civil Service "related to merit proved immense," Margaret Thatcher was later to write, recalling that "we made progress, but it took several years and a lot of pushing and shoving" (Thatcher 1993: 46).

The Megaw Report on Civil Service pay was published in July 1982. And the sole trade unionist on the Committee, John Chalmers, issued a Minority Report (Cmnd 8590, 1982: 102–115) which kept the Priestley system, the recommendations in the Megaw Committee's Majority Report represented a compromise with the market (Fry 1985: 90–96, 115–119). The Majority Report argued that: "The governing principle for the Civil Service pay system in the future should be to ensure that the government as an employer pays civil servants enough, taking one year with another, to recruit, retain, and motivate them to perform efficiently the duties required of them at an appropriate level of competence" (Cmnd 8590, 1982, para. 91). The Majority Report used the argument of the comparability principle: "Civil Service pay increases and level of remuneration, including fringe benefits, should in the longer term broadly match those available in the private sector for staff undertaking jobs with comparable job weight ... the main comparisons used in the system would be of the trends of percentage increases in comparator pay rates in the current pay round. This information would be supplemented as soon as possible, and thereafter every fourth year, as a check, by information on levels of local remunerations... The data collection analysis would be carried out under the supervision of an independent Board" (ibidem, para. 101). The Civil Service Pay Information Board (ibidem, para. 125) consisted of five "independent-minded persons" appointed by the Prime Minister (ibidem, para. 128) and "to maintain demonstrable independence from the Civil Service management and unions, surveys, data collection, and analyses should be undertaken by management consultants on behalf of the Board" (ibidem, para. 129). What was named "informed collective bargaining" (ibidem, para. 9) was to be involved when the board presented the negotiating parties with its findings. The limits within which a pay settlement could be researched would be "the inter-quartile range," meaning the middle ranges of outside pay. Though the parties "would need to give weight to management needs" (ibidem, para. 102), the majority of the Megaw Committee believed that "the Government should regularly make it clear, as it has done to us, that the cash limit system does not necessarily imply a completely rigid control of pay increases on the basis of the initial assumptions" (ibidem, para. 219). The majority of the Megaw Committee recommended too that more emphasis needed to be placed on internal relativities, which had been the case under the Priestley system (ibidem, para. 195), involving discussions of them between management and unions against the background, where appropriate, of job evaluation information (ibidem, para. 103).

It was these observations that aroused the interest of the Institution of Professional Civil Servants, representing specialist groups, which, differently from the other unions, pointed out "the Megaw Report as the foundation on which a new pay system can be built." Another recommendation was that the Civil Service Arbitration Agreement should be revised to put the government and the unions on a more equal footing (Cmnd 8590, paras. 269–270). The Megaw Majority Report favoured too "arrangements to encourage more active departmental and line management involvement in relating pay to management needs and efficiency, and measures to relate performance directly to pay" (ibidem, para. 104). Incremental scales were only to be retained for grades below Principal and its equivalent (ibidem, para. 335), and even then related to performance as measured in annual reports (ibidem, para. 339). For grades from Principal to below Under Secretary, incremental pay should be replaced by merit rangers, again on the basis of annual report (ibidem, para. 344). The salaries of civil servants at Under Secretary level and above should continue to be settled without negotiation, after the receipt of the report of the Review Body on Top Salaries (ibidem, para. 355). As for index-linked pensions, the Megaw Majority did not need to replicate the work of the Scott Committee and restricted itself to recommending that civil servants' pension contributions should be made more explicit (ibidem, paras. 163–164). Both the Majority and the Minority Reports of the Megaw Committee were essentially Conservative in that they acted as if centralised pay determination and grading for the Civil Service as a whole would continue in broadly the same form, whereas decentralised arrangements encouraged by "business methods" had been already introduced with FMI.

The Megaw Majority Report did seem to make a concession to business philosophy in embracing merit pay, an idea of Sir Derek Rayner (CAB 164/1740, MPO Report, January 1983). There were, in fact, few new ideas in the world of Civil Service pay. Though it came to be largely forgotten later, the Fulton Committee, for instance, had recommended the introduction of performance pay, while at the same time endorsing the Priestley System (Cmnd 3638, 1968, paras. 226–229). The intellectual coherence of the Priestley Report was attributed to Barbara Wootton, who had a clear, socialist position she believed to be rational (Wootton 1955). She was alarmed at the variations in public sector pay, and the expression of the need "to bring order out of the present chaos" (Kahn 1962: 10) was a catchphrase to condemn pay based on "business methods" lines. Despite these criticisms, what the Thatcher Government wanted was to draw a line under the Priestley era and its "rationality." Obviously, there was not to be a clear resolution. That the Review Body on Top Salaries survived the Megaw Majority Report underlines the Report's conservatism. The Civil Service's pay arrangements had been developed with an intricate evolution during the 1980s, but the CCSU at least found the way for a new interpretation, as it made clear in a paper submitted to the TUC Public Services Committee in 1989: "Since the Government unilaterally abandoned pay research in 1981, the Treasury's pay strategy has been to continue to screw down Civil Service pay in the interest of containing public expenditure. In effect, annual pay reviews since 1981 had been cash limit driven at the expense of meaningful negotiation. As chronic problems of recruitment and retention and low morale emerged, the Treasury resorted to the pursuit of the flexibility, through ad hoc arrangements such as Special Pay Addition and Local Pay Additions, and ill-fated performance bonus schemes, generally with little or no consultation. These ad hoc pay arrangements failed to solve the problems and the Treasury was forced to discuss implementing long-term pay determination. The Treasury's general approach to the non-industrial Civil Service's emerging pay system is to promote a more selective approach, whereby pay is targeted at groups and areas where it considers there are problems, that is grades where there are recruitment and retention difficulties, or skill shortages." As the aim of the

Civil Service unions was to ensure a "settled, orderly, and fair national pay system for all non-industrial civil servants," the conclusion of long-term pay agreements was preferable to "the haphazard and disjointed arrangements" that had proceeded them, especially as the agreements involved union participation. All the agreements reached included a spinal pay structure, performance pay and a system for pay determination in the long period based on annual pay movements surveys conducted at least every four years of the levels of pay and benefits of jobs outside the Civil Service. All the arrangements also contained provisions for extra pay to be agreed for posts where there were recruitment and retention difficulties (CCSU Bulletin, May 1989: 69). It was in the autumn of 1985 that the Treasury proposed outline ideas for a long-term Civil Service pay agreement, nearly three years after the then Chancellor of the Exchequer, Sir Geoffrey Howe, had announced both the government's acceptance of the Megaw Report and the intention to seek an agreement.

The new system, established by the Government through a series of agreements with the unions in 1986 and 1987, involved the introduction of the pay spine and of pay spans. The pay spine was a sequence of pay points, arranged to provide suitable incremental progression, on which all staff covered by the agreement were to be paid with effect from 1 September 1987.

A pay span consisted of a number of consecutive pay points on the pay spine which were available for paying staff occupying posts within that span. Posts were to be allocated to spans according to their job weight and there was to be one span for each grading level thus determined. Categories, classes and grades as such were to be abolished and occupational groups were to be redesigned. Pay spans would be divided into scales and ranges. A pay scale or scales would form the lower part of a pay span, and provided that they were efficient, staff would normally progress in annual steps up the spine to the maximum of their scale. Staff who received a "Box 1—outstanding" rating for overall performance in their annual report and who were below the maximum of the scale were eligible to receive an immediate extra increment. They would then receive their normal increment on their incremental date. The provision was to apply within the limits of the maximum of the scale. Increments could also be withheld or withdrawn in accordance with the agreements set out in paragraphs 1247 and 1248 of the Civil Service Code.

The pay range was to consist of at least three points on the spine. Progression up the range was to be discretionary in the sense that it would not be automatic, but it would be in accordance with strictly defined rules and criteria. Increments in the pay ranges would depend on performances as assessed in the annual reports over a period of time. Staff would be eligible for consideration for an increment in the range in accordance with the following criteria: receipt of at least one Box 1 (outstanding) marking after reaching the maximum of the scale; receipt of at least three consecutive Box 2 (performance significantly above requirements) markings after reaching the maximum of the scale; receipt of at least five consecutive markings of Box 3 (performance fully meets normal requirements) or above after reaching the maximum of the scale; and if in the view of management, they merit such an award for consistently producing valuable and effective work. Further increments could be awarded after the elapse of further similar periods.

It was expected that if reporting and marking criteria were properly observed the staff who received range points would constitute no more than 25% of the staff at each grading level in each department. Range points could be withdrawn on a mark time basis where performance was deemed to have fallen off over a prolonged period. Additionally, range and scale points could also be used for other purposes: where, for example, particular and special difficulties of recruitment and/or retention would arise, they could be dealt with by identifying the group of posts concerned on the basis of function and/or discipline and/or location, and advancing pay for the staff occupying these posts up the span. Their pay scales would be adjusted accordingly. Other arrangements could be made to deal with particular problems when the other provisions of this agreement were unsuitable or inappropriate. There was to be an appeals procedure in accordance with paragraph 9973 of the Civil Service Code.

Between November 1987 and July 1989, the government made new long-term pay agreements with the unions that included the pay-for-performance mechanism.

The long-term pay agreement that the Treasury had secured for grades 5, 6 and 7 had involved over 20,000 staff. The agreement made with the IPCS had covered 60,000 civil servants as had that with the Inland Revenue Staff Federation (IRSF), while the agreements with the National Union of Civil and Public Servants (NUCPS) have embraced 100,000 civil servants and that with the Civil and Public Services Association (CPSA) approximately twice as many.

The CCSU observed: "All five agreements make provision for performance pay. In all five cases, however, the agreements have preserved existing pay scales and normal incremental progression. Performance criteria have been introduced only in respect to additional payments above the old scale maximum, and any pay achieved by performance is extra money on top of existing scales. The agreements have also been successful in eliminating many unacceptable features of the government's earlier experiments in performance pay in the Civil Service. In particular in place of a wholly discretionary system—with the dangers of favouritism and abuse—the agreements tie the performance pay to annual markings under the established Civil Service staff reporting system. The agreements also provide for an appeals system and for joint monitoring and review." The award of performance pay was introduced in order to limit the overall cost. The Council stated that: "Regional pay variation is not a feature of any of the agreements. Indeed, for the unions concerned, the agreements provide a framework for a measure of control over the Treasury's recent propensity to impose a non-negotiable flexibility, for example, Local Pay Additions" (CCSU Bulletin, May 1989: 69–70).

The extension of departmental discretion in determining pay and the resulting variation in the pay of officials of the same grade in differing towns and sometimes in the same one had alarmed the CCSU, which described the outcome of this "saga" as a "dog's breakfast" (CCSU Bulletin, July 1988: 97). More dispassionately, the NAO later concluded that "on the available evidence from the Treasury and the Department for Trade and Industry, Local Pay Additions are an effective, cheap, and flexible response to staff recruitment problems" but that "this is not so strongly the case for retention." "The future long-term pay of non-industrial civil servants will be determined by a system of informed collective bargaining," the Council argued to the TUC Public Services Committee in May 1989, believing that "provisions on pay flexibility do not run counter to agreements providing for a national framework for bargaining and the preservation of national pay rates" (CCSU Bulletin, May 1989: 70). Regional pay was not the only attack to the tradition of the Civil Service pay system.

From that perspective, performance pay had gained the unions' early opposition, and with provisions for its award reaching all the way up the service to Grade 2 and Grade 3 levels, its further application was easier to accept even for unions because it seemed to guarantee a greater uniformity in rewards. And for these reasons, the reform of Civil Service pay and structure became irreversible and permanent in the coming decades.

Changes in the Civil Service's Recruitment and Training

The real changes in the mission of the Civil Service Commission began in the 1980s when this had translated itself into a highly professional central recruitment agency. The 10% of recruitment that was carried out directly by the Commission was to the grade of Executive Officer and above to the equivalent grades in other administrative groups and classes. Writing in 1981, the then First Civil Service Commissioner stressed that departmental recruitment was subject to at least formal Civil Service Commission supervision (Allen 1981: 22–23). Following the amendment of the Civil Service Order in Council of 1978, this was no longer the case by 1982 (CAB 164/1587, "The Centre: Transfer of functions order," 16 November 1981).

In 1985 and 1986, experiments were made in the local recruitment of Executive Officers by the Board of Inland Revenue and the DHSS (Civil Service Commission 1987: 17). Departmental recruitment would seem to promote greater flexibility, and in the economic climate of that time, it could be expected that national pay scales would enable government departments with offices in the relatively depressed parts of Britain to locally recruit potentially very able people, even of university entrance standard as defined, and sometimes with the fundamental skills already developed, for even basic clerical work. In the more prosperous regions, the Civil Service was less well placed.

There was a high wastage rate in the clerical grades in such areas, and the reason for the local recruitment experiments mentioned earlier for the Executive Office Grade was that "the biggest problem in filling vacancies remains in London and the South East where unemployment is relatively low; the cost of living, particularly housing, relatively high; and competition from employers at its fiercest" (Civil Service Commission 1987: 14). Few observers seemed interested in the career Civil Service below its higher grades, despite the need to achieve efficiency also in the lower grades, and despite the fact that in modern times the Civil Service has always placed great emphasis on promotion from below.

In 1985, the MPO conducted a review for identifying and developing internal talent in the Civil Service (Eland Report 1985). The Civil Service Commission highlighted two years later that "we remain anxious to develop in-Service talent to the full; the aim is for the 50 percent of the fast stream to come from internal sources" (Civil Service Commission 1987: 16). This was at the same time that the Commission was turning down literally thousands of outside applicants for the fast stream. The abandoning of the wider graduate entry also determined that "for the first time Oxbridge candidates made up a minority of those appointed" to the fast stream when the results were declared in 1986 (Civil Service Commission 1987: 14–16). It might well have been a worrying sign that in the competition for the best graduate, the severity of which showed no signs of abating, as the Atkinson inquiry testified (Atkinson Report 1983: 6), the Career Civil Service was losing out.

No recruitment system can be better than the men and women presenting themselves for appointment, but it was evident that "research in 1970s established that the CSSB method had effectively predicted long-term potential for senior posts in the Civil Service," and a further statistical study of candidates selected between 1972 and 1981 and recorded as "fast streamers" and still in post at the beginning of 1992 came to the same conclusion (Clements Bedford Report 1992: 2–4).

Another innovation established by the Fulton Report of 1968 was the Civil Service College. After a decade of debate among civil servants and academics, the idea was to create a sort of ENA (École Nationale d'Administration) patterned on the French model to produce the new higher civil servants. However, this project never achieved this aim for several reasons. A Civil Service Department review team identified one reason in 1974: "The College, unlike the justly esteemed École Nationale d'Administration, is not an elitist institution. If it had been, it might have found it easier both to establish its repute with some of its more demanding critics and to fulfil the research and promotional roles proposed for it. On the contrary, it was proposed by the Fulton Committee and accepted by two successive governments that it should be a large-scale and broad-based institution. As such, it has been expected to provide a very widely assorted range of courses, more varied, probably, than those of any comparable institution in this country and of such divergent nature as to generate not a little ambiguity, and even some inner contradictions in its role. All this for a very large and constantly changing body of trainees of very widely varying abilities, experience, and degrees of commitment and enthusiasm" (Heaton–Williams Report 1974: 14).

Hence, the Civil Service College was supposed to cater for everybody, and in its early years at least it ended up pleasing very few people, including its first Principal, who was drawn from academic life and who wanted an elitist institution rather like the London School of Economics of Laski's time, to which the Civil Service unions were opposed.

As performance at the College was not important for their careers, the training provision for the Administration Trainees attracted criticism (Fry 1995: 267–272). The post of Principal went to senior civil servants from 1976 onwards, and the Civil Service College gradually established a role for itself as an efficient provider of Civil Service training. In terms of overall provisions, it was a minor role as, for instance, the College's Report for 1982–1983 made clear: "Departments rightly continue to provide the great bulk of Civil Service training from their own internal resources. Most have their own training centres and they were responsible ... for 75% of the total training (measured in trainee days). A further 20 percent was provided by external institutes—local authority night schools, further education institutes, polytechnics and universities, and business schools. The remaining 5 percent was the College's share" (TNA, JY/13, "Civil Service College Annual Report and Accounts," 13th Report, 1982–3: 3).

From September 1981, a modular system was introduced to meet formal training needs of the different phases of the early career of those in Administration Trainee and Higher Executive Officer grades. The induction courses were concerned with communication skills, with Parliament, Government and the Civil Service, and with Finance and Control of Public Expenditure. There were six modules available at the next level, including essential quantitative skills and also economics, government and the administration; later still, further modules were presented, notably Staff Management (Thompson 1984: 48–54). The continued prominence of economics and its related subjects reflected the subject matter of most administrators' work, and the supposed flexibility of modularisation did not disguise the lesser commitment of resources (Fry 1995: 95). Training in the non-industrial Civil Service in the late 1980s was reviewed by the National Audit Office (NAO), which observed that: "This compares favourably with the volume of training per person in the private sector. But a review of good practice in the private sector, carried out by the NAO in parallel with the Civil Service study, showed that in a sample of leading firms the training is differently distributed, with senior staff and high fliers receiving most training. In the Civil Service, junior and middle managers receive the most" (National Audit Office 1990: 1). This was despite the Coster Report of 1984, and the following Development Programme for staff between Principal (Grade 7) and Assistant Secretary (Grade 5) was started in September 1985 because "formal training had been neglected" and intended to be on a scale "well above the average for British managers" (Coster Report 1984; Coster 1987: 293).

Earlier in 1985, a six-week Top Management Programme for newly appointed Under Secretaries had been established (TNA/Civil Service College, Fifteenth Report, 1984–5: 5). The Senior Professional Administrative Training Course, designed for specialists transferring to administrative work, dated from as early as 1972 (Fry 1985: 49–50, 67–68). Sixteen weeks of early career formal training for administrators, though, was never going to impress those who were aware of the ENA arrangements and that institution's type of direct entry.

The Fultonite vision, at least presented by John Garrett 25 years on, was that the Civil Service College had become "gentrified" in "the way that educational institutions in Britain always go in that they always begin as technical colleges for ordinary people and end up as universities" (HC 390-II, 1992–3, q. 647). Garrett described the Civil Service College as having facilities that were "gold plated" (ibidem, q. 648) and as being like "Oxbridge with rhododendrons," enforcing "the mandarin image" (ibidem, q. 666). While the ENA might well aspire to a social status comparable with that of Christ Church or All Souls, Oxford College, the Civil Service College has never been in this league, and, though definitions of what constitutes a university keep changing, for most of its existence the College has had more in common with a technical college. The Fulton Committee neither sought such status for the Civil Service College nor did it do much to prevent it. Some of the Committee's members were interested in the ENA, presumably with the idea to import it, but this advocacy process failed, even because the Fulton Report itself was dependent on the Treasury's Osmond Report for the main body of such ideas as it had on post-entry training (Fry 1995: 207–214, 221–225). Far from having a mandarin image then or later, the Civil Service College always seemed abandoned in its early years, before designing for itself a role more coherent with the new Civil Service, to which was added the managerial approach that the Thatcher Government required even in the College's dealings with the Service. The Fulton Committee certainly wanted the career Civil Service to persist, but it also believed that it needed to be opened up to more later recruitment than had been common, which has occurred, and also to secondments, which occurred following the Fulton Report in 1968. The next step was in 1977, when the then government decided to seek a "sharp and significant increase" in the number of civil servants seconded to business organisations. In March 1989, Lord Young and Richard Luce, as members of the Thatcher Government, initiated the Bridge Programme "to build more bridges between government and industry," the aim of which was to further encourage secondments and job exchanges between civil servants and business people, the scheme being run by individual departments. Prior to this programme, targets were set for the Civil Service as a whole (250 outwards and 200 inwards). Under the Bridge Programme, an overall doubling of secondments took place (Gosling and Nutley 1990: 3).

A follow-up study found that civil servant secondees were regarded by private sector organisations as being "excellent ambassadors for their departments," and that, while the Bridge Programme might well lead to the formalisation of procedures, previously these had been haphazard (ibidem: 92). As far as civil servants' careers were concerned, the study concluded: "There was evidence from line managers and other departmental representatives that the idea of a lifetime career was changing. The 'velvet drainpipe' was leaking at all levels, through secondment, and through early leaving (sometimes as a result of secondment). This was not regarded as a particular problem, as a well-trained and informed civil servant would benefit the private sector. However, three large companies were very concerned lest the civil servants might be 'testing the water' before taking the plunge into the private sector. They saw their role as training bureaucrats for the Government" (ibidem: 91). Greater movement in and out of the Civil Service had long since become a familiar part of the reformer's agenda. Yet when Peter Levene was appointed to the Ministry of Defence from private industry in 1985 at a salary twice that of his Civil Service counterparts (FDA News, April 1985: 1–2), there was unease, which caused the Civil Service Commission to express the need to get the procedures right (Civil Service Commission, 119th Report, 1986: 7–9), a vision also present in several critical House of Commons reports about the dangers of higher civil servants taking up outside appointments (HC 216, 1980–1; HC 302, 1983–4; Cmnd 9465, 1984; Cmnd 585, 1989). However, the trend for external appointments would increase inexorably in the following years because of the Next Steps effect and because of the rise of special advisers' power in central government.

COMPLETING THE PUZZLE: TOWARDS NEXT STEPS REFORM. WORKING PATTERNS AND ADMINISTRATIVE AGENCIES

The New Civil Service Working Patterns: The Mueller Report

"Examination of working patterns outside the Civil Service shows that many people do not work from 9am to 5pm, 5 days a week with the prospect of a lifetime's employment and career advancement. Non-standard and alternative working patterns are increasing and becoming more widespread. The most significant trends are the wider and more imaginative use of part-time work, varieties of temporary work, shift-working, and sub-contracting, and the reduction of systematised overtime. The primary reason for this development is the economic pressure to reduce running costs by matching staff costs with work as closely as possible. The secondary reason is the availability of labour prepared, and sometimes demanding, to work non-standard patterns. Managers at local level have generally had the freedom and the incentive to respond by developing individual schemes which, taken cumulatively, amount to a significant change in employment practices." This was the theory, in a report called Working Patterns, explained by a study team led by Anne Mueller of the former MPO, that summarised some recent developments in the private sector (Mueller Report 1987, paras. 2.1–2.2), set out in a document dated September 1987 and circulated by the Treasury within the Civil Service and its unions two months later.

The Mueller team's examination of "alternative patterns of work being evolved by business and industry" was accompanied by a consideration of "what benefits these might have for the Civil Service and for the customers of the various services which are provided" (ibidem, para. 1.2). What was imagined in Working Patterns was what in effect would be a two-sided Civil Service, with a core Civil Service that would enjoy job security and career prospects, and a peripheral Civil Service that would be employed on a wide range of conditions of employment. These contracts would permit the introduction on a large scale of recurring temporary contracts; nil-hours contracts, which mean people being available for work but with no guarantee of it; annual-hours contracts, which state the agreed number of guaranteed hours an employee is contracted to work through a 12-month period; widespread part-time employment; part-time work for individual senior staff; fixed-term contracts; and provision for home working (ibidem, para. 7.1).

The benefits that followed from new working patterns of this kind were said to be the opportunities given for the better use of new technology (ibidem, para. 3.14), the greater ability to respond to fluctuations in workload and enhanced capacity to adapt to new demands in the labour market (ibidem, para. 2.4), notably by recruiting staff with low skills (ibidem, para. 3.21). The study team recognised that "some outside employment conditions and practices that are favourable to alternative working patterns are at odds with those that are generally regarded as essential elements of the Civil Service employment/career package or a distinctive characteristic of a 'good employer'" (para. 6.9). In the Civil Service as currently organised, the study team said "some regulations, such as those covering shift disturbance allowance, travel, and subsistence, superannuation and maternity leave, can constrain the efficient management of working time," adding that "the rules of annual leave, overtime, and substitution may not always operate to make sure that the needs of the work take precedence" (ibidem, para. 4.9). Substantially, what the study team which produced Working Patterns was pointing out was that the career Civil Service with its characteristic bureaucratic professionalism tends to make for staff costs to be effectively treated as if they were fixed costs, while the philosophy of the FMI was to treat them as running costs.

Hence, given the Conservative Government's will to persist with the FMI, the scale of the career Civil Service had to be considerably reduced, eventually down to a core. The study team argued against using the terms "core" and "periphery" on the grounds that "in general successful outside firms do not have one set of terms and conditions from which all alternative working patterns are seen as derogation" (ibidem para. 7.8). The career Civil Service possibly had as much standardisation as its necessarily complex structure could sustain, and the Mueller team recognised that maintaining the core of the career Civil Service and eventually developing alternative working patterns elsewhere risked "creating two classes of employee—the 'haves' and the 'have nots'." In Civil Service terms, any such move would be redolent of the worst features of established and unestablished service before the 1971–1972 pension reforms and would rightly be resisted (ibidem, para. 7.7).

The establishment issue was to do with security of tenure and associated rights, and the Working Patterns reforms were directed towards restricting tenure and rights. If the norm was substantially changed, then appeals against aberrations lost their force. "Working Patterns is a programme for revolutionary changes in Civil Service conditions of employment," declared the IPCS, accompanying its analysis with a picture of "the original nil-hours contract—dockyard labourers waiting to be offered work 'on the stones' in London Docks in 1931." The IPCS observed: "The Working Patterns programme of 'reforms' would sound the death knell for the role of government as a 'good' employer. In pay terms that has already been the case since 1980. The Cabinet Office Report would now kill off any remaining pretension that the government's own employment policies should set an acceptable standard for the rest of the community" (IPCS Bulletin, 2/88: 8–9). The unwillingness to consult the unions before the circulation of the Mueller Report seemed to offend the FDA as much as that document's "emphasis on cost cutting." The FDA could not see how adopting alternative working patterns that had the effect of diminishing job security would attract people to the Civil Service, but it gave a positive evaluation of some of the Mueller proposals because "we have a long-standing commitment to the extension of part-time work, which can play an important part in helping a civil servant to combine a career with domestic responsibilities; and we favour flexible working hours." The FDA then prepared a set of guidelines for negotiators which seemed designed to negate the exercise (FDA news, March 1988: 7).

The CCSU, in its response to the Mueller Report, sent to the Treasury in March 1988 research findings to challenge the evidence of changing working patterns outside the Service on which the Mueller proposals were based, before going on to give details of a "real alternative," meaning the further improvement of conditions of service (CCSU Bulletin, July 1988: 101–111). In the meantime, however, the main attention had turned to the Next Steps Report, in which proposals formulated in the Mueller Report found a definitive implementation.

The Birth of the Next Steps Report

"It was only towards the end of my time in government that we embarked upon radical reforms of the Civil Service which were contained in the Next Steps programme. Under this programme much of the administrative—as opposed to policy-making—work of government departments is being transferred to agencies, staffed by civil servants and headed by chief executives appointed by open competition. The agencies operate within frameworks set by the departments, but are free of detailed departmental control. The quality of management within the Public Service promises to be significantly improved," Margaret Thatcher wrote in her memoirs (Thatcher 1993: 49). The official history recorded that when, in the autumn of 1986, her Adviser on Efficiency, Sir Robin Ibbs, presented a critical review of progress in Civil Service reform since 1979, "the Prime Minister ... was disappointed to discover that, after seven years of effort to improve management in the Civil Service, so much still needed to be done. She commissioned Sir Robin to find out why, and to suggest how to move matters on." So "at the beginning of November 1986, Sir Robin Ibbs and the Efficiency Unit—a small team of civil servants and people from industry—began an intensive fact-finding exercise" (Goldsworthy 1991a: 3–4).

The scrutiny project was led by Kate Jenkins, a member of the Efficiency Unit and later its chief of staff. That team was given 90 days to complete the scrutiny. This involved conducting more than 150 interviews, including 21 ministers, 26 permanent secretaries, 26 grade 2/deputy permanent secretaries, a number of personnel and financial directors, nationalised industry chairmen and staff in local and regional office (Panchamia and Thomas 2014). The team collected opinions on how effective previous initiatives had been in improving managerial tasks, what measures had helped the most, what obstacles remained, and what future improvements were needed (Haddon 2012: 17). Following the scrutiny process, the team led a collaborative process with civil servants. A group of six most senior permanent secretaries, led by Sir Robert Armstrong, then Head of the Civil Service, was entrusted with testing and developing the new administrative structure. It included Sir Kenneth Stowe (DHSS to 1987, then Cabinet Office), Sir Brian Cubbon (Home Office) and Sir Clive Whitmore (Ministry of Defence). At this point, many senior officials didn't seem to understand the full implications of the process and where it was going. The Next Steps report seemed a standard research and it was not threatening in its methods, and for this reason they allowed the team access to information they might not otherwise have disclosed. The Efficiency Unit presented its report *Improving Management in Government: the Next Steps* to the Prime Minister in March 1987. The report argued early for a better organisation that resulted from the breaking-up of the Civil Service unity: "The Civil Service is too big and too diverse to manage in a single entity. With 600,000 employees it is an enormous organisation compared with any private sector company and most public sector organisations. A single organisation of this size which attempts to provide a detailed structure within which to carry out functions as diverse as driving licensing, fisheries protection, the catching of drug smugglers, and the processing of Parliamentary Questions is bound to develop in a way which fits no single operation effectively" (para. 10). So, in explicit contrast with the Fulton Committee, which recognised that the work of government departments might be better organised if each department employed its own staff independently, and built its own grading system, but then went on to endorse a unified Civil Service (Fulton Report 1968, para. 196), the Efficiency Unit was prepared to urge the breaking-up of the career Civil Service into many administrative agencies. "At present the freedom of an individual manager to manage effectively and responsibly in the Civil Service is severely circumscribed," the Ibbs Report observed. "There are controls not only on resources and objectives, as there should be in any effective system, but also in the way in which resources can be managed. Recruitment, dismissal, choice of staff, promotion, pay, hours of work, accommodation, grading, organisation of work, the use of IT equipment are all outside the control of most Civil Service managers at any level. The main decisions on rules and regulations are taken by the centre of the Civil Service. This tends to mean that they are structured to fit everything in general and nothing in particular. The rules are therefore seen primarily as a constraint rather than as a support, and in no sense as a pressure on managers to manage effectively. Moreover, the task of changing the rules is often seen as too great for one unit or one manager or indeed one department and is therefore assumed to be impossible" (para. 11). Then, as in the report of 1987 by the NAO and the Public Accounts Committee before it, the Efficiency Unit underlined the ineffectiveness of the FMI in the long term and that much more could be done. The price to achieve more efficiency and effectiveness would have been the changes to the Civil Service framework and organisation.

The Efficiency Unit reported that "it was clear the advantages which a unified Civil Service is intended to bring are seen as outweighed by the practical disadvantages, particularly beyond Whitehall itself. We are told that the advantages of an all-embracing pay structure are breaking down, that the uniformity of grading frequently inhibits effective management, and that the concept of a career in a unified Civil Service has little relevance for most civil servants, whose horizons are bounded by their local office, or, at most, by their department" (ibidem, para. 12).

The report outlined three types of activity: the "need to focus on the job to be done," staff should have relevant experience and skills, maintaining constant pressure for improvement. The implications of the report were long term and permanent. First, it recommended hiving off the delivery of functions of Whitehall into autonomous arm's-length agencies, which would involve transferring around 75–95% of the existing Civil Service out. Second, it recommended changing the skills and management of what remained of the machinery of government. Third, it recommended retaining a unit in the centre of government to maintain an institutional pressure for reform (Panchamia and Thomas 2014: 25).

Together, these solutions implied fundamentally changing the "genetic structure" of Whitehall and transforming the way officials conceived of their core functions and responsibilities. While progress was made on all three recommendations (e.g. the Top Management Programme was established to train Whitehall officials in management), only the first point, agencification, was pursued with success. The agencification process dealt with the concerns of middle managers and articulated their frustration with constraining central rules, but generated ambiguity, resistance and even opposition by other civil servants. The environment of Whitehall was cautious around the reform, primarily because of the enormity of the proposed change and the prospect of Treasury hostility (Panchamia and Thomas 2014: 26).

Margaret Thatcher supported the project in its aims. In the end, prime ministerial approval meant that Ibbs and Jenkins had significant influence to drive through the conclusions of the scrutiny process (Kandiah and Lowe 2007: 121). The Treasury was highly resistant, fearing a loss of control over public finances and upward pressure on agency expenditure. The first protest came during the phase of writing of the draft in February 1987, and the issue became discussed seriously in the summer of 1987 when the Treasury suspended cooperation with the process, causing something of a break. Nigel Lawson, the Chancellor, and Sir Peter Middleton, the Permanent Secretary of the Treasury, campaigned hard to block the publication (Kandiah and Lowe 2007: 126). Opposition was not limited to the Treasury, but came from different parts: the No. 10 Policy Unit, Thatcher's principal private secretary and press secretary, some ministers, unions and permanent secretaries. While some senior officials welcomed the opportunity to free themselves from management and delivery concerns, others feared the consequences of losing control over whole sections of their department. Unions were similarly divided: some concerns were that it was another step towards extensive privatisation, while others saw it was a chance to renegotiate management on staff and pay conditions, as the Treasury feared (Panchamia and Thomas 2014: 29).

Treasury support was fundamental to carry the reform on. However, Thatcher, under the advice of Ibbs and Armstrong, refused advice from the Head of the No. 10 Policy Unit, her chief of staff and her principal private secretary to make any significant step forward that would change the bulk of the report. This resulted in a long battle with the Treasury, which delayed the publication of the report by nearly one year. Lawson was eventually won round when he began to be convinced that Next Steps fitted with political commitment of using market models for public services delivery and it was a first step towards an extensive privatisation. Middleton remained sceptical for a long time and had to be "talked and drafted around" (Kandiah and Lowe 2007: 112). Finally, only minor wording and emphasis changes were made to the final report. This expressed clearer lines of accountability and slowed down the pace of reform by downgrading it to a pilot project (ibidem: 119).

At the ministerial meeting in July 1987, Thatcher asked all ministers to put forward candidates for the pilot stage. Although this stage was voluntary, departments were expected to produce at least two candidates, which "gave scope to enthusiasts and embarrassed others … into action" (Jenkins 2010: 118). Departments then analysed their functions and identified areas where agencies could be set up. Initially, departments put forward fairly modest candidates who already had a degree of autonomy. There was a conclusive effort to create an agency in more autonomous areas first and leave the more politically sensitive ones for later, when experience had been reinforced. During this time, wider developments could have distracted attention and stalled progress, including a general election in 1987 and a change in the leadership of the Civil Service that passed from Armstrong to Sir Robin Butler in 1988. This period has been considered a crucial time that, if not handled well, could easily have led to a disempowered agenda. However, the Efficiency Unit made a significant effort to communicate the importance of Next Steps to the Labour opposition to prevent it being abandoned if Labour came to power (Haddon 2012: 20). Important efforts were also carried on by the TCSC, which published its first, very supportive report in July 1988 when the Next Steps reform was considered as permanent (HC 494, 1988).

Considering the main managerial features introduced by the Next Steps report, it can be pointed out that the Efficiency Unit found that the pressures on departments were mainly on expenditure and activities, and that there was too little attention to results and value for money (para. 8). The management and staff concerned with the delivery of government services, which involved some 95% of the Civil Service, were generally convinced that the developments towards more clearly defined and budgeted management had been both positive and constructive (para. 3). At the higher levels of the Civil Service, though, the Efficiency Unit argued "senior civil servants inevitably and rightly respond to the priorities set by their Ministers which tend to be dominated by the demands of Parliament and communicating government policies" (para. 6).

Ministers, feeling themselves overloaded, complained to the Unit that, provided no major political risk was involved, they would be enthusiastic to improve managerial tasks. The Efficiency Unit stated "better management and the achievement of improved performance is something that the Civil Service has to work out largely for itself" (para. 7), but it would be "unrealistic to expect Ministers to do more than give a broad lead" (para. 7). The Unit knew the limits of the higher Civil Service and it noticed that "senior management is dominated by people whose skills are policy formulation and who have relatively little experience of managing or working where services are actually delivered." One Grade 2 official told the Unit "the golden route to the top is though policy not through management," and this was reflected by the early experience with the agencies system and the need for training for officials. The Unit argued "this kind of signal affects the unwritten priorities of a whole organisation, whatever the formal policy may be" (para. 4), and it added that "managing large organisations involves skills which depend a great deal on experience; without experience, senior managers lack confidence in their own ability to manage. Although, at the most senior levels, civil servants are responsible for both policy and service delivery, they give a greater priority to policy, not only because it demands immediate attention but because that is the area in which they are on familiar ground and where their skills lie, and where ministerial attention is focused. A proper balance between policy and delivery is hard to achieve within the present framework" (para. 5).

The Efficiency Unit concluded that the structure needed to be revisited: "The aim should be to establish a quite different way of conducting the business of government. The central Civil Service should consist of a relatively small core engaged in the function of serving Ministers and managing departments, who will be the sponsors of particular government policies and services. Responding to these departments will be a range of agencies employing their own staff, who may or may not have the status of Crown servants, and concentrating on the delivery of their particular service, with clearly defined responsibilities between the Secretary of State and the Permanent Secretary on the one hand, and the Chairmen or Chief Executives of the agencies on the other. Both departments and their agencies should have a more open and simplified structure" (para. 44).

By the spring of 1988, the Ibbs Report implementation to create executive agencies was added to the Mueller Report on working patterns, starting a process of changes in the Civil Service conditions, structure and organisation that would last for the next decades.

Implementing the Report and Building the Agencification (1988–1990)

The phase of implementation was embedded in the Next Steps Report to the Prime Minister. On the day of presentation, Margaret Thatcher spoke in the House of Commons supporting the report's recommendations and suggesting that the agencies should be created "to the greater extent," a statement that did not establish any limits for the agencification process (Drewry 1994: 583–595). Between 75 and 95% of civil servants would be hived off to executive and autonomous agencies focusing on service delivery. Central government would lose some of the detailed controls it held so that senior officials would have more time to concentrate on policy, while agencies would have more freedom to adopt business-like management practices. It was hoped that this would lead to more accountable management with specific targets, customer-focused services and better value from public expenditure. The underlying intention was to separate delivery from policy in order to realise better linkages between them (Kandiah and Lowe 2007: 108).

By 1988, even the Treasury was committed to realising this project. More generally, the aims corresponded with the traditional attitude that saw civil servants as highly effective as policy analysts, but as needing "to be preserved from doing what they were very, very bad at, such as the delivery of services" (Kandiah and Lowe 2007: 117). The entire environment was more supportive than it had been, but not completely aligned with what was to come. Having considered the challenging objectives of the reform, Thatcher appreciated that it was vital to have it project-managed by a Permanent Secretary, directly answerable to her. Peter Kemp, a Treasury senior official, was appointed the project as project manager and became a Permanent Secretary in the Cabinet Office. He was identified for the role because of his accountancy background and his hard-working mentality (Jenkins 2010).

While Kemp's role, experience and style gave him some strength, some senior officials were essential. In this sense, Robin Butler was hugely important in managing internal Civil Service tensions and gaining access to the Prime Minister when needed. Thatcher didn't offer high-profile support or a significant amount of her time, but made it clear that she supported the agenda and she would not tolerate continued opposition (Kandiah and Lowe 2007: 128). The combination of support gave Kemp the authority to complete the changes and that meant that no other departments, especially the Treasury, could stop him. The operating model was shaped by an analysis of previous reforms. The scrutiny process had revealed that an "initial flurry of ministerial activity was likely to fade, and implementation unlikely to be carried through, without a dedicated central unit" (ibidem: 128). Accordingly, a Next Steps Unit (NSU) was created, which led the reform strategy and had access to the Prime Minister and her staff, when needed. The Unit was composed of ten motivated and skilled people, including a Grade 3 director, a Grade 5 day-to-day manager and junior account managers. This model was inspired by the Efficiency Unit created in 1979 by Derek Rayner, which demonstrated that a small, focused organisation would create value and results, while a large one would only "add bureaucracy." The NSU was seen as a small team comprising "misfits," "slightly awkward people" and, unusually, a few outsiders, many of whom had a strong understanding of service delivery (Panchamia and Thomas 2014: 27). Following the leadership of Kemp, they were seen as "disruptive mavericks armed with an unwavering commitment to change things" (ibidem). The team worked towards a numerical target of 75% of civil servants into agencies and developed a clear set of processes around which a new agency would be established, and it later developed into a thirteen-point checklist of essential characteristics to create an agency. This involved conducting a review of pre-agency functions to control what was supposed to be delivered, what management techniques would make it work better, and how performance would be improved if the function was privatised, abolished or established as an agency.

Then, considering this review, the team would shape the relationship between the parent department and the agency in a carefully crafted, custom-made framework agreement, which set out the objectives, performance targets and resources assigned to each agency. This was drafted in consultation with the Treasury, and single negotiations would take place on any proposed changes to staff pay and conditions (NAO 1989: 3).

Finally, each agency was formally launched with a public statement from the relevant minister. A few years into the reform, the Treasury devolved more financial flexibility to agencies and an important element of this was the trading fund model. This gave agencies greater control over how they spent the money that they received from customers. The expectation was that profits would be reinvested into service improvements that customers would recognise, thereby improving how agencies related to customers.

Responsibility for the day-to-day operations of each agency was delegated to a chief executive. For these ideas, Kemp was particularly focused on recruiting outsiders such as accountants with experience in financial management. They would be held accountable for performance by a minister, who in turn would be held to account by Parliament for the agency's performance (NAO 1989: 12–13). During this development phase, the team invested an immense amount of time in briefing all those who were involved, coordinating networks, creating champions for reform and devising a communications programme, including booklets, public reports and a video which communicated that the reform was succeeding. Kemp ran regular meetings with agency chief executives to discuss common challenges and provided updates to permanent secretaries at the weekly Wednesday morning meeting, and he always had clear support from Butler, which ensured that the initiative wasn't seen as a revolution against the Civil Service but as a normal process of modernisation to cooperate with (Panchamia and Thomas 2014: 30). The Unit's primary measure of success was progress against coverage targets, which was published in an annual report.

External accountability for progress was largely provided by the Treasury Commons Select Committee (TCSC), which published annual reports in the first few years of reform. The TCSC could easily have sabotaged the programme, but Kemp, and later project managers, understood the need to keep it on side (ibidem). A significant amount of time was spent discussing recommendations openly and honestly, such as the need to strengthen accountability to Parliament, soon fulfilled though the creation of agency accounting officers. The TCSC became an important "reforming partner," playing a key role in publishing the changes more widely. Given that very few ministers were interested, and the opposition didn't really express a view, the only parliamentary voice was "intelligent and supportive" (Kandiah and Lowe 2007: 122–123). The day of the Next Steps presentation, Prime Minister Margaret Thatcher stated: "The Government will develop a continuing programme for establishing agencies, applying progressively the lessons of the experience gained" (127, HC Deb. 6s.c.1149).

The Next Steps Report considered the Boards of Customs and Excise and of Inland Revenue to be non-ministerial bodies with a defined statutory autonomy. In addition, the Prison Service Agency, the Defence Procurement Executive and the National Health Service Management Board were agencies within departments, and then there were some non-departmental bodies such as the Manpower Service Commission. As far as concerned accountability, officials with operational responsibility would be liable to appear before Select Committees of the House of Commons (Annex A, para. 8), and the powers of the Parliamentary Commission for Administration would be brought to bear on the agencies.

During the first series of inquiries by the Treasury and Civil Service Committee, Sir Peter Kemp stated: "I am Central Department Project Manager and I had a very small team—initially only three people—to help me" (HC 494-II, 1987–8, evidence, q. 9). In addition to this Project Team and the influence of osmotic discussions with the world of academia, think tanks and other professions, the Project Manager was supported by two other groups, as Diana Goldsworthy pointed out: "Closest at hand was the Project Executive, a small working group from the central departments—the Treasury, the Efficiency Unit, and the OMCS—which met weekly to think through some of the across-the-board issues as they came up, and to make sure that there was agreement about the way that progress was being made. The Project Manager also met informally each month with the Project Liaison Group, composed of senior representatives from the main departments. Here, ideas could be exchanged before they were worked up into firm principles. This helped to involve departments in the process of developing Next Steps policy and to get endorsement of the Project Manager's ideas. The aim was to foster support for and a sense of purpose about Next Steps at senior level" (Goldsworthy 1991b: 21–22).

Goldsworthy remarked, "Although the Government was firmly committed to implementing Next Steps, the policy itself was not publicly set down anywhere in any detail," and he continued: "Indeed, Sir Robin Ibbs's Report had described an idea, and sketched out, but no more, how it might be put into effect, so the policy had to be developed in the light of progress" (ibidem: 34). Peter Kemp, when asked in a session of Treasury and Civil Service Committee in May 1988 what percentage of the Civil Service he expected would be in agencies in ten years, answered: "I would be personally sorry if we did not get to at least three-quarters." As the agencies comprised "11 or 12 percent so far" of the Service, Kemp said that meeting his target meant that "the very large battalions like the DHSS, which has something like 90,000 people, come into the reckoning" (HC 494-II, 1987–8, evidence, q. 23).

In some cases, Kemp's plan in creating agencies in some areas of government was not shared by ministers. Nigel Lawson, the Chancellor of the Exchequer at the time, later wrote that he had "volunteered three of my outlying departments, the Stationery Office (HMSO), the Royal Mint, and the Central Office of Information, as executive agencies," but that "I did not, however, support Kemp's desire to convert the Inland Revenue and the Customs and Excise into agencies. These politically sensitive departments, with a small but important policy role, had long enjoyed a high degree of autonomy from political control so far as their executive functions were concerned, and converting them into agencies would have created no discernible advantage. Moreover, the only way in which it could have been achieved would have been to transfer their policy role to the Treasury, leaving them as purely tax-collecting agencies. This was something to which the Chairmen of the two Revenue departments were implacably opposed, arguing with some plausibility that policy advice was improved if it was informed by practical experience on the ground" (Lawson 1992: 392–393). Despite these arguments, the Boards of Inland Revenue and of Customs and Excise were designed by the Next Steps programme and, in June 1989, A.W. Russell, an official from the Board of Customs and Excise, made it clear to the Treasury and Civil Service Committee that the aim would be achieved (HC 217, 1988–9, evidence, q. 116).

In May 1989, Peter Kemp clarified that, even though the initial Next Steps target of creating 16 agencies by April 1989 had not been met, the target to move at least 75% of civil servants into executive agencies remained. "In fact about eight are now likely to be set up by July 1989," the Comptroller and Auditor General had stated in a report published 6 June 1989 (HC 420, 1988–9, para. 58). Peter Kemp replied in an evidence: "The unpublished report, although obviously available to the National Audit Office, I made to the Prime Minister in July 1988 did suggest that we might have expected 16 to be set up. In fact only five were set up. We now have seven. We did one last month, the Resettlement Agency of the Department of Social Security, and only yesterday the Civil Service College was set up as an agency. I am hoping very much there will be one more: the QEII Centre will be set up before we get to the end of July. You are quite right that makes eight out of 16" (HC 420, 1988–9, evidence, q. 4016). "We have not been able to go quite as fast as Peter Kemp had hoped," said G. H. Phillips, the senior official at the Treasury with whom Kemp had most regular contact, in evidence to the Treasury and Civil Service Committee, arguing, "First of all, it is important when you are starting off a new enterprise—and here we agree completely with Peter Kemp—that you set yourself an ambitious target in order to get things moving, in the knowledge that you may not be able quite to meet it. Secondly, in the process of dealing with the first few agencies we have obviously come across a number of across-the-board issues which have needed to be settled in relation to these particular agencies but which might then have application across government. Therefore it has been right to take time over doing them." Then, "in departments there has been a recognition that perhaps their timetables on some occasions were over ambitious" (HC 348, 1988–9, evidence, q. d263). The Treasury and Civil Service Committee argued for "an improvement in the pace at which executive agencies are created" (HC 348, 1988–9, para. 12).

"The Project Manager's judgement is that by next summer at least 20 agencies will have been established, with more to come," the Conservative Government reported in October 1989 in response to the Treasury and Civil Service Committee (Cm. 841, 1989: 3). "There will be 30 agencies established by the end of the next week," Richard Luce, a Minister of State involved, informed a Tory MP on 2 April 1990, adding, "We expect more to be set up by the summer" (170 HC Deb. 6s. Written Answer, c.386). In July 1990, the Treasury and the Civil Service Committee reported that "the situation this year is very different: 33 agencies have been established compared to eight a year ago" and "not only have more agencies been created: larger numbers are now involved. The largest agency created in the first year of the programme was the HMSO, with 3250 staff. In the past few months the Employment Service (35,000) and the Land Registry (11,000) have been launched. The total number of staff now in agencies is about 80,000" (HC 481, 1989–1990, paras. 8–9). The first Next Steps review was published in October 1990 and reported that "there are now 34 agencies ... by next summer we expect that there will be around 50 agencies up and running, covering 200,000 people" (Cm. 1261, 1990: 7). The reform was on its way and it was becoming permanently institutionalised, creating a new framework for the Civil Service.

CONCLUSIONS: FROM REDUCING WASTE AND MANPOWER TO A NEO-MANAGERIAL BUREAUCRACY

To conclude on this period, when on 28 November Margaret Thatcher left Downing Street in favour of John Major, the administrative reform of the Civil Service was running and a turning point towards modernisation in the history of this institution had been definitely reached. The yearly spending review, manpower reduction, executive agencies creation and functions hived off, new arrangements in the Civil Service pay, recruitment and framework, budgeting devolution, a new development of managerial skills and techniques and separation of policy-making and policy implementation had become regular and permanent. Probably, there was not an initial "grand strategy" by Thatcher Governments for the Civil Service reform, but the objective was to build a government that "works better and costs less" (Hood 2015). To achieve this result, there was a first "emergency" phase that lasted until 1983 and focused mainly on waste, costs and manpower reduction, considered as priorities to reduce public expenditure and to respect cash limits. The second "managerial" phase (1984–1990) was characterised by the shaping of a new administrative structure based on privatisations, contracting out, executive agencies, performance measurements and merit pay. In the following government, led by John Major, the breach in the traditional structure of the Civil Service opened by Mrs. Thatcher widened, managerial reforms continued to be implemented, and the traditional organisation of the Civil Service continued to be overhauled.

REFERENCES

Books, Journals, and Articles

Allen, F. H. (1981). The basis and the organization of recruitment. *Management Services in Government, 36,* 21–28.

Buchanan, J. M. (1960). *Fiscal theory and political economy.* Chapel Hill: University of North Carolina Press.

Buchanan, J. M. (1975). *The limits of liberty: Between Anarchy and Leviathan.* Chicago: University Press of Chicago.

Buchanan, J. M., & Tullock, G. (1962). *The calculus of consent.* Ann Arbor: University of Michigan Press.

Buchanan, J. M., & Wagner, R. E. (1977). *Democracy in deficit: The political legacy of Lord Keynes.* New York: Academic Press.

Burnham, J., & Pyper, R. (2008). *Britain's modernized civil service.* Basingstoke: Palgrave Macmillan.

Cassels, J. S. (1983). *Review of personnel work in the civil service: Report to the Prime Minister.* London: HMSO.

Chipperfield, G. H. (1983). *RIPA management information and control in Whitehall* (p. 2). London: RIPA.

Cosgrave, P. (1985). *Thatcher: The first term.* London: The Bodley Head.

Council of Civil Service Unions. (1988/89/90). *Bulletin.* London.

Drewry, G. (1994). The civil service: From the 1940s to "next steps" and beyond. *Parliamentary Affairs, 47*(4), 583–596.

Drewry, G., & Butcher, T. (1991). *The civil service today.* Oxford: Blackwell.

Drucker, P. (1977). *Management.* London: Pan Books.

Dunleavy, P. (1986). Topics in British politics. In H. Drucker, P. Dunleavy, A. Gamble, & G. Peele (Eds.), *Development in British politics* (pp. 329–372). Melbourne: Macmillan.

First Division Association. (1984–1989). *News.* London: FDA.

Flynn, A., et al. (1988). Accountable management in British central government: Some reflections on the official record. *Financial Accountability and Management, 4,* 169–189.

Friedman, M. (1962). *Capitalism and freedom.* Chicago, IL: The University of Chicago Press.

Fry, G. K. (1985). *The changing civil service.* London: Allen & Unwin.

Fry, G. K. (1995). *Policy and management in the British civil service.* Hemel Hempstead: Prentice Hall.

Gamble, A. (1986). The political economy of freedom. In R. Levitas (Ed.), *The ideology of the New Right* (pp. 25–44). Cambridge: Polity Press.

Gamble, A. (1994). *The free economy and the strong state.* Basingstoke: Palgrave Macmillan.

Garrett, J. (1980). *Managing the civil service.* London: William Heinemann.

Gibbon, S. G. (1943). The civil servant: His place and training. *Public Administration, 21*, 85–90.

Goldsworthy, D. (1991a). *Setting up next steps.* London: HMSO.

Goldsworthy, D. (1991b). *Setting up next steps: A short account of the origins, launch, and implementation of the next steps project in the British civil service.* London: HMSO.

Gosling, R., & Nutley, S. (1990). *Bridging the gap: Secondments between government and business.* London: Royal Institute of Public Administration.

Haddon, C. (2012). *Reforming the civil service. The efficiency unit in the early 1980s and the 1987 next steps report.* London: Institute for Government.

Hancock, C. J. (1974). MBO in the government service. *Management Services in Government, 29*(1), 16–26.

Hayek, F. (1944). *The road to serfdom.* Abingdon: Routledge.

Hayek, F. (1960). *Constitution of liberty.* Abingdon: Routledge.

Heclo, H., & Wildavsky, H. (1981). *The private government of public money.* Melbourne: Macmillan.

Hennessy, P. (1990). *Whitehall.* London: Fontana Press.

Heseltine, M. (1987). *Where there's a will.* London: Bloomsbury Reader.

Hewart, Lord B. G. H. (1929). *The new despotism.* London: Ernest Benn.

Hood, C. (1995). The "New Public Management" in the 1980s: Variations on a theme. *Accounting, Organizations and Society, 20*(2/3), 93–109.

Hoskyns, J. (1983). Whitehall and Westminster. An outsider's view. *Parliamentary Affairs, 36*, 137–147.

Hunt, J. (1986). *Managing people at work.* Maidenhead, Berkshire: McGraw Hill.

Jenkins, K. (2010). *Politicians and public services: Implementing change in a clash of culture.* Northampton: Edward Elgar Publishing.

Johnson, N. (1985). Change in the civil service: Retrospect and prospects. *Public Administration, 63*, 415–433.

Kandiah, M., & Lowe, R. (Eds.). (2007). *The civil service reforms of the 1980s.* London: CCBH Oral History Programme.

Kahn H. R. (1962). *Salaries in the public services in England and Wales.* London: Allen & Unwin.

King, A. (Ed.) (1976). *Why is Britain becoming harder to govern?* London: BBC.

Lawson, N. (1992). *The view from No. 11: Memoirs of a Tory radical.* London: Bantam Press.

Likierman, A. (1982). Management information for ministers: The MINIS system in the department of the environment. *Public Administration, 60*(2), 127–142.

Lowe, R. (2011). *The official history of the British civil service*, Vol. I (1966–1981). Abingdon: Routledge.

Marshall, G. (1984). *Constitutional conventions: The rules and forms of political accountability.* Oxford: Clarendon Press.

Metcalfe, L. (1993). Conviction politics and dynamic conservatism. *International Political Science Review, 14*(4), 351–371.

Metcalfe, L., & Richards, S. (1987). *Improving public management.* London: Sage.

Niskanen, W. A. (1971). *Bureaucracy and representative government.* Chicago: Aldine.

Niskanen, W. A., et al. (1973). *Bureaucracy: Servant or master?* London: Institute of Economic Affairs.

Panchamia, N., & Thomas, P. (2014). *The next steps initiative.* London: Institute for Government.

Parris, H. (1969). *Constitutional bureaucracy. The development of British central administration since the eighteenth century.* London: Allen & Unwin.

Pliatzky, L. (1982). *Getting and spending: Public expenditure, employment and inflation.* Oxford: Basil Blackwell.

Ponting, C. (1986). *Whitehall: Tragedy and farce.* London: Hamish Hamilton.

Pyper, R. (1985). Sarah Tisdall, Ian Wilmore and the civil servants' right to leak. *Political Quarterly, 56,* 72–81.

Pyper, R., & Robins, L. (2000). *United Kingdom governance.* Basingstoke: Macmillan.

Ramsden, J. (1980). *The making of conservative party policy: The conservative research department since 1929.* London: Longman.

Richards, S. (1987). The financial management initiative. In J. Gretton & A. Harrison (Eds.), *Reshaping central government* (pp. 22–41). Oxford: Policy Journals.

Richards, D. (1993). *Appointments in the higher civil service.* Strathclyde papers in government and politics, no. 93. University of Strathclyde, Glasgow.

Richards, D. (1997). *The civil service under the conservatives, 1979–1997.* Brighton: Sussex University Press.

Rothschild, N. M. V. R. B. (1977). *Meditations of a broomstick.* New York: HarperCollins.

Thatcher, M. (1993). *The downing street years.* London: HarperCollins.

Theakston, K. (1995). *The civil service since 1945.* Oxford: Blackwell.

Thompson, J. W. (1984). Fast-stream training at the civil service college. *Management Services in Government, 39,* 48–54.

Tullock, G. (1965). *The politics of bureaucracy.* Washington, DC: Public Affairs Press.

Tullock, G. (1976). *The vote motive: An essay in the economics of politics. With applications to the British economy.* London: The Institute of Economic Affairs.

Vinen, R. (2009). *Thatcher's Britain.* London: Simon & Schuster.

Wildavsky, A. (1979). *The politics of budgetary process.* Boston: Brown.

Wilding, R. W. (1983). *The need for change and the financial management initiative* (pp. 39–51). London: HM Treasury, Peat Marwick/RIPA.

Woodhouse, D. (1994). *Ministers and parliament: Accountability in theory and practice.* Oxford: Clarendon Press.

Wootton B. (1955). *The social foundations of wage policy.* London: Alllen & Unwin.

Zifcak, S. (1994). *New managerialism: Administrative reform in Whitehall and Canberra.* Philadelphia: Open University Press.

Archive Sources, Parliamentary Papers, and Official Publications

Atkinson Report. (1983). *Selection of fast stream graduate entrants to the home civil service, the diplomatic service, and the tax inspectorate; and of candidates from within the service.* London: Civil Service Commission.

Cabinet Office. (1979). *Standing order No. 152.* London: HMSO.

Civil Service Commission. (1986). *119th Annual report.* London: HMSO.

Civil Service Commission. (1987). *120th Annual report.* London: HMSO.

Clements Bedford Report. (1992). *Fast stream cohort research: Ten to twenty year follow up. Analysis of the relationship between CSSB procedures and subsequent job performance.* London: Recruitment and Assessment Service.

Cmnd 78. (1986-7). *Accountability of ministers and civil servants: Government response to the first report from the treasury and civil service committee and to the first report from the Liaison committee, session 1986-87.* London: HMSO.

Cm. 841. (1988-9). *Developments in the next steps programme: The government reply to the fifth report from the treasury and civil service committee.* London: HMSO.

Cm. 1261. (1990). *Improving management in government: The next steps agencies review 1990.* London: HMSO.

Cmnd 1432. (1961). *Control of the public expenditure.* London: HMSO.

Cmnd 3638. (1968). *Report of the committee of the civil service* (Fulton Report). London: HMSO.

Cmnd 4506. (1970). *The reorganization of central government.* London: HMSO.

Cmnd 7797. (1979). *Report on non-departmental public bodies.* London: HMSO.

Cmnd 8590. (1982). *Report of the (Megaw) inquiry into civil service pay.* London: HMSO.

Cmnd 8616. (1982). *Efficiency and effectiveness in the civil service: Government observation on the third report from the treasury and the civil service committee,* session 1981-2, HC 236. London: HMSO.

Cmnd 9058. (1983). *Financial management in government departments.* London: HMSO.

Cmnd 9297. (1984). *Progress in financial management in government departments.* London: HMSO.

Cmnd 9465. (1983–4). *Acceptance of outside appointments by crown servants: Government observations on the eighth report from the treasury and civil service committee.* London: HMSO.

Cmnd 9841. (1986). *Civil servants and ministers: Duties and responsibilities. Government response to the seventh report from the treasury and civil service committee, session 1986–87.* London: HMSO.

Cmnd 9916. (1985–6). *Westland plc: The defence implications of the future of Westland plc. The government's decision-making: government response to the third and the fourth reports from the defence committee, session 1985–6.* London: HMSO.

Conservative Party, Conservative General Election Manifesto. (1979, April). *Margaret Thatcher Foundation Archive.*

Coster, P. R. (1987, June). The civil service senior management programme. *Employment Gazette,* 291–300.

Coster Report. (1984). *Training for senior management study: Outline proposals for a senior management development programme.* London: Management and Personnel Office.

Eland Report. (1985). *Scrutiny of the means of identifying and developing internal talent. Central report and action plan.* London: MPO.

Financial Management Unit. (1983). *Report by MPO/Treasury financial management unit.* London: MPO, HM Treasury.

Financial Management Unit. (1984a). *Budgetary control system.* London: MPO, HM Treasury.

Financial Management Unit. (1984b). *Top management system.* London: MPO, HM Treasury.

Financial Management Unit. (1985a). *Resource allocation in departments: The role of the principal finance officer.* London: MPO, HM Treasury.

Financial Management Unit. (1985b). *Top management systems.* London: MPO, HM Treasury.

Financial Management Unit. (1985c). *Policy work and the FMI.* London: MPO, HM Treasury.

HC 38. (1982). Debate 6 s.c. 918. London: HMSO.

HC 54. (1980–1). *First report from the treasury and civil service committee: The future of the civil service department.* London: HMSO.

HC 61. (1986–87). *The financial management initiative. Thirteenth report from the committee of public accounts.* London: HMSO.

HC 92. (1985–6). *Seventh report from the treasury and civil service committee: Civil servants and ministers, duties and responsibilities. Vol. I Report. Vol. II Annexes, Minutes of evidence and Appendices.* London: HMSO.

HC 216. (1980–1). *Fourth report from the treasury and civil service committee: Acceptance of outside appointments by civil servants.* London: HMSO.

HC 217. (1988–9). *Sixth report from the treasury and civil service committee: Presentation of information on public expenditure.* London: HMSO.

HC 236. (1981–2). *Third report from the treasury and civil service committee: Efficiency and effectiveness in the civil service. Vol. I, Report; Vol. II, Minutes of evidence; Vol. III, Appendices.* London: HMSO.

HC 302. (1983–4). *Eighth report from the treasury and civil service committee: Acceptance of outside appointments by crown servants.* London: HMSO.

HC 348. (1988–9). *Fifth report from the treasury and civil service committee: Developments in the next steps programme.* London: HMSO.

HC 420. (1988–9). *Thirty-eighth report from the committee of public accounts: The next steps initiative.* London: HMSO.

HC 481. (1989–90). *Eighth report from the treasury and civil service committee: Progress in the next steps initiative.* London: HMSO.

HC 494. (1987–8). *Eighth report from the treasury and civil service committee: Civil service management reform: The next steps. Vol. I, Report. Vol. II, Annexe, Minutes of evidence and Appendices.* London: HMSO.

HC 519. (1985–6). *Fourth report from the defence committee: Westland plc: The government's decision-making.* London: HMSO.

HC 588. (1986–7). *The financial management initiative: Report by Comptroller and Auditor–General/National audit office.* London: HMSO.

Heaton–Williams Report. (1974). *Civil service training: Report by R.N. Heaton and Sir L. Williams.* London: Civil Service Department.

HM Treasury. (1984). *Civil service statistics 1984.* London: HMSO.

HM Treasury. (1986). *Multi departmental review of budgeting: Executive summary.* London: HM Treasury.

Mueller Report. (1987). *Working patterns: A study document by the cabinet office (management and personnel office).* London: HM Treasury.

National Audit Office. (1989). *The next steps initiative,* HC 410 (1988–9). London: HMSO.

RIPA Working Group. (1987). *Top jobs in Whitehall: Appointments and promotions in the senior civil service.* London: RIPA.

The National Archives (TNA), Kew, UK

TNA, CAB 128/66.
TNA, CAB 128/70.
TNA, CAB 128/76.
TNA, CAB 164/1587.
TNA, CAB 164/1588.
TNA, CAB 164/1628.
TNA, CAB 164/1629.
TNA, CAB 164/1709.
TNA, CAB 164/1740.
TNA, Civil Service College, Fifteenth Report, 1984–5.

TNA, JY/13, Civil Service College Annual Report and Accounts, 13th Report, 1982–3.
TNA, PREM 19/5.
TNA, PREM 19/6.
TNA, PREM 19/60.
TNA, PREM 19/62.
TNA, PREM 19/147.
TNA, PREM 19/148.
TNA, PREM 19/152.
TNA, PREM 19/243.
TNA, PREM 19/244.
TNA, PREM 19/245.
TNA, PREM 19/250.
TNA, PREM 19/679.
TNA, PREM 19/680.
TNA, PREM 19/1175.
TNA, PREM 19/Civil Service long-term manpower policy.
TNA, PREM 19/Civil Service, Annual Scrutiny of Departmental Running Costs.
TNA, PREM 19/Government Machinery.
Treasury. (1987). *Agreement on the pay, pay system, organization and personnel management agreements for grades and groups represented by the institute of professional civil servants*. London: HM Treasury.
Wardale Report. (1981). *Chain of command review: The open structure*. London: HMSO.

CHAPTER 3

Focus on Policy Implementation, Consumer Service and Marketisation: Civil Service Reform in the Major Government (1990–1997)

CONTINUITY AND IMPLEMENTATION: THE EXECUTIVE AGENCIES

On 28 November 1990, John Major succeeded Margaret Thatcher both as Prime Minister and Conservative Party leader, and he established a new Conservative Government as a result of a new political balance inside the party. As far as concerns the bureaucratic organisation that we are investigating, the main feature was a strong continuity with Thatcher's reforms. Furthermore, the influence of new managerialism in central government practices, and within it in particular New Public Management's doctrine (Hood 1991, 1995; Pollitt 1990), was becoming more widespread and influential.

The executive agencies were implemented and the Next Steps programme completed, privatisations and contracting out were widened to local public services, the Civil Service's manpower reduced, market testing was introduced in Whitehall, greater attention was concentrated on public services and delivery with the Citizen's Charter initiative, and a new system of recruiting was established with the idea of achieving more flexibility and opened the Civil Service to outsiders. Despite some differences in style, leadership and political environment, Major's government could be considered the continuation and the natural developer of Thatcher's programme and ideas on the public sector.

© The Author(s) 2018
L. Castellani, *The Rise of Managerial Bureaucracy*,
https://doi.org/10.1007/978-3-319-90032-2_3

123

Implementing Next Steps Agencies

By the early 1990s, the political context had become highly unstable and risky: the poll tax riots exploded, Thatcher left government after a revolt in her party and she was replaced by John Major, the Gulf War began, and a general election occurred in 1992, giving Conservatives another victory. Alongside this, many reforms were put onto the agenda, including the Citizen's Charter and Competing for Quality Programme in 1991, and they were announced by the new Prime Minister, speaking to the Conservative Central Council on 23 March 1991.

Peter Kemp, Next Steps project manager, was particularly conscious that these initiatives were a direct contest for the implementation of Next Steps reform. There was a strong effort to manage the effect produced by the programmes of the new government. Kemp and Robin Butler, the Cabinet Secretary, met the shadow Cabinet in the run-up to the general election and convinced them that "Next Steps was a transferable technology that could deliver a better model for whoever formed the government" (Panchamia and Thomas 2014a: 7).

In May 1991, John Smith, the shadow Chancellor, gave a speech committing the Labour Party's cooperation to the reforms. Butler worked to ensure that a possible change in the party government in the 1992 elections did not undermine the progress, by introducing new administrative interests for John Major such as increasing transparency and accountability through the Citizen's Charter into the narrative of the Next Steps (Haddon 2012: 20). By May 1991, 50 agencies had been established, including 50% of civil servants; 60–70% of chief executives had been appointed following an open competition; and about 35% came from outside the Civil Service.

In November 1991, the second Next Steps Review was published and it highlighted that the most important change of the year had been the creation of the Social Benefits Agency in April 1991, which employed around 70,000 staff (Cm. 1760, 1991: 57).

The Next Steps model began to spread more awareness of financial and budgetary issues, as well as an acceptance of external recruitment, normalising a process that just a few years before was seen as highly radical. However, some unsolved problems remained around accountability, especially about the relation between CEO and Ministers, as well as performance measurement (Panchamia and Thomas 2014a: 8). These concerns created the occasion for the Fraser review, which criticised the fact that there was no one in department responsible for controlling agencies, and it recommended a senior department sponsor for each agency to act as consultant on agency performance (Efficiency Unit 1991). In September 1992, Kemp left the Civil Service after a clash with William Waldegrave, then Minister for Public Services, and Richard Mottram replaced him as project manager. This change in leadership provided an opportunity to implement and enforce the reform programme. Mottram was a policy director at the Ministry of Defence and he had shown little interest in the implementation of the Next Steps report until his appointment as project manager in 1992, when he was appointed Permanent Secretary. In December 1992, Mottram's team reported the third Next Steps review, which recorded: "There are now 76 executive agencies, of which 20 have been launched in the last year together with 30 Customs and Excise Executive Units and 34 Inland Revenue Executive Offices working on Next Steps lines. Between them, they employ just over 290,000 civil servants, or slightly more than half the total" (Cm. 2111, 1992: 6). The fourth Next Steps Review, published in December 1993, stated: "Since the publication of the last Review ... 6 new agencies have been launched. These include HM Prison Service, the third largest agency, whose Director General (Chief Executive) is responsible for managing a mix of directly managed and contracted-out facilities, and the Child Support Agency, and the Northern Ireland Child Support Agency, the first official bodies to be established, from the outset, as agencies" (Cm. 2430, 1993: 6). Furthermore, the Review reported that "there are currently 92 agencies. Together with the 31 Executive Units of HM Customs and Excise and the 33 Executive Offices of the Inland Revenue, working fully on Next Steps lines, they employ 60 percent of the Civil Service" (ibidem: 6).

Mottram established a strong relationship with the Cabinet Secretary and he frequently accessed the Prime Minister. At this stage, Treasury resistance was "no longer an issue" (Panchamia and Thomas 2014a), even if Nigel Lawson, the Chancellor of the Exchequer, was sceptical about the appointments of the chief executives in the agencies, stating that "most of the Chief Executives are still drawn from the Civil Service" and denouncing the lack of openness and outsiders. The fourth Next Steps Review, of December 1993, stated: "Chief Executives are normally appointed through open competition to get the best person—whether a civil servant or an outside appointee—for the job. Of the 98 Chief Executives and Chief Executive-designate appointments made so far,

65 have been recruited via open competition. Of those, 35 have come from outside the Civil Service, from a wide variety of backgrounds including the private sector, local government, the National Health Service, and the academic world" (Cm. 2430, 1993: 8).

The government was slow in implementing open competition and the Treasury and Civil Service Committee repeated its view on open competition (HC 481, 1989–90, para. 28), hence in May 1990, the government made clear its position in a Parliamentary Answer by the Economic Secretary of the Treasury: "The first priority in selecting Chief Executives and other key staff for agencies must be to get the right person for the job ... Open competition will be considered in every case as a potential means of attracting talented people from inside and outside the Service." The Minister argued that "pay is usually based on normal Civil Service arrangements but more is offered if this is necessary to secure the right person" (HC 173 Deb. 6s, Written Answers, c.192).

The Treasury and Civil Service Committee pointed out in 1990 that "the Chief Executive's job at the Social Security Benefits Agency carries a salary about half the going rate in a private financial institution with a network of high-street outlets" (HC 481, 1989–90, para. 29). Chief executives were appointed on the basis of fixed-term contracts, which were not the same in each case, and Peter Kemp underlined that if they were responsible for major mistakes the consequence should have been their dismissals, because the government had "to fire the people in charge" (ibidem, q. 162).

About appointments for particular jobs in agencies, Kemp argued that: "These will be people with grades, because we are that sort of animal. There must be benchmarks for pay and that sort of thing, but they are still not in the hierarchical situation as they might previously have been. These are very special jobs and responsibilities delegated by the Minister personally ... they will be individually graded posts, but they will be rather more loosely graded" (ibidem, q. 175). As far as concerned the chief executive's responsibility, the Treasury argued in 1989 that "the Chief Executive's authority is delegated to them by Ministers who are and will remain accountable to Parliament and its Select Committees" (Cm. 914, 1989, para. 5.3), and it clarified that "A key feature of Next Steps is the personal accountability of Chief Executives to their Ministers for the discharge of their responsibilities as set out in an agency's framework document and for the achievement of performance targets" (ibidem).

The Treasury also stated that: "The Government therefore believes that the general rule must continue to be that civil servants who give evidence to Select Committees do so on behalf of their Ministers. In practice, where a Committee's interest is focused on the day-to-day operation of an agency, Ministers will normally regard the Chief Executives as best placed to answer on their behalf. The Chief Executive will be able to inform the Committee how his agency has performed its responsibilities. Ministers themselves will remain fully accountable for all Government policies. Agency Chief Executives will in addition be appointed Accounting Officers or Agency Accounting Officers ... Where the agency has its own vote, the Treasury will appoint the Chief Executive as Accounting Officer under existing procedures ... the Government also accepted that where an agency does not have its own vote and is financed by one or more sub-heads the departmental Accounting Officer will designate the Chief Executive as Agency Accounting Officer" (ibidem, para. 5.4–5.5).

In September 1990, the Thatcher Government feared that Next Steps could fail in its development; for this reason, Sir Angus Fraser, the successor of Sir Robin Ibbs as Adviser on Efficiency for the Prime Minister and the Efficiency Unit were asked to lead a study on the executive agencies "to investigate, in the context of development of the Next Steps Programme, the relationship between individual departments and their agencies, taking account of the responsibilities of the central departments to consider how departments ought to adapt their structure, size, and methods of working and to make recommendations" (Efficiency Unit 1991: 29). This work was completed in May 1991 and titled *Making the Most of Next Steps*, and it was also known as the Fraser Report.

The paper selected three areas in which the development of executive agencies could be improved. The first concerned the mission of any agency, and it argued: "Departments and agencies must develop and maintain a clear and shared vision of what an agency is there to do and of what its priorities and objectives should be. This is particularly important at the three-year review. The Project Manager should continue to monitor progress on these issues in his reports to the Prime Minister" (ibidem: 3). The Report also recommended: "We would expect departments and agencies to give a high priority to improving target setting. The aim should be for each agency to have a handful of robust and meaningful top-level output targets which measure financial performance, efficiency, and quality of customer service, over and above whatever subsidiary performance indicators are required for the agency's internal management purposes" (ibidem: 3). And it added: "There should be a firm timetable agreed between the agency, the department, and the Treasury for ensuring that all agencies have, by the time of the three-year review of their framework document, financial regimes suited to their business needs, including the associated accounting and financial management systems. The Project Manager should continue to monitor progress on these issues in his reports to the Prime Minister" (ibidem: 4).

As noted, the passage from the Thatcher to the Major Government didn't change the approach to public management. The Fraser Report focused on management by objectives, accounting and performance evaluation, tracing continuity in implementation with the previous government. The second area of development outlined in the report involved "empowering the Chief Executive," and it argued that "the objective should be to move to a position where agency framework documents establish that, with the overall disciplines of the cash limits and targets set, managers are free to make their own decisions on the management of staff and resources except for any specifically reserved areas. The exclusion of any area from the Chief Executive's authority should be positively justified. In order to achieve further progress in delegation, a first objective should be to revise framework documents on these lines at the first three-year review of each agency. This does not rule out an earlier review if the Chief Executive or sponsor department considers it timely. The Order in Council should be amended at the earliest opportunity to permit such delegation" (ibidem: 5).

The Report stated that "open competition should continue to be the conventional route for filling Chief Executive posts. Departments should develop for all Chief Executives, including those from inside the Service, schemes for remuneration which offer significant rewards for achieving results and clear and effective penalties for failure" (ibidem: 5–6). And it continued: "All departments should examine the full range of internal services they provide (including consultancy, inspection, and review services) and, in the context of their next annual plan, set out a timetable for moving to the provision and procurement of as many of them as practicable on a full costs basis. This would leave chief executives—and where appropriate budget holders within the department—free to decide where they can obtain best value for money. Where they continue to use HQ resources or expertise, whether or not on a charging basis, costs and quality of services should be clearly specified. It would be primarily

3 FOCUS ON POLICY IMPLEMENTATION, CONSUMER SERVICE ...   129

for the Treasury to monitor progress in this area in its discussions with departments on their plans" (ibidem: 6).

Here is reaffirmed the original idea of the Financial Management Initiative of 1982 in order to complete the process of budgetary delegation-setting constraints for departments and to let the chief executive free to manage the resources available. The third point of the Fraser Report was about the role, the organisation and the size of departments: "As the Next Steps initiative develops, departments should formulate a clear statement of their evolving role and the part their agencies play in the delivery of their policy objectives. The statement of the agency's strategic purpose can then be expressed in the context of the department's aims and objectives and become part of a shared vision" (ibidem: 7). The Report argued, "Departments should consider how best they can support Ministers in their roles in relation to agencies and identify a focal point at senior level for their dealings with each agency. The arrangements adopted should be clearly set out in the framework document and their effectiveness evaluated as part of the three-year review of the framework document ... The Accounting Officer Memorandum ... should be amended to clarify the respective Accounting Officer responsibilities of Chief Executives and Permanent Secretaries" (ibidem: 7–8).

It continued arguing that departments should agree with Treasury a timetable for establishing target staffing levels, preceded, as necessary, by a detailed review of their headquarters' functions, which needed to include the relevant posts in the Senior Open Structure. These reviews should be informed by wider advice from within the Service, including the Next Steps Project Manager, and by experience from the private sector and other parts of the public sector (ibidem: 9). The idea to open up the Civil Service continued to dominate the process of implementation of the Next Steps initiative, marking a change in the history of the British bureaucracy.

As far as concerned the role and organisation of central departments, the Fraser Report stated: "As the initial work demanded by the establishment of agencies declines, the central departments should review their changing roles in the light of the Next Steps and set new staffing levels for these functions. It will be even more important than in the past that criteria for selecting people to staff these functions should include experience of working in other parts of government, including agencies directly concerned with the provision of services" (ibidem: 9). The Treasury and the Office of Public Service and Science were worried about the implementation of the Fraser Report, and they asked a French official for a study to evaluate progress in the implementation of the Next Steps Initiative. The name of the official was Sylvie Trosa, and the Trosa Report was published in February 1994, six years after the Next Steps report. The Trosa study recognised the need to make order: "There was a need to make certain changes to the current arrangements" in the executive agencies' design in order to "avoid day-to-day interference in management issues; define a clear role for the centres of departments; and plan the evolution of the human resources of the departments" (Trosa Report: 1). It pointed out: "Those recommendations are as relevant now as they were when the Report was issued. That raises the question of why very little progress has been made on these issues since the Report was published. Several hypotheses might be made, but what seems clear is that one of the major reasons that relatively little has happened is that departments have not felt that it was in their interests to implement the changes. Given that part of the Fraser recommendations was for a 25% reduction in departmental staff dealing with central functions, perhaps this is not too surprising" (ibidem: 72). Then, the Trosa Report focused on the management of the agencies and it noted that there existed a considerable cultural gap on both sides, with chief executives often believing that departments' management was a bureaucratic obstacle, and departments viewing agencies as a little fortress following their own aims regardless. Too often senior managers in a department had no experience in man management. The fact was that many agencies bought fewer services from the centre and were more concerned with creating closer relationships with their clients. In that case, if a department does not make a special effort (such as an effective Advisory Board) to keep a certain unity, the divergence between agencies and parent departments can only grow (ibidem: 6).

The report aimed to create "more interchange of staff through mobility (still minimal), common training, networking etc., and the extension of Next Steps principles to the remaining parts of a department (probably fewer financial targets but more quality and improvement targets). Otherwise the fact of having two categories of staff (Ibbs Report) and two completely different ways of working can only create resistance and inertia (to go back to Trevelyan, the intellectual and the executive functions will remain separate)" (ibidem: 7).

Despite these reports on the implementation of the executive agencies, the Major Government focus had shifted from the executive agency towards the Citizen's Charter and the *Competing for Quality White Paper* by 1991. These occurred after the new general direction of the Next Steps reforms, but represented a challenge in terms of priorities since Major had never shown much interest in the agenda. Things became more complicated when in 1992, a Conservative counter-attack began immediately after the general elections. Backbenchers and radical voices of the party began to argue that public servants were escaping into agencies, which formed a barrier for privatisation, contracting out, or for the dropping out of functions (Kandiah and Lowe 2007).

It was crucial that the Citizen's Charter and Competing for Quality were tied in with Next Steps to ensure continued prime ministerial interest. Mottram made a great effort to achieve better coordination of these policies among civil servants employed in different departments and agency staff (Panchamia and Thomas 2014b). Eventually, all the reforms were integrated into the same narrative, giving the impression that the Prime Minister was absolutely focused on the reform, a behaviour that encouraged all the Permanent Secretaries, including the most reluctant, to implement the Next Steps (ibidem). By the mid-1990s, Next Steps had become a permanent reform and part of a very supported set of policies, which made it easy to underestimate how it had been contested a few years before. The Next Steps Unit developed the agencification process as a standard procedure; it was well experienced in implementing it and over the years it required less day-by-day attention. Agencies were created at a faster pace and in higher-profile areas, such as customs and revenue, defence, child support and prisons; by 1994, 99 agencies had been created, comprising 65% of the Civil Service (Richards 1997: 44).

With time, the process changed its pace, becoming slower and more ritualised (Panchamia and Thomas 2014b). On the other hand, the process of agencification began to stabilise and the agencies were considered as an institution of the Civil Service; in other words, they were considered the normal way things were done. The exact number of agencies meant that departments and ministers were less engaged in the design, approval and monitoring of agencies, and some Fraser suggestions, such as the use of external consultants to supervise the process, were never really put in practice. As some officials argued, with this method, numbers became the priority and they prevailed over quality. By the mid-1990s, the government understood that the framework agreements for individual agencies were not an incentive to improve performance. So in July 1995, Michael Heseltine was appointed Deputy Prime Minister and focused on the reform of public services. He fostered the development of a major public sector benchmarking project that would be able to compare performance of different agencies. However, these experiments were stopped by resistance from the Treasury and individual agencies, and they were never really implemented (James et al. 2011). In broader terms, this loss of focus on agency performance led to some high-profile IRA prisoner escapes, which led Michael Howard, then Home Secretary, to fire the agency chief executive, Derek Lewis. The case underlined the confusion in the roles and accountability of ministers and chief executives, as well as problems arising from a lack of support for agencies, poorly designed policies and underestimation of the resources required to set up an agency.

Prior to the 1997 election, Labour had publicly committed to the Next Steps programme, despite problems that derived from the erosion of ministerial responsibility. Once in power, David Clark, then Minister for the Cabinet Office, declared that "delegation is here to stay" and that Labour would not repeal the reform (Theakston 1995: 45–59). Soon after, the 1997 Next Steps report stated that more than 75% of the Civil Service was now working for the agencies. As a result, it announced the end of the main creation phase and closure of the central unit (Next Steps Report 1998). In the end, the reform resisted and the continuity was guaranteed by maintenance that introduced simplification and reduction in the number of agencies. Departments now had sole responsibility for their agencies, with little external support from a central unit. To conclude, the Next Steps initiative was a successful attempt to refresh and reinvent an existing Civil Service reform intervention such as Rayner's scrutinies and lasting reforms. It began ambitiously with the target of hiving off between 75 and 95% of the Civil Service to executive agencies and immediately had a huge impact on the framework of the central government. But the discipline and the cautiousness gradually decreased over time as agency creation became standardised and normalised. As political, and therefore official, the attention of the government focused on other initiatives such as the Citizen's Charter and Competing for Quality.

THE CITIZEN'S CHARTER INITIATIVE: TOWARDS CUSTOMER SERVICE IN CENTRAL GOVERNMENT

The White Paper that presented the Citizen's Charter opened with this statement: "All public services are paid for by individual citizens, either directly or through their taxes. They are entitled to expect high-quality services, responsive to their needs, provided efficiently at a reasonable cost. Where the state is engaged in regulating, taxing, or administering justice, these functions too must be carried out fairly, effectively, and courteously" (Cm. 1599, 1991). With these words was presented Major's big idea on public services known as "The Citizen's Charter," whose aim was to improve value for money for taxpayers, now called "consumers" or "customers," and also for public sector activities. A "lexical revolution" underlined how managerial culture was pervading the higher echelons of the British state.

The bulk of it was in a different concept of public sector organisation: "Choice can also be extended within the public sector. When the public sector remains responsible for a function, it can introduce competition and pressure for efficiency by contracting with the private sector for its provision." It continued: "Finally, choice can be restored by introducing alternative forms of provision, creating a wider range of options wherever that is cost-effective." It added: "Through the Citizen's Charter the Government is now determined to drive reforms further into the core of the public services, extending the benefits of choice, competition, and commitment to service more widely. The Citizen's Charter is the most comprehensive programme ever to raise quality, increase choice, secure better value, and extend accountability" (ibidem).

Indeed, Mr. Major's willingness to be personally identified with the Charter, and his determination that it had a high profile, was a consistent theme in the Charter's development. The Citizen's Charter Unit, which was responsible for the implementation, development and coordination of the Charter initiative, was part of the Cabinet Office. One of its tasks was to agree on the exact wording of any given Charter with the public service concerned. It should be pointed out that although the privatised utilities, as well as the Post Office, issued standards of service agreements, these were not counted as part of the Charter initiative itself.

The 1991 White Paper was a wide-ranging document, discussing, among other things, existing practices in the public sector, the powers of regulators over the privatised utilities, the use of market testing and contracting out to improve the quality of public services and future legislation to privatise some parts of the public sector. Arguably the most distinctive aspect of these proposals concerned the creation of Charters. Each public service would be required to issue a Charter, with two linked aims: first, to enable consumers to determine what were acceptable standards of service for that particular institution; and, second, to tell them how to go about complaining, and obtaining redress, if the service they were given fell below this benchmark. In short, Charters would empower those who relied on public services to ensure they obtained the standard of service they were entitled to receive (Seely and Jenkins 1995).

Inside the Charter

The first part of the Citizen's Charter was presented by the Major Government in July 1991. The Command Paper that established the initiative was about the key principles for the public services to raise the standards and quality. The general premise of the government was to promote "more privatisation" and "wider competition," using "further contracting-out," monitoring civil servants' work with "more performance-related pay" and "published performance targets." The guarantees to the citizens–consumers were based on the principles of "comprehensive publication of information," "more effective complaints procedure," "more independent inspectorates" and "better redress for the citizens when the services go badly wrong." The Citizen's Charter Programme spelled out six key "principles of public services" which every citizen was entitled to expect (Cm. 2101, 1992). They were: (a) Standards—the setting and publication of explicit standards for services and the publication of actual performance against these standards; (b) Information and openness—information and openness in the provision of services; (c) Choice and consultation—the provision of choice wherever practicable, together with regular and systematic consultation with the users of services; (d) Courtesy and helpfulness—courteous and helpful service from public servants; (e) Putting thing right—redress and well-publicised and easy-to-use complaints procedures; and (f) Value for money—the efficient and economical delivery of services within the resources the nation can afford.

From Charter to Charters

The implementation of the Citizen's Charter proposed by the White Paper provided for the creation of many Charters, one for every issue considered by the government. The aim of the Charter covered all the public services as well as services delivered by the Civil Service.

By 1993, there were over 30 Charters in the different branches of the public sector. The taxpayer Charter established what taxpayers could expect of the services provided by the Inland Revenue and by Custom and Excise, and targets were set for the time taken to reply to a customer's letter. The Benefits Agency and the Employment Service also produced Charters. These Charters gave an interesting framework for the Citizen's Charter's "big ideas." Here are some examples from the health care and transport sectors: "If you need to call an emergency ambulance, it should arrive within 14 minutes if you live in an urban area, or 18 minutes if you live in a rural area, or 21 minutes if you live in a sparsely populated area" and "On the London Underground, if you wait more than 20 minutes for a train, you should receive a refund voucher." About roads: "Contractors of road repairs will incur a financial penalty if they cone off more of the motorway than is strictly needed to do the repairs" (Cm. 1599, 1991).

The first Parent's Charter too was issued in 1991. It signalled the start of an information revolution to extend parental choice and to raise standards. It promised parents five key documents: "a report on their child's progress at least once a year; regular reports on their child's school from independent inspectors; performance tables for local schools; a prospectus or brochure about individual schools; and an annual report from the school's governors" (ibidem, 1991). As we will see below, these were not legal entitlements for the citizens, but they provided principles for the Civil Service and other administrative bodies to deliver better services. All these Charters were coordinated by the Prime Minister's Office as outlined by the 1991 White Paper: "The Prime Minister will appoint a panel of advisers for the Citizen's Charter initiative. A Unit will be set up in the Cabinet Office to coordinate the programme of action arising from the White Paper" (ibidem: 7).

To conclude on this point, it has to be pointed out that some organisations were not covered, such as universities, and even a number of private sector organisations were seeking to employ the Charter technique.

The government said it was reluctant to force Charters on the privatised utilities, but the Charter principles were to be pressed on the utilities via the regulatory offices. A number of local authorities had already been using Charter documents to set out standards of service. In each case, the Charter documents were to set out the standards of service that the user could expect, but the precise status of these documents was difficult to ascertain. Formally, Charters had not legal effectiveness, but these documents could be characterised as customer service contracts or customer guarantees and, as such, they clarified the standard of service which the customer was entitled, in principle, to receive (Barron and Scott 1992).

The Citizen's Charter and Its Relationship with Government Departments and Next Steps Agencies

A few days after 22 July 1991, the date of the official launch, the Citizen's Charter Unit was established in the Cabinet Office. The unit was responsible for examining draft Charters, it had 30 staff, and it was directed by Diana Goldsworthy (1991–1993), a civil servant of the Ministry of Defence, and Genie Turton (1993–1997), a deputy secretary from the Department of Environment. The unit worked in parallel with an Advisory Panel chaired by the chief executive of Boots plc, which reported to the Prime Minister. After the launch of the Citizen's Charter, a number of individual Charters were written by several departments and Next Step Agencies.

In 1992, the Prime Minister's Office developed the Charter Marks award, described by the Citizen's Charter Unit as "the Oscar for public services." The winners of these annual awards, who met the goals established and reached high levels of customer satisfaction, were entitled to use the Charter Mark logo for three years.

The Charter Unit also ran different activities promoted to exchange information and ideas across the public services, including Charter quality networks and seminars. Another step towards the implementation was in 1993 when the Citizen's Charter Complaints Task Force was created under the leadership of Lady Wilcox. The Task Force included members from the public and the private sectors, and they examined how complaints systems in the public services were working. The Task Force published its report in July 1995, and it wrote a *Good Practice Guide* for use by public service managers and staff (Seely and Jenkins 1995). Interactions between programmes and continuity with the past became evident in the case of the Next Steps programme and the Citizen's Charter. As we have seen, the Next Steps Initiative resulted in substantial hiving off of government functions from the Whitehall departments to executive agencies. In the early nineties, the Civil Service was "federalised" into these independent executive agencies with their own budget and functions in providing public services. This fragmentation of the Civil

Service was the premise to develop further reforms such as privatisations, contracting out, performance management and measurement. Indeed, within each executive agency, these new policies were easier to promote and to manage compared to large departments. The key aspect of this innovation was the separation of policy-making from service provision, a principle embodied in reforms throughout the public sector. The main objective was to further devolve managerial freedom subject to strict financial constraints, thus creating a working environment for managers equivalent to that of a private sector business. All services to the new agencies were to be properly costed and financed, whether coming from within other government agencies or the private sector. Thus, the incentives towards meeting the requirements of economy, efficiency and effectiveness were similar to those in the private sector.

This new organisational framework was functional to progressively shift the focus of administrative reforms from departmental organisation to public services delivery managed by smaller administrative units. This was even the case of the Citizen's Charter initiative. For this reason, each executive agency established its Charter, fixing the standards of the specific public service they provided. This process was named "charterism" to point out the flourishing of Charters drafted by executive agencies and to enhance the new polycentric and pluralist organisation of the public sector.

The Results of the Charter

The most detailed information on the operation of the Citizen's Charter lies in the two Citizen's Charter Reports, prepared by the government and published in November 1992 (Cm. 2101) and March 1994 (Cm. 2540). There was no fixed timetable for the publication of these Reports, and, as yet, a third report was never produced. Both Reports contain a great deal of information on how individual public services implemented the principles of the Charter in practice, though, as it has already been pointed out, neither the 1991 White Paper, nor any other publication, had set down a single set of tools for judging all public sectors' performance in this respect. It was argued that the production of this information is, in itself, proof of the Charter's success; the idea of the public services publishing their own standards was an innovation. Of course, the opposite vision had been argued: that by requiring services to publish measurable standards, performance would be turned towards certain types of activities, practically those that are easiest to measure or improve. Aside from this, it had proved more difficult to use this type of information in assessing the quality of public services themselves.

A success for the Major Government, it was the impact that the Charter had had, since its inception, on public expenditure. This aim was discussed in the first report, though efficiency gains were linked, not with the initiative of Charters themselves, but a much wider set of policies intertwined with the Charter initiative in broader terms: namely privatisation, market testing, improving management and performance-related pay (first report). By means of the first two policies, some activities would be hived off by the public sector, since they could be done more efficiently by private companies. For those areas that remained in the public sector, the first report stated that efficiency would be maximised by devolving management responsibility and ensuring that each individual's rewards were related directly to their individual performance.

In December 1994, the report on maladministration and redress by the Select Committee on the Parliamentary Commissioner for Administration made criticism about standards and compensation in the public services affected by Charters. In its summary, the Committee reported the views of the National Consumer Council (NCC) on the standards set out in the individual Charters: "The NCC has claimed that there is some confusion among the Charters in their use of language" and "... the language of Charters is sometimes vague and ambiguous. It can be difficult to tell which statements involve enforceable standards as distinct from unenforceable 'targets,' 'aims' and so on. The term 'standard' is sometimes unhelpfully used when all that is being promised is that the organisation will aim to achieve a certain level of service—and there is no guaranteed redress in the event of failure to do so" and "The Committee focused on the lack of attention given to redress for consumers and it recommended that a 'Redress Team' be established within the Charter Unit to monitor and advise on the granting of redress within departments and agencies ... Such a team would be able to advise on improvements in Charter standards and conduct selective and specific audits of departmental practice" (HC 112, 1994).

The government's reply to these recommendations was published in March 1995. There was agreement on the need for "close co-operation between the Treasury and the Citizen's Charter Unit in advising departments and agencies on questions of redress and compensation." The government promised to consider the recommendation to form a Redress Team "in light of the forthcoming Report from the Citizen's

Charter Complaints Task Force, which is undertaking a wide-ranging review of public service complaints systems" (HC 316, 1995).

About the more general recommendation that existing Charters should have to improve the forms of redress, and that a survey be conducted of public services to help in this matter, the government's statement was: "The Government agrees that Charters should make clear that users of the service in question are entitled to redress, appropriate to the circumstances and from the appropriate authority, when Charter standards are not met. It will seek to ensure that this is made clear when new Charters are produced, or existing ones revised. Some form of redress should in principle be available in response to a failure to meet any Charter standard, but the nature of that redress (including whether it be non-financial or financial) may depend on other factors, e.g. the extent to which there has been a failure to meet a standard; whether the complainant has suffered financial loss as a result; whether the handling of the original complaint has been maladministrative. It would not therefore be useful or cost-effective to revise every Charter in order to list standards in the manner proposed. On the proposed survey of public services, the government will consider this recommendation further in the light of the final report of the Complaints Task Force, which is itself carrying out a wide-ranging review of the systems for complaints and redress in public services" (ibidem, 1995).

A poll carried out for the Trades Union Congress by National Opinion Polls in autumn 1994 found that two-thirds of the 1000 people asked saw the Charter as a public relations exercise. One in three had seen either a copy of the Charter, or one of the individual Charters, but only 2% of respondents had used a Charter. Of course, this type of response may simply reflect the fact that the Charter was a long-term programme. Moreover, consumer rhetoric and delivery results to individuals did not follow the same pace. While the first became immediately a government catchphrase, the second was much slower and it faced, as seen below, implementation problems and even some failures as the Charterline.

Charter Mark and Charterline: A History of One Success and One Failure

The Charter Mark Scheme was first discussed in the Citizen's Charter (Cm. 1599). The scheme established that public organisations which satisfied selected criteria in their provision of public services were awarded with the Mark. This Mark certified excellence in the public sector. The scheme was formally launched in January 1992, and 36 Charter Marks were awarded in September that year. The functioning of the Charter Mark was explained in the first report on the Citizen's Charter, published in November 1992:

> Winners had to satisfy the judges—the Prime Minister's Citizen's Charter Advisory Panel—that they met the Citizen's Charter principles for delivering quality in public services. The winners also had to provide evidence both of customer satisfaction and of measurable improvements in quality of service. And they had to have plans to introduce or have in hand at least one innovative enhancement to their services which could be or is being introduced without increasing the cost either to the taxpayer or to those who use the service. Charter Mark winners can now use the Charter Mark on their products and equipment, on stationery, vehicles, and promotional material to show that their achievements have been recognised. (Cm. 2101)

The control of the process was organised and supervised by independent consultants and, in 1994, this role was taken by the Touche Ross company. A team of Charter Mark assessors, chosen from within the public services providers, evaluated the applications for awards submitted by the organisations concerned. Furthermore, the Advisory Panel considered comments received from, among others, government departments, independent regulators and the Audit Commission. A shortlist of the best applications was compiled and visited by either members of the Advisory Panel, one of the Charter Mark assessors, or senior staff from the Cabinet Office. The Advisory Panel then drew up a final list of winners, with the commitment of the Citizen's Charter Minister, and the list was approved by the Prime Minister (Seely and Jenkins 1995).

In 1993, the government doubled the number of awards deriving from the model of the scheme from 50 to 100. The Charter Marks were given to 93 organisations in October 1993. In October 1994, 98 awards were conferred, and 123 organisations received commendations; overall, 523 organisations had applied that year for consideration for a Charter Mark ("98 services get their reward," Cabinet Office Press Notice, 21/10/1993). In January 1995, during a debate on the Charter, David Hunt, Minister for the Citizen's Charter and Chancellor of the Duchy of Lancaster, announced that the scheme would be enlarged so that members of the public could make a direct contribution to the selection of winners: "I believe that we must make the Charter Mark award much more the property of the public and that we must involve many more members of the public in the system. With the introduction of public nominations for honours, the Prime Minister has set up a system which has been a remarkable success. I want to extend that principle. I am pleased to announce that in 1995, for the first time, we will ask the public—the users of public services—to nominate organisations for a Charter Mark award" (HC 20 Deb. 13.01.95, c.364).

In the second report on the Charter, published in March 1994, it was argued that "the award of a Charter Mark is not a final stamp of approval. Charter Mark winners are expected to go on raising their standards of service year by year and Charter Marks can be taken away if standards fall. Charter Marks are held for three years, and then winners must reapply with evidence of how their service has improved" (Cm. 2540). David Davis, the then Parliamentary Under-Secretary of State for the Office of Science & Technology, in a written answer given in June 1994 explained the process of withdrawing a Charter Mark from an organisation that didn't maintain or improve their standards: "No organisations have had their Charter Marks taken away, although the Citizen's Charter Unit reserves the right to take away a Charter Mark from an organisation whose performance subsequently falls significantly below standard" (HC 38 Deb. 14.06.94, c.433W).

The Charterline was an experiment launched on 19 May 1993; it was a telephone helpline to supply information about the status of public services to residents in Nottinghamshire, Derbyshire and Leicestershire. The government had announced its intention to pilot such a scheme in its first report on the Charter:

> The Government intends to pilot a telephone helpline, the 'Charterline,' to help people who find it daunting or frustrating to get information from large bureaucracies. Charterline will be an advice and information service. It will give: information about the Citizen's Charter and about the other Charters and statements of Charter standards that have been published; contact numbers to help people to find out more about public services; contact numbers for making complaints about services. There are already many successful telephone helplines in service and Charterline will link in with these. It will also direct people to other sources of help such as the various Ombudsmen. We aim to launch the Charterline pilot in 1993. If successful, Charterline will eventually cover all public services nationwide. (Cm. 2101: 49)

The next month, the results of a survey commissioned by the Citizen's Charter Unit were published on the public's view about this scheme. It concluded that "Charterline would be widely welcomed. Nine in ten respondents said it was a good idea and should be set up" (The Charterline Service, Research International, December 1992: 8). In February 1993, the pilot area chosen for the scheme covered Leicestershire, Nottinghamshire and Derbyshire; this area was selected on the basis of its being broadly representative of the entire country, in terms of its population and its area of public services ("Pilot Area Chosen for Charterline," Cabinet Office press notice, 17 February 1993). It was stated that the experiment would run for six months, and, if successful, would be extended to cover the whole country during 1994. At that time, the average number of calls received was around 200 per day, but this figure dropped dramatically over the six-month trial, fuelling speculation that the whole scheme would be scrapped (Seely and Jenkins 1995).

In May, the minister William Waldegrave announced the failure of the scheme and that it would not be extended on a national basis. The Cabinet Office improved the distribution of existing helpline numbers to the general public ("Better access to public services information," Cabinet Office press notice, 6 May 1994).

The failure of Charterline, and the public's presumed preference for taking complaints or inquiries directly to the particular public service involved, seemed to underline this trend in the Charter's character, away from national initiatives affecting public services generally, and towards local or regional developments within individual services.

THE RISE OF MARKETISATION: MARKET TESTING, CONTRACTING OUT AND COMPETING FOR QUALITY

As we have seen, the replacement of Mrs. Thatcher with Mr. John Major in November 1990 did not arrest the Conservative Government's pace in reforming the Civil Service. The implementation of the Next Steps programme continued fast, and the Citizen's Charter proved that the aim of the government for radical change in the Civil Service was one of the priorities for the new premiership. In particular, attention was focused on delivery of public services and promotion of free market competition. As the Cabinet Office explained, "We believe that the process of buying public services from private contractors is still only in its infancy" and "We propose to move the process decisively forward. There are great potential benefits to be had, both in improved quality and lower costs." It was a governmental aim to "subject much more work each year to market testing than has ever been the case before" (Cm. 1599, 1991: 33).

There was a clear attention to Civil Service numbers, pay levels and conditions, as stated in the White Paper of November 1991, *Competing for Quality*: "Market testing so far has been largely concentrated on traditional support services. The government wishes to build on this by opening up to competition new areas, closer to the heart of government: Departments, executive agencies, and contribution to the delivery of, for example, clerical and executive operations, specialist and professional skills, and a wide range of facilities and management approaches" (Cm. 1730, 1991: 12).

The government was determined to give a "new impetus" to market testing and to the contracting out of functions and to establish further targets for departments and executive agencies for measuring performance and progress. The targets were set up with the contribution of special advisers from the private sector, and a continuing programme was established under the control of central monitoring (ibidem: 8–9). The procedures for market testing existing services had to move faster. After a "decade of efficiency reform," the government believed the existing practice of allowing time for the in-house operation to gain maximum efficiency before competitive tendering could begin should be discontinued (ibidem: 11). The government stated that "departments which achieve savings through market testing and contracting out" would be able to apply these savings for "the benefit of their programmes"; it also considered that "for competition to be possible, managers need to know the full cost of providing services in-house. Often overhead costs fall on central budgets and appear free to the user." It continued: "Where a manager's budget is fully charged for all the goods and services used, the incentive to increase efficiency is maximised for costs and savings directly affecting the budget. Increasingly, services provided by one department to another are being charged for. The Government is also encouraging charging for services supplied within departments" (ibidem: 9–10).

The second annual report on the Citizen's Charter reported "a step change in central government's market testing activity." By the end of 1993, 389 individual market tests had been made, and "in most individual cases where comparisons are possible savings of over 25 percent have been made," and it added, "the overall average saving was over 22 percent." In-house teams had gained 68% of the work when they had been allowed to compete, which was not the total because "113 activities were contracted out as a result of a strategic decision to employ an outside employer" (Cm. 2540, 1994: 93).

The market testing was then supported by provisions in the Deregulation and Contracting Out Act of 1994 which established the opportunity for the civil servants to exercise a Minister's government functions on his behalf, was extended to private contractors. Obviously "those (functions) transferred out from the Civil Service had to be given comparable terms and conditions of service" (Fry 1995). Furthermore, the Conservative Government had continued to reform the Civil Service's pay arrangements. For Major Government, long-term pay agreements should be reached considering principles of private business practices, and the Citizen's Charter too underlined that in future "a larger proportion of pay would be linked to performance," adding that "we will encourage the drive towards greater delegation and flexibility in the Civil Service" (Cm. 1599, 1991: 35).

The Chancellor of the Exchequer, Norman Lamont, wanted to renegotiate the long-term pay agreements, and on 24 July 1991, he proposed to introduce "three new elements into Civil Service pay structures. The first is to put in place a range of forms of performance-related pay in order to achieve a closer link between performance and reward, both for individuals and for groups of staff. This will be an important means of securing the objective of improving the quality of public services, which is at the heart of the Citizen's Charter Programme. Over time, performance will come to determine a larger portion of the pay bill without performance pay becoming a disguised way of providing unacceptably high increases in the pay bill. The second is to further enable responsibility for pay bargaining to be delegated to Civil Service departments or agencies to allow them wider discretion in relation to their pay and grading regimes. Alternative pay and grading structures will be approved where they are expected to produce value for money benefits greater than through centrally controlled negotiation. The third is to give an option to those departments and agencies for which such extensive discretion is not appropriate to negotiate for themselves flexibilities of their own within the total of the overall central pay settlement agreed by the Treasury" (HC 195 Deb. 6s. Written Answers, c.604–605).

The idea of the Chancellor was to secure the confidence of the staff that their pay would be determined fairly. The government withdrew from a previous pay agreement in January 1992, and this withdrawal was extended to the agreement of 1925 that provided for arbitration in Civil Service pay and related matters. A new Civil Service Arbitration Agreement was signed in October 1992 which "does not provide for unilateral access to arbitration as did the old one" (CCSU Bulletin, October/November 1992: 148–149). In the first report on the Citizen's Charter initiative, it was recorded that "new performance pay schemes have been put in place for half a million civil servants. These provide for an individual's pay to reflect his or her performance against objectives set each year" (Cm. 2101, 1992: 67). The changes were concentrated mainly in the lower grades of the Civil Service; indeed, the pay proposal for Grades 5, 6 and 7 was "dramatic evidence of the Government's ambitions for performance-related pay. The scale max and all centrally determined spine points disappear to be replaced by a pay range. Between the min and the max of the range departments will be allowed to pay staff on intermediate points, negotiated with their trade union side. Range quotas and restraints are abolished." In September 1992, the new pay arrangements for Grades 5, 6 and 7 were published and stated "all increases will be performance related" (Treasury 1992). Similar statements were made for other grades, manager and specialist, clerical and secretarial grades. It survived the adjustment to the interquartile range of pay and conditions of relevant jobs outside the public sector, and this arrangement tended to be seen by the unions as a very important element of the pay determination system. In November 1992, the then Chancellor of the Exchequer stated that "in the coming year pay settlements in the public sector should be restricted to a maximum 1.5 percent ... without exception, regardless of whether pay is negotiated, recommended by review bodies, or subject to formula calculations" (HC 213 Deb. 6s. c.996).

The Civil Service (Management Functions) Act of 1992 crystallised important changes that had been made in the last decade between central government, departments and agencies. William Waldegrave, then Chancellor of the Duchy of Lancaster, argued: "In the present organisation the Treasury is given the responsibility for determining pay, grading, expenses, allowances, holidays, hours of work, and other related personal matters. The Minister for the Civil Service regulates the conduct of civil servants and those other conditions of service which are not allotted to the Treasury … As things stand … the Treasury and the Prime Minister cannot lawfully delegate those functions to the departments and agencies; they cannot be delegated to another Minister—the relevant Secretary of State, for example—let alone to agencies which are responsible for the day-to-day management of the staff that they employ. Whether it is sensible or not—I do not think that it can be—decisions affecting the working conditions of all 560,000 or so civil servants must conform to rules laid down by the two central departments, and those rules, like the laws of the Medes and Persians, must then be obeyed" (HC 213 Deb. 6s. c.458).

Waldegrave underlined that these arrangements were now "wholly inappropriate," constituting as they did "an immensely complicated system of hurdles set up when the Treasury was, in effect, the personnel department of a small Civil Service." The Cabinet pushed "to introduce … more variegated styles of employment in our great Public Service," Waldegrave added, and the 1992 Civil Service Management Functions Act was approved to delegate Civil Service for personnel management functions previously exercised from the ministers to departments and agencies officials and these functions were to be "progressively devolved" (ibidem, c.464). Contrary to how it was presented at the House of Commons, this Act was not just a technical Bill with a restricted scope. As John Garrett declared, the legislation had great potential: "The big change embodied in the Bill is the end of the national Civil Service. That is the point of the Bill: agency employees—at present, civil servants—will be subject to terms and conditions, employment regulations, recruitment and training policies and rights peculiar to the agency concerned. Instead of having a national Civil Service, we shall have a conglomerate of agencies, all with different terms and conditions" (HC 213 Deb. 6s. c.451).

Furthermore, the Mueller Report was implemented in the early nineties by the Major Government. A 1990 Treasury report stated that "the standard pattern of working" was being increasingly displaced by a much wider range and diversity of working arrangements, and it added: "Part-time working, for example, has grown tremendously over the last few years" (Treasury 1990: 1). It was later reported by the Civil Service Statistics that "between 1984 and 1992 the number of non-industrial part-timers has increased from 16,029 to 43,590. Nearly 16% of all women non-industrial staff now work part-time. While the proportion of men working part-time is still low—0.9%—the number working part-time has risen from 954 in 1984 to 2377 in 1992" (HM Treasury 1992: 14). In April 1992, of the 368,045 staff in all departments excluding agencies, 7% were part-timers and 2% were causals, and in the agencies were, respectively, 11 and 5% (Treasury and OPPS 1993, Annex X). This document underlined that most civil servants worked with permanent contracts and it highlighted that "full-time permanent employment was easier to manage" (ibidem, section 8).

In July 1992, Sir Robin Butler, Cabinet Secretary and Head of the Home Civil Service, and Sir Peter Levene, the Prime Minister's Adviser on Efficiency and Effectiveness, established a commission to make a point on the Civil Service reform and to study future personnel arrangements in central government. John Oughton, the Head of the Efficiency Unit, was appointed to supervise the report that was published in November 1993, and it was called the Oughton Report. This study considered "current arrangements in departments for identifying and developing those with potential, for appointing to top posts, and the tenure under which staff are currently employed" (Efficiency Unit 1993: 1).

The report reaffirmed traditional principles of the British Civil Service: "the key principles of recruitment through fair and open competition, promotion though merit, the emphasis on integrity, objectivity, and impartiality and non-politicisation as the foundation for a permanent Civil Service continue to remain valid and should be preserved" (ibidem: 7). A Permanent Secretary who worked on the Report observed the lack of coordination created by years of reform, but he commented positively "we often need to create order out of chaos—indeed that is often what effective public administration is" (ibidem: 15). This Report showed how the perception of civil servants was changed, from a cultural point of view, after nearly 15 years of Conservative reforms in search of more efficiency and effectiveness. One Grade 2 official interviewed told the study team: "The drive should be to find people who can show added value, not ask clever questions" (ibidem: 22). The report launched an offensive against the top grades, considering that "Grade 1s and 2s need to be persuaded to leave their rooms. They see themselves as top policy advisers to Ministers, not managers" (ibidem: 24).

The study argued that one of "the biggest weaknesses of the Civil Service was in the fact that people tend to stay in a particular job for only a relatively short period of time before being moved to another post" (ibidem: 49), an opinion supported also by a Permanent Secretary, who argued that "the current caricature of a successful career is to get yourself whizzed around as many posts as possible, rubbing shoulders with very senior people. In reality, people need at least a couple of specialisms" (ibidem: 50). An agency CEO added that "high flyers should be identified on the basis of their achievements (as they come through the organisation), not a specially watered flowerbed" (ibidem: 31).

The Oughton Report made specific recommendations and one of the most impressive was: "The Treasury should work up proposals for alternative contract terms of employment for the Senior Open Structure, so that the costs and benefits can be assessed, which would safeguard against politicisation, but which would strike an appropriate balance between risks and rewards ... We recommend a contract of indefinite term but with a clear, specific period of notice" (ibidem: 81). The report pushed for more openness and it looked to the model of private organisations "in which 80 percent of their vacancies were filled from within and the remaining 20 percent through open advertisement, from which they might expect to fill som vacancies from outside their organisation and some from insiders who matched the best outsiders. This does not compare too starkly with recent Civil Service experience. Over the last three years, 14 percent of the vacancies in the Senior Open Structure have been openly advertised and that has led to 10 percent of the vacancies being filled by people who were not career civil servants" (ibidem: 55).

These were the recommendations promoted by the Oughton team that showed how the interest of the government was to open up the Civil Service and to contract out most of the public services, ensuring competition. At the same time, to preserve good morale and to make acceptable these changes, the government reaffirmed traditions and "classic" principles of the Civil Service in more than one executive paper. Indeed, it needed another two government papers to further change the Civil Service organisation.

THE CIVIL SERVICE: CONTINUITY AND CHANGE—THE RESILIENCE OF TRADITIONS

A crucial step to consolidate the reforms, started in 1979 by Margaret Thatcher's government and continued by Major's government, was the White Paper published in July 1994 and titled *The Civil Service. Continuity and Change* (Cm. 2627, 1994). The White Paper was commissioned by minister William Waldegrave, and it was assessed by Sir

Peter Kemp, the manager who developed the Next Steps initiative and retired in 1992.

Sir Peter Kemp's radical beliefs on public management and entrepreneurial approach to government could not be doubted. Indeed, one of the central ideas of the paper was closely related to agencies, and it was to establish by April 1996 a Senior Civil Service from Grade 5 level and above, including all agency chief executives, and for its members new pay and contractual arrangements. The White Paper stated that: "The new Senior Civil Service that would emerge from this process would be broader than the existing Senior Open Structure, which is confined to the current Grades 1–3. The government believes there is merit in such a development. It would strengthen the cohesion not only of the senior management of departments, but also of the wider Senior Civil Service. Entry to the Senior Civil Service from within a department or agency would be marked for the individual concerned by leaving negotiated group pay arrangements and moving to individually determined pay, and by acceptance of a written contract of service. It would be a signal to the individual and to his or her senior managers of the need to think more broadly, both in respect of the job to be done and, potentially, in career management terms, looking across the Civil Service and at opportunities for experience outside. The Report noted a step change in responsibility between the current Grade 7 and 5—requiring the ability to manage through others and a greater role in representing the organisation externally that accords with the Government's perception—and reinforces the case for extending the scope of the Senior Civil Service to encompass that level of responsibility" (para. 4.18).

The paper pointed out progress made by 1979: in the highest three grades numbers were cut by 20% in 15 years, and departments had eliminated unnecessary layers of management (para. 4.19). To complete this process of modernisation, the government asked departments to arrange a Senior Civil Service structure that "matches the need of the organisation and is not driven by a formal Service-wide grading system; and informing the process of moving senior staff on to new pay and contractual arrangements" (para. 4.20). These senior management reviews were created to continue the trend that had seen more than 50% of the individuals who had left the Senior Open Structure in the previous seven years doing so before the normal retirement age, 30% of them having departed as the result of voluntary or compulsory early retirement brought about by management. The White Paper suggested introducing a "privatisation" of contract for the new Senior Civil Service. Indeed, new written contracts would specify the terms and conditions of employment for members of that Service, with specified periods of notice.

The government did not favour fixed terms or rolling contracts, but it argued that "there could not be a single comprehensive contract applicable to everyone," and this option was introduced to give more freedom to agencies and departments that "would have discretion to use either of these alternative forms of contract as they judge best in the circumstances" (para. 4.31–4.35). Here the government proposed an adjustment of the Senior Civil Service contractual conditions to any similar contracts in the private sector, and more flexibility was introduced along with personalisation of pay and conditions. The idea of Major's reform was to create "a smaller but better paid Senior Civil Service." A single pay range was established for all Permanent Secretaries up to and including the Head of the Home Civil Service, with the level and extent of the range being determined on the basis of the advice of the new Review Body on Senior Salaries. A remuneration Committee was to establish the position of individual Permanent Secretaries within this range.

The target of a smaller Civil Service was achieved; indeed, the paper reported: "The size of the Civil Service will fall below 500,000 over the next four years." The means of doing this would be to continue the control of running costs (para. 3.33), and a special provision was established for the short-term funding of any resulting early retirements (para. 3.34). The White Paper explained the government's policy of monitoring departmental functions in order to drop, privatise, market test, contract them out or organise an agency for which the set-up was extended from three to five years (para. 3.22).

This slowdown was part of a precise strategy of the government, which wanted to give departments and agencies "greater freedom and flexibility to develop programmes for improving efficiency which best meet their own needs" (para. 3.20). These programmes had a role to play in the Efficiency Plans that departments and agencies were to be required to draw up each spring to show how they were to stay within their running costs limits over the next three years (para. 3.21). Proposals for disaggregating the Civil Service pay and grading were made clear both by the White Paper and more precisely by the Office of Public Service and Science. From April 1996, existing national pay arrangements were replaced by a single agreement for each department and the government reserved the autonomy to agencies for having responsibility for its own pay and grading (para. 3.26). The aim was that departments could develop a "flatter management structure" (para. 3.29).

Preserving Traditional Values: The Role of the Civil Service

After the White Paper *The Civil Service: Continuity and Change*, a new phase was opened by the Major Government. On 1 November 1994, the Treasury and Civil Service Committee published its fifth report, *The Role of the Civil Service* (HC 27, 1993–4), focused mainly on constitutional aspects of the Service and the problems of accountability that derived from a long path of reforms during the last 15 years.

The last three years of Major's office were used by government and Parliament to manage legal and institutional ambiguities that characterised the modernised Civil Service. The report largely endorsed the government's reforms, in particular, the development of the Next Steps Initiative and the Citizen's Charter. However, the Committee was hesitant and doubtful on one specific issue: accountability.

The report expressed the confusion over the dividing line between government ministers and agency chief executives and particularly as it influenced the relationship between control of policy and operational control. The constitutional convention of ministerial responsibility, by which a minister is responsible for the actions of all officials under his or her control, remained theoretically in force. Yet the question remained as to how far ministers could be held responsible for the actions of government agencies that have been given a considerable degree of autonomy and that are often expected to respond to the demands of market forces (see Chapter 5).

The new convention grew that ministers are responsible for policy matters while chief executives are responsible for operational matters. The problems arose when all questions posed by the parliament concerned operational matters made by agencies, for which minister had no responsibilities. One of the recommendations made by the Committee to resolve this dilemma was that officials in charge of government agencies should be made accountable to a parliamentary select committee rather than to a departmental minister. The Committee was concerned about the erosion of the traditional values of the Civil Service such as impartiality and integrity owing to innovations introduced by the Next Steps programme and strategies to increase efficiency of civil servants.

The report recommended that a new Code of Conduct for the Civil Service should have been introduced by the government to spell out in concrete terms just what was to be expected of the Service. This crystallisation of traditional values would have helped, in the argumentation of the Committee, to preserve the unity and integrity of the Service in the ongoing managerial revolution. It was also proposed that there should be a new appeals procedure whereby breaches of the new code could be reported to the Civil Service Commissioners.

The government drafted a new code in the Command Paper of 1995, *The Civil Service: Taking forward Continuity and Change*, but both Parliament and government were unwilling to accept any moves which were intended to make agency chief executives directly accountable to Parliament. The government was determined to maintain the convention of ministerial responsibility as the sole garrison of accountability.

Taking Forward Continuity and Change

The recommendations of *The Role of the Civil Service* were received by the government with the Command Paper *The Civil Service: Taking Forward Continuity and Change* in January 1995 (Cm. 2748, 1995). This document was particularly important to set the basis for updating constitutional status of the Civil Service. Indeed, in the first chapter the Command Paper stated its mission: "The Command Paper indicates the government's acceptance of the proposal, recommended by the Select Committee, for a new Civil Service Code, to apply all civil servants, summarising the constitutional framework within which they work and the values they are expected to hold and incorporating a new, independent line of appeal to the Civil Service Commissioners in cases of alleged breaches of the Code or issues of conscience which cannot be resolved through internal procedures" (para. 1.5).

A draft of the Code was attached to the Paper. However, the government wanted to ensure a better accountability for the Civil Service and the document announced "the Government's intention to enhance the role of the Civil Service Commissioners as guardians of the principle of selection on merit, and its decision that the next First Civil Service Commissioner will have a new role in monitoring internal appointments and consequently should not hold the post as a serving civil servant" (para. 1.5).

The paper confirmed the government's intention to proceed with the other approaches set out in *Continuity and Change* to improve the efficiency and effectiveness of the Civil Service, including delegation of pay and grading below senior levels to departments, and the introduction of Efficiency Plans in place of the centrally driven *Competing for Quality Programme*. The paper reaffirmed the idea of carrying out senior management reviews in all departments, to introduce new pay arrangements for the Senior Civil Service, including Permanent Secretary, and to introduce contracts for all senior civil servants. The Paper was a compromise between the necessity to continue the process of modernisation and the defence of traditional values of the Service.

To accomplish this mission, a new Civil Service Code was fundamental. As the document argued: "The aim of this new Civil Service Code will be, as the Select Committee recommended, to set out with greater clarity and brevity than existing documents the constitutional framework within which all civil servants work and the values which they are expected to uphold." It continued, "It must also reflect the existing constitutional position rather than seek to change it, and provide a clear and more accessible expression of duties and responsibilities which are already a condition of employment in the Civil Service" (para. 2.8).

The role of Commissioners was enforced as far as concerned open competition. The paper stated that "the Civil Service Commissioners will in the future be responsible for the interpretation of the principles of fair and open competition on merit for all Civil Service recruitment—not, as now, only for senior appointments." The government established a simple but binding Code issued by the Commission that set out principles and exceptions for recruitment addressed to departments and agencies. Moreover, the Commissioners became responsible also for approving all appointments from outside the Civil Service to the new Senior Civil Service. Major's government decided that "a new Code could also be promulgated as soon as it had been agreed, without waiting for a legislative opportunity" and this was possible because "the management of the Civil Service is one of the aspects of the Prerogative which is exercised by Ministers on behalf of the Crown" (para. 2.15).

Here was expressed a very traditional constitutional position that denoted a certain amount of "conservatism" in approaching legislation about the Civil Service. Indeed, the Paper argued, "the Government is, however, cautious about the prospect of opening up the possibility of change in the constitutional position of the Civil Service, and thereby risking its politicisation. It would not introduce or support legislation which ran such risks or specified in detail the employment rights of the civil servants, conferring on them privileges or disadvantages relative to other employees, or inhibiting effective and efficient management. Before introducing a Civil Service Bill the Government would, therefore, need to be satisfied that there was a broad measure of agreement on legislation which sustained rather than altered the existing constitutional position of the Civil Service, retained the flexibility of the existing arrangements for regulating the terms and conditions of civil servants, and did not change the position of civil servants under general employment law" (para. 2.17).

The third chapter of the Paper focused on performance. It confirmed the government's attention to "clear standards of service for users and to a clearer definition of output targets" and to "tight control of the costs of running the Civil Service" (para. 3.1). The control of running costs included a cut of 10% in real terms and the elaboration of Efficiency Plans that included privatisation, strategic contracting out, market testing and application of Next Steps principles, together with techniques such as benchmarking and business process re-engineering. As far as concerned recruiting and training of civil servants, the White Paper confirmed the strategy of Continuity and Change with "maintaining of a predominantly career Civil Service, providing the opportunity for a full career for those whose performance continues throughout to meet requirements" (para. 3.5) and the government "also proposes to revise the fast-stream entry scheme along the lines proposed in the Review of arrangements for the Fast Stream entry into the Civil Service, which was published in July 1994 at the same time as Continuity and Change" (para. 3.6). The Cabinet used a very linear approach on the issue of recruitment and training, coherent with historical development of the institution. By 1992, 5000 posts in the Civil Service had been eliminated through privatisation, and value for money continued to be significantly improved as the result of reviewing activities and exposing them to competition under the Competing for Quality programme. The White Paper reported that "between April 1992 and September 1994, over £2 billion of activities were reviewed under this programme, producing annual cost savings of £400 million (average cost savings of 20 percent), with a reduction of 27,000 in Civil Service manned posts" (para. 3.9). Then, the Major Government announced the intention to carry out a policy evaluation of the first three years of Competing for Quality and to continue to promote contracting out. Regarding Next Steps agencies, the White Paper argued: "A key task for the next two years will, therefore, be to continue the programme of agency creation for this function where agency status is found to be the best approach" (para. 3.13).

The government set out its strategy to improve managerial tasks for executive agencies in *Taking Forward Continuity and Change*. It pursued arrangements for the strategic monitoring of agencies by departments, strengthening the departmental control on performance, and it promoted maximum clarity about objectives and targets, delegation of management responsibility and a clear focus on outputs and outcomes. Departments and agencies were being given greater freedom and flexibility to develop programmes for improving efficiency which best met their own needs. Responsibility for pay and grading of staff below senior levels was delegated to all departments by 1 April 1996. As far as concerned the management information systems, the White Paper established: "the Efficiency Unit scrutiny of management information systems, aimed at determining departmental and agency needs in the light of best practice in the public and private sectors, will be completed at the end of February 1995. The report will be submitted to the Prime Minister's Efficiency Adviser, who will then advise Ministers on the recommendations" and "OPSS/Treasury will be working with departments to share examples of best practice in management techniques—for example, benchmarking, and business process of re-engineering—with applications in Government departments, agencies, and public bodies" (para. 3.16).

The White Paper summarised the results of the government's plan for the Civil Service. The size of the institution had fallen by over 40,000 posts since January 1993, from 565,000 then to 524,000 in January 1995. The plan was to reduce Civil Service manpower to significantly under 500,000 by 1997, a mission that would be accomplished by Major's Cabinet through privatisation and contracting out, early retirement policy, working methods and pay and grading arrangements. The fourth chapter of the paper was focused on the new Senior Civil Service. It reaffirmed policy options chosen in Continuity and Change, establishing "leaner, flatter management structures with less emphasis on working through hierarchies and more scope for talented individuals to make their mark; explicit, written employment contracts for senior civil servants; and better, more flexible pay arrangements which recognise increased levels of personal responsibility, reward successful performance, and assist in retaining high-performing staff with the greatest potential" (para. 4.6).

The government established six objectives: "to end the traditional grading systems at these levels and to have a pay system which does not impose an organisational pattern but encourages senior structures tailored to departmental requirements, with the minimum necessary management layers; to provide better rewards within a smaller Civil Service for those who contribute most to policy formation and management objectives in departments and their agencies; to give flexibility to Heads of Department to reflect levels of responsibility and of individual performance; to ensure that the pay system supports cohesion across the Senior Civil Service and helps to encourage free movement between departments; to establish a system that is fair and transparent in operation; and to maintain the role of the SSRB, to whose advice the Government attaches continuing importance" (para. 4.13). As it can be noticed, the Senior Civil Service reform of the Major Government represented another step towards managerialisation of the public sector. It was not a revolution, but an incremental reform that started in the early 1980s and continued until the end of the 1990s. It ensured more flexibility, performance measurement and openness in the profession in return for the end of the "job for life" regime, a reduction of Civil Service intervention in policy-making in favour of a greater attention of civil servants on public services delivery, and the introduction of a new appointment style directly inspired by private sector practices.

Conclusions: The Friction Between Management and Tradition at the End of the Twentieth Century

Two trends for the Civil Service during Major's era can be identified. The first was the progress of market-oriented and managerialisation reforms that moved from administrative organisation, with the completion of the Next Steps programme, towards contracting out, performance measurement, more attention for delivery and public services. The second was the rise of regulation in the Civil Service. In this area, the problem was mainly related to accountability and responsibility of civil servants and, in particular, of Chief Executive Officers of Next Steps executive agencies. As far as concerned the first aspect, the Civil Service was smaller after the seven years of Major's government: staff numbers decreased from 553,863 in 1990 to 475,340 in 1997. In the last year of Conservative Government (1996–1997), 77% of civil servants were working in an executive agency, and the continuous process of agencification set up 110 agencies from 1988 to 1997 (Office for National Statistics 1997).

As far as concerned codification, the government drafted in 1992 the document *Questions of Procedure for Ministers*, and in 1995, it proposed a new Civil Service Code. The pressure of managerialisation, market testing and media exposure, as well as the openness of the Service, necessitated stronger legislation to bind and to ensure preservation of traditional values of the British Central Government bureaucracy. The government showed an eagerness to reaffirm traditional principles of this institution in its documents, especially in those where the pressure for changes in the Civil Service career and structure was heavier. The tension between tradition and managerialisation in the Service was not reduced in Major's period, but in some ways increased. The Cabinet justified reforms with the need for better services, more efficiency and less waste, and it strove to enforce traditional principles of the Civil Service to reassure civil servants while reaffirming their legal position.

On 15 March 1995, the government fixed by statute the traditional principles of the Civil Service, the new arrangements of the Civil Service Commission established in 1991, and it established basic rules for special advisers' appointments with the Order in Council 1995. It set the basis for further developments both in public services and in the institutional framework. Continuity in "constitutional resilience" that meant the effort to preserve traditional values and change with "managerial revolution" introducing new tools and organisation for civil servants continued to be, as in the Thatcher era, in rhetoric and practice the "swinging pendulum" of government.

References

Books, Journals, and Articles

Barron, A., & Scott, C. (1992). The Citizen's Charter Programme. *Modern Law Review, 55*(4), 526–546.

Fry, G. K. (1995). *Policy and management in the British civil service.* Hemel Hempstead: Prentice Hall.

Haddon, C. (2012). *Reforming the civil service. The efficiency unit in the early 1980s and the 1987 next steps report.* London: Institute for Government.

Hood C. (1991). A public management for all seasons? *Public Administration,* *69*(1), 3–19.

Hood, C. (1995). The "New Public Management" in the 1980s: Variations on a theme. *Accounting, Organizations and Society, 20*(2/3), 93–109.

James, O., Moseley, A., Petrovsky, N., & Boyne, G. (2011). Agencification in the UK. In K. Verhoest, S. van Thiel, G. Bouckaert, & P. Laegreid (Eds.), *Government agencies in Europe and beyond: Practices and lessons from 30 countries.* Hampshire: Palgrave Macmillan.

Kandiah, M., & Lowe, R. (Eds.). (2007). *The civil service reforms of the 1980s.* London: CCBH Oral History Programme.

Panchamia, N., & Thomas, P. (2014a). *The next steps initiative.* London: Institute for Government.

Panchamia, N., & Thomas, P. (2014b). *Civil service reform in the real world. Patterns of success in UK civil service reform.* London: Institute for Government.

Pollitt, C. (1990). *Managerialism and the public services: The Anglo-American experience.* Oxford: Blackwell.

Richards, D. (1997). *The civil service under the conservatives, 1979–1997.* Brighton: Sussex University Press.

Seely, A., & Jenkins, P. (1995). *The Citizen's Charter* (Research Paper 95/66). House of Commons Library.

Theakston, K. (1995). Continuity, change and crisis: The civil service since 1945. *Public Policy and Administration, 10*(3), 45–59.

Archive Sources, Parliamentary Papers, and Official Publications

Cabinet Office. (1994, May 6). *Press notice.* "Better access to public services information." London: HMSO.

Citizen's Charter Unit. (1992). *The Charterline Service.* London: Research International.

Cm. 1599. (1991). *The Citizen's Charter: Raising the standard.* London: HMSO.

Cm. 1730. (1991). *Competing for quality: Buying better public services.* London: HMSO.

Cm. 1760. (1991). *Improving management in government: The next steps agencies. Review 1991.* London: HMSO.

Cm. 2101. (1992). *The Citizen's Charter: First report.* London: HMSO.

Cm. 2111. (1992). *The next steps agencies: Review 1992.* London: HMSO.

Cm. 2430. (1993). *Next steps agencies in government: Review 1993.* London: HMSO.

Cm. 2540. (1994). *The Citizen's Charter: Second report.* London: HMSO.

Cm. 2627. (1994). *The civil service: Continuity and change.* London: HMSO.

Cm. 2748. (1995). *The civil service: Taking forward continuity and change.* London: HMSO.

Cm. 3880. (1998). *Next steps report 1997.* London: Stationery Office.

Efficiency Unit. (1991). *Making the most of next steps: The management of ministers' departments and their executive agencies. Report to the Prime Minister* (Fraser Report). London: HMSO.

Efficiency Unit. (1993). *Career management and succession planning study* (Oughton Report). London: HMSO.

HC 27 (1993–4). Treasury and civil service committee. *Fifth report. The role of the civil service,* Vol. I. London: HMSO.

HC 112. (1994). *First report select committee on the parliamentary commissioner for administration.* London: HMSO.

HC 195. (1992–3). Deb. 6s. Written answers, c. 604-5. London: HMSO.

HC 213. (1992–3). Deb. 6s. c. 451-458-996. London: HMSO.

HC 316. (1995). *Government response to the first report from the select committee on the parliamentary commissioner for administration.* London: HMSO.

HC 481. (1989–90). *Eighth report from the treasury and civil service committee: Progress in the next steps initiative.* London: HMSO.

HM Treasury. (1992). *Civil service statistics 1992.* London: HM Treasury.

Office for National Statistics. (1997). *Civil service statistics.* London: HMSO.

Treasury. (1990). *Made to measure: Patterns of work in the civil service.* London: HM Treasury.

Treasury. (1992, October). *New pay arrangements for grades 5, 6 and 7: Text of the agreement between HM treasury and the association of first division civil servants, the institution of professionals, managers and specialists and the national union of civil and public servants.* London: HM Treasury.

Treasury and OPPS. (1993). *A picture of flexible working in government departments and agencies.* London: HM Treasury.

CHAPTER 4

1997–2007: Coordination, Consolidation and Delivery in Blair's Government

NEW LABOUR, THE THIRD WAY AND THE CONSOLIDATION OF PUBLIC MANAGEMENT

The New Labour Party won the 1997 general election, and their leader Tony Blair became Prime Minister on 2 May. Labour's 1997 Manifesto made no explicit references to the public sector and the Civil Service, but broad ideas about the reform of the central government were pointed out: "Over-centralisation of government and lack of accountability was a problem in governments of both left and right. Labour is committed to the democratic renewal of our country through decentralisation and the elimination of excessive government secrecy." Then, the manifesto focused on the coordination between state and market. The aim was to find a "the Third Way" between neoliberalism and socialism, a vision elaborated by Anthony Giddens (1998), one of the inspirers of New Labour's political proposal. The manifesto argued: "The old left would have sought state control of industry. The Conservative right is content to leave all to the market. We reject both approaches. Government and industry must work together to achieve key objectives aimed at enhancing the dynamism of the market, not undermining it." This statement effectively influenced the new government's approach to administrative reforms and public services organisation. The commitment expressed by New Labour to the New Public Management ideas was confirmed during the first years in government, and a series of clues proved it.

© The Author(s) 2018
L. Castellani, *The Rise of Managerial Bureaucracy*,
https://doi.org/10.1007/978-3-319-90032-2_4

First, Tony Blair's government didn't repeal any substantial administrative reforms made by the previous Conservative Governments: the Next Steps agencies reform was completed; the open structure was not re-arranged; competitive tenders were maintained; performance-related pay and performance evaluation were enforced. As we will observe, the managerialisation process was taken even further with some adaptations to the changed political environment. Second, some more innovations were introduced as a symbol of trust in new managerialism. For example, in one of the towers of Whitehall traditionalism, the Foreign Office, Robin Cook started up a process of organisational rebranding by publishing a "mission statement." Other ministers followed his example, introducing motivational techniques in order to encourage civil servants to take "ownership" of departmental and agency objectives (Painter 1999: 99–100). The Prime Minister introduced the practice of a business-style annual report to inform citizens about the progress achieved with the public-sector reform. Beyond these communication skills, other developments indicated a firm commitment to new public-management-oriented reform. The government quickly dropped its proposal on market testing in favour of a more selective use of the policy within the framework of *Best Value* in local government, and *Better Quality Services*, its Civil Service equivalent. These initiatives' objective was to replace the law of compulsory competitive tendering and market testing with a more pragmatic approach. The aim was to find the best provider of a public service through consideration of competitive tendering, although, contrary to the previous system, there would be no obligation to do this, provided solid internal reviews of service provision were sufficient to have satisfied the external audit and the Cabinet Office, the Treasury and Cabinet Committee in the case of the Civil Service.

The procedures of the most controversial form of contractualisation of the last years, the Private Finance Initiative, were reformed, but basic principles resisted despite growing criticism within the New Labour Party. The privatisation process was not reversed. For example, the government's plans for the London Underground and the air traffic control system were based on public–private partnership but definitely introduced significant elements of privatisation. Another important aspect of the public-sector reform agenda was the continuation of the emphasis on consumerism.

The Labour Government's position was initially expressed in 1997 by David Clark, the Chancellor of the Duchy of Lancaster and Public Services Minister, when he announced that the Citizen's Charter would continue, soon after relaunching and refocusing it. The new programme was renamed Service First, and its aim was to improve "quality" and "performance" of the public services. The programme included the People's Panel, a 5000-strong nationally representative group charged to tell the government "what people really think" about public services and the efforts taken to improve them. This New Labour experiment was adopted in mid-1998 and was ended by the Cabinet Office in 2002. The Cabinet Office argued that government did not still need a central initiative because in 2002 agencies and departments had developed their own customer polling system (Burnham and Pyper 2008: 143). Furthermore, the government clearly showed its willingness to use managerial techniques such as benchmarking, the practice of comparing processes and procedures between administrations and transferring the best practices from one to others, performance indicators and public service agreements (PSAs), introduced to set out what taxpayers could expect in return for public expenditure on specific services.

All these improvements were illustrated in several governmental papers and, as we will see in the next paragraphs, summarised in the *Modernising Government White Paper* published in March 1999. This paper put together many of the managerial issues and processes which had been deploying piecemeal during the life of the Blair administration and even before. This document was, in some respects such as clarity, shortness and simplicity, a typical Blair product centred on communicative approach. However, the White Paper's contents underlined the government's philosophy and emphasised the significance and the centrality of the new public management in the New Labour project. The pace of reform was very tight, but only two years after its launch the Modernising Government initiative incorporated the practical concepts of the new "focus on delivery" and "reforming public services agenda" (Massey and Pyper 2005). However, while it was a political necessity for New Labour in government to adopt phraseology and techniques of the new public management, it was not necessarily the case that this approach to governance, even supported by the philosophy of the Third Way, would facilitate a real transformation of the public services invoked by its proponents. During the Blair era, "administrative crisis" in providing public services didn't disappear, such as the ones of the Child Support Agency and the Passport Agency with the collapse of their services in 1999, nor did the policy failings of the Foreign Office, such as the "arms to Sierra Leone" affair. For these reasons, some observers (Painter 1999; Horton and Farnham 1999) have recognised that the political claims for the virtues of the new public management and modernisation were often inflated.

The political leaders tended to emphasise the benefits of the New Public Management without focusing on policy implementation, impact and outcomes evaluation (Barber 2007, 2015). In government, the New Labour Party attempted to differentiate its approach from that of the previous Conservative Governments and effectively gave its managerialism a softer, friendlier and more accommodating image. Furthermore, the focusing on constitutional and political reform rather than economy reform was the strategy to enhance citizenship. As Painter (1999: 100) noted, the concepts of communitarianism and stakeholderism were initially stressed as means by which the harshness and rigidity of market solutions and naked competitiveness might be alleviated, but the currency of these concepts was fairly limited, and they were superseded, in time, by the Third Way, a much broader set of ideas. The debates about the Third Way approach involved a large number of issues (Giddens 1998, 2000, 2002), and the Third Way presented itself as a path between rampant free market capitalism and state socialism. However, it offered a linkage with the early manifestation of new managerialism and the New Labour modernisation programme (Newman 2001).

Third Way initiatives included partnerships in delivering public services, inclusion in policy formulation and coordination or join-up between government agencies and markets as the route to modernise governance and reform the Civil Service. However, as some authors noted (Horton and Farnham 1999: 225–228), the concept of the Third Way and its rhetoric decreased a few months after the victory in the 1997 general election. Indeed, Prime Minister Tony Blair and his ministers opted to develop the broader concept of modernisation as the key of the managerial reforms. In the end, the differences between the New Labour and Conservative Governments' approaches to public management and the Civil Service in some respects at least did not appear to be fundamental or striking. Indeed, "more significant, perhaps, are the areas of similarity" (Horton and Farnham 1999: 255).

A New Governmental Style: The Reorganisation of the Central Government

The first priority for the Blair Government was to introduce a new arrangement of the central government in order to start the programme of public-sector reforms illustrated during the electoral campaign of 1997. The first working paper was *The Government Expenditure Plans 1998–1999*, and it was published in April 1998 (Cm. 3920). The first chapter of the paper, called "Departmental Report," is particularly significant to understand the public policy approach used by the New Labour Government that was based on a "Unitisation" of the central government that meant a creation of different units composed by civil servants for policy-making on the principal social issues of the public debate. The paper opened with the appointment of the new Cabinet Secretary and Home of the Civil Service, Sir Richard Wilson, on 3 January 1998, which ended the ten years of his predecessor Lord Robin Butler.

After that, it showed the principal changes introduced by the new government, such as the creation of the Social Exclusion Unit, based in the Cabinet Office, to tackle the problems associated with unemployment, low incomes, poor housing, family breakdown and crime. In June 1997, the Better Government Team was set up; its aim was to produce a White Paper that formulated the vision of the new government on public services along with a programme of work to be taken forward together with government departments and partners. In May 1997 was created a Freedom of Information unit to set out proposals for a Freedom of Information Bill as proposed by the Prime Minister in his first Queen's speech. In the meantime, a Strategic Communications Unit was created at 10 Downing Street to coordinate the government's strategic messages across departments. Then, the Deregulation Unit was renamed the Better Regulation Unit; its aim was to cut the red tape for business and to ensure a right balance between costs and risks of regulation. In 1997–1998, this Unit led a review of 60% of administrative forms in government, reducing them by 18% in 1998 (ibidem: 27).

The Citizen's Charter Unit and the Charter Mark Unit were maintained in order to relaunch the initiative for improvement of public services. The Efficiency and Effectiveness Group was set up to improve performance of departments and agencies "by securing better value for money for the resources they use and by improving management of their business, to assist in carrying out the Government's programme to provide high-quality and efficient public services, at the lowest cost to the taxpayer" (ibidem: 7). The Efficiency and Effectiveness Group was formed by civil servants of the Efficiency Unit and the Next Steps Unit. A new agency called the Government Car and Despatch Agency was created on 1 April 1997 under the supervision of the Office for Public Service to secure transport, distribution and mail-related services for central government departments, the public sector and other approved customers. In the end, a Cabinet Office Secretariat was created "to support efficient, timely, and well-informed collective determination of Government policy and to drive forward the achievement of the Government's agenda" (ibidem: 16). The reorganisation was completed on 1 April 1998.

A major role in the policy management was played by the Office of Public Service in the Cabinet Office (OPS). The purposes of the OPS were: modernising and simplifying government so that it works more effectively for the benefit of the people; implementing a key government programme to improve the accessibility and quality of public services for citizens and business; and providing the central strategic supervision for the Civil Service (ibidem: 20). Six executive agencies were associated with the OPS and these were: the Central Computer and Telecommunications Agency; the Civil Service College; the Government Car and Despatch Agency; Property Advisers to the Civil Estate; the Buying Agency; and the Security Facilities Executive. In addition, the Central Office of Information was transferred to the Duchy of Lancaster under the responsibility of his ministry. The Report showed the results of the first year of the Blair Government, such as the Charter Unit major consultation to find out what people wanted of the Charter Programme, in preparation for the relaunch of the Charter as part of the Better Government programme; furthermore, the Charter Unit ran the 1997 Charter Mark Awards Scheme, with a record 947 applications and 365 awards. More than 28,000 nominations were received from members of the public. The contract for the Government Secure Internet was awarded in June 1997, and the service was operational from January 1998. The Efficiency Unit played a full part in the Comprehensive Spending Review (CSR), participating in the steering groups of all departmental reviews and in the cross-cutting reviews of many areas of government pursuing the Prime Minister's requirement that the spending review should include rigorous scrutiny of the scope for increasing efficiency. Twelve new agencies were created in the first year of government, meeting the target of more than 75% of civil servants employed by agencies. The plan of government was to implement a second phase to benchmark agencies against the Business Excellence Model, involving more than half of all executive agencies, 15 of the largest NDPBs, the Metropolitan Police, and six units from core departments and including in all some 360,000 staff. The Information Officer Management Unit (IOMU) developed its services and systems to enable it to take on a much wider strategic role, and the Senior Civil Service (SCS) Group implemented and monitored a common pay, appraisal and evaluation system across departments and established an Interchange Unit to monitor performance of departments and provide advice (ibidem: 21).

The last organisational change in the government system was introduced in the 2004 Budget speech by the Chancellor Gordon Brown, who announced that the government would merge HM Customs & Excise with the Inland Revenue to form a single department: Her Majesty's Revenue and Customs (HC Deb 17 March 2004 c. 331). This followed the recommendation of a review chaired by Gus O'Donnell, permanent secretary to the Treasury, which had been set up in July 2003 to review the three organisations dealing with tax policy and administration: Customs & Excise, the Inland Revenue and HM Treasury (HM Treasury press notice 78/03, 2 July 2003). The Commissioners for Revenue and Customs Bill was passed in 2005, before the general election. The Explanatory Notes to the Bill stated that the merger would enable the new department to meet its demanding PSAs and realise efficiency savings, with integration contributing 3000 posts towards total savings in HMRC of 16,000 posts by 2007/2008 (Revenue and Custom Bill 2005).

The objectives of the new government became clear after the first report and paper: focusing more on social issues with the creation of specialised units in government to pursue policy targets, taking forward a long-term spending review, improving public services and giving continuity to the initiatives such as the Citizen's Charter and Next Steps agencies started by the previous Conservative Governments to implement managerial techniques and skills in the Civil Service and to provide the introduction of new regulations such as the Freedom of Information Act and the Civil Service Code and Bill.

SWEEPING AWAY THE QUANGO STATE? CONTINUITY WITH MIXED RESULTS

The analysis of central government's changes under the Blair Government would be incomplete without a focus on quangos (quasi-non-governmental organisations). As we have seen, Thatcher's government attempted to reduce and rationalise these bodies but the result was not completely satisfying in terms of numbers (they decreased but many quangos were born as well in the Thatcher era) and the use of them, particularly in local government, was never repealed by the Conservative Governments of the 1980s and the 1990s.

In 1995, the then leader of the opposition Tony Blair pledged to "sweep away the quango state" should Labour be elected to power at the following election. This appeared to suggest an intended strategy of central reform with practical measures to increase the accountability of quasi-state institutions. After a few months in Downing Street, the Labour Government then published a document, which was considered less radical than its pre-election comments. The consultation paper *Opening Up Quangos*, published in June 1997, suggested some reforms:

(a) increasing the upwards accountability of quangos to ministers through the doctrine of ministerial responsibility to Parliament, as well as to higher-level bodies, such as government departments, regulators and larger quangos; (b) reinforcing this upwards accountability through fair and accessible complaints mechanisms, plus tightened relations with ministers, higher-level bodies, and, in more cases, the Ombudsman service; and (c) increasing quangos' "responsiveness" to the needs of local communities through increased "openness," enforced largely through voluntary codes based on the government's code on access to official information.

Following answers to this consultation paper, in June 1998, the government published *Quangos: Opening the Doors*, which set out its proposals for a non-statutory guidance framework for non-departmental bodies. The paper advised that: NDPBs should hold annual open public meetings, where practicable and appropriate, and where practicable, NDPBs should release summary reports of meetings; NDPBs should invite evidence from members of the public to discuss matters of public concern; NDPBs should aim to consult their users on a wide range of issues by means of questionnaires, public meetings, or other forms of consultation; executive NDPBs and advisory NDPBs that have direct dealings with members of the public should be brought within the jurisdiction of the Parliamentary Ombudsman; parliamentary select Committees should be invited to take a more active role in scrutinising the work of NDPBs; the close cooperation between local authorities and NDPBs with local offices should be encouraged; board members' codes and registers of interest, which were already mandatory for executive NDPBs, should be extended to all advisory NDPBs; and all advisory and executive NDPBs should produce and make publicly available annual reports.

Furthermore, the Public Administration Select Committee (PASC) published a report on quangos in 1998–1999 which recommended further action in increasing the transparency of local public spending bodies, while acknowledging that progress had been made: "Many NDPBs now publish a wide range of information about themselves either on paper or on the Internet. The evidence we requested from each department which sponsors NDPBs shows how far most quangos have implemented the recommendations in *Quangos: Opening the Doors*. It is now common for NDPBs to issue Annual Reports, minutes, or summary reports of meetings" (Quangos Public Administration Select Committee, HC 209-I 1998–99).

Through a series of reforms documented in reports from the Public Accounts Committee, the National Audit Office's responsibility for auditing was extended to all executive NDPBs. The Government Resources and Accounts Act 2000 enabled the government to make Orders to provide the Comptroller and Auditor General with statutory rights of access and to enable his appointment as auditor on behalf of Parliament to those non-departmental public bodies currently audited by auditors appointed by ministers or the bodies themselves.

In July 1998, the government published *Quangos: Opening Up Appointments*, which included a commitment to the equal representation of women in public appointments and a proportionate representation of ethnic minority groups. Of particular significance was the extension of the Commissioner for Public Appointments' remit to include ministerial appointments to the boards of public corporations, nationalised industries, utility regulators and advisory NDPBs from 1 October 1998.

Hence, there were four key documents produced by the Blair Government: *Opening Up Quangos* (11 November 1997), *Responses to the Consultation Paper: Opening Up Quangos* (May 1998), *Quangos: Opening the Doors* (29 June 1998) and *Quangos: Opening Up Appointments* (5 July 1998).

Following the 1997 election, the Labour Government brought more bodies under the jurisdiction of the Commissioner for Public Appointments, but it resisted broader changes to local public spending bodies. There had been occasional suggestions of elections for local bodies, such as police boards, but no general policy to introduce electoral principles. Statutory rights to inspect agendas and minutes of local government meetings, and to attend such meetings, were not extended to quangos until the implementation of the Freedom of Information Act 2000 in January 2005. This now offers the public opportunity to gain more information on quangos, particularly with regard to publication schemes, but a series of exemptions means that public bodies may resist disclosure in certain instances (Skelcher et al. 2001: 13; Parliament and Constitution Centre 2005).

Parliamentary debates on the subject of quangos indicated that political interest and the previously felt urgency for widespread reform then declined. Tony Wright, Chairman of the PASC, noted at the start of a Westminster Hall debate:

> One would have thought that with all the attention focused on quangos in recent years, there would have been queues at the door for our debate this afternoon with people wanting to weigh in with their views on something that has been a running theme in our political life for a long time. It is distressing and revealing that this is not the case. (HC 346 Deb 16 March 2000 c115WH)

Then, in 2003 the PASC published the report *Government by Appointment: Opening Up the Patronage State* (2003). The conclusions drawn by the Committee were: there was a basic lack of information about the quango state, including which bodies exist, their roles and powers, and their formal organisational status. Lists currently in circulation (such as the Cabinet Office publication Public Bodies) did not include all bodies and commonly included errors and omissions; there was poor public understanding of the process by which department ministers and officials decide whether a given body should become a NDPB, executive agency, non-ministerial department, or another "unrecognised" form of quango, and the implications of this categorisation in terms of the accountability frameworks that pertain to each type; public mistrust in the quango state remained and while the proportion of women, people from ethnic minorities, and people with disabilities in public bodies had improved, further increases were necessary to ensure the boards of quangos were representative of the public they served (MacLeavy and Gay 2005).

In response to these findings, the PASC pointed out some recommendations: "The Government should create a comprehensive 'Directory of Government' that would set out the topography of the state and be available online for use by members of the public. This would improve the transparency of the quango state and raise the public's perception of its legitimacy; the Government should ensure clarity of quangos' status and the process by which this is determined. This ought to improve intelligibility of the overall system and thus raise its strategic capacity within any given policy field; the Government should extend the remit of the Commissioner for Public Appointments. This should help increase the public's faith in the appointment process; and the Government should continue with programmes that aim to increase proportions of women, members of ethnic minorities, and people with disabilities within the quango state. This will help diminish the view that quangos are the domain of a privileged elite and that members are only appointed as a result of political patronage" (HC 165-I, 2003).

In its formal response to the 2003 PASC Report, the government accepted the recommendation for a "Directory of Government" and the need for increased transparency and it promised a review of quangos, to be conducted by the Cabinet Office, and proposed initiatives to allow local government some supervision over local public spending bodies. The government planned to maintain its investment in programmes that helped to further increase the representation of minority groups on the boards of quangos (MacLeavy and Gay 2005).

At the end of the Blair premiership, the issue remained under discussion, especially as concerned accountability and representativeness of these non-governmental bodies. Regarding numbers of quangos, public bodies showed a decline in total NDPB numbers, from 1128 in 1997 to 849 in 2003. However, NDPBs which are the responsibility of devolved administrations haven't been included since 2002. Excluding NDPBs sponsored by the Scottish Office, Welsh Office and Northern Ireland Office, in 1997 there was an overall total of 880. In the case of the Conservative Governments as well as the Blair administration, the divergence between government aims and final results in reducing these spurious bodies was consistent.

THE COMPREHENSIVE SPENDING REVIEW: ROUTINISING PUBLIC SPENDING CONTROL IN THE CIVIL SERVICE

In July 1998, the government launched the CSR initiative (Cm. 4011, 1998). In the introduction, the Prime Minister wrote, "This Government will spend only what it can afford, and will spend wisely to achieve specific outcomes" (Cm. 4011: 5). Then he explained the mission of the spending review: "This White Paper sets out the overall plans for each department for the next three years and the Government's new, strategic approach to public spending. In each area, it reflects detailed public service agreements between departments and the Treasury about how these overall totals will be spent, with clear objectives and output and efficiency targets that departments have agreed to meet." The PSAs were one of the most important innovations introduced by Blair's Cabinet during his first term in office and, as we will see, the PSA would have been the pillar of the public service reform.

The new strategy of government was illustrated by the Prime Minister's introduction: "That is why we insist on a new principle for funding public services: 'money for modernisation'. 'Money for modernisation' is a contract. It says we will invest more money but that money comes with strings attached. In return for investment there must be reform" (ibidem: 5). In the General Overview of the White Paper, the spending plans showed how the government would combine prudent spending plans with stability (three years—long-term plan), separating capital investments and budget in order to avoid the squeeze out of investment in the short term, and flexibility, which meant the central government could act as enabler, promoter, owner, and controller depending on the opportunities and needs. The paper continued setting out the departmental plans: "Reforms across departments will result in:

- resources being reallocated from bureaucracy to front-line services;
- services being targeted more effectively where they are most needed;
- greater emphasis on prevention rather than simply dealing with the symptoms of deep-rooted social problems;
- and wasteful expenditure and subsidies being cut, and the commitment to competition enhanced" (ibidem: 10).

It further proclaimed: "The Government will ensure that the policy reforms and targets are delivered by:

- monitoring closely each department's PSA;
- regular reporting of progress on the main departmental targets and manifesto commitments, including in the Government's Annual Report;
- monitoring progress on the growth and employment strategy in the Economic and Fiscal Strategy Report; reporting annually on poverty trends and the delivery of the main anti-poverty measures;
- keeping Departmental Investment Strategies under review to ensure the Government's investment strategy as a whole is being delivered; requiring outstanding reviews to deliver against tight timetables and maintaining the pressure on departments to secure further service improvements" (ibidem: 16).

The CSR was the first step towards a further modernisation of central government: monitoring progress, reporting results, control of investment and strategy, attention to delivery were the new issues established by Blair's Cabinet and the PM's advisers that informed a new approach particularly for civil servants.

PUBLIC SERVICES FOR THE FUTURE: THE PUBLIC SERVICE AGREEMENTS

In December 1998, the Chief Secretary to the Treasury presented Command Paper 4181, titled *Public Services for the Future: Modernisation, Reform, Accountability*, to explain the concrete effects of the PSAs in the governmental departments. The commitment to achieve and monitor results continued: "The amount spent or numbers employed are measures of the inputs to a service but they do not show what is being achieved. [...] What really matters is the effectiveness and efficiency of the service the public receives" (ibidem: 2). PSAs were a single document in which each department wrote some important information about the public service offered. The elements established by the White Paper were: an introduction setting out minister's commitments on behalf of all the administrative bodies of the ministry; the aims and objectives of the department or cross-cutting area focusing in particular on growth and employment, promotion of fairness and opportunity, delivery and efficiency; the resources which have been allocated to it by the Treasury with the CSR; key performance targets for the delivery of its service, together with, in some cases, a list of key policy initiatives to be delivered (SMART—Specific, Measurable, Achievable, Relevant and Timed); a statement about how the department had increased the productivity of its operations (Cm. 4181).

The paper showed how the Cabinet was committed to enforcing managerialism through spending reviews and performance management, and how governmental papers were becoming more usable and simple to communicate outside the Civil Service. The aim was to enforce responsibility of competent ministers for each public service towards performance monitoring; indeed, "The publication of PSAs is of course only the beginning. The Government will be monitoring performance against individual PSAs" and "if progress is slipping, a Cabinet Committee chaired by the Chancellor of the Exchequer will look with the relevant Minister or Ministers at ways of getting performance back on track" (ibidem: 2), and this control by the Treasury was meant, as well, to strengthen its role in controlling governmental activities. The government committed itself to giving regular information to Parliament and to writing a public annual report on general progress.

This approach by the government was unavoidable because the PSAs covered all departments and agencies right across government and set out the aims and targets the government had established for the rest of the Parliament and beyond.

Modernising Government: A New Focus on Public Services Delivery for the Civil Service

In April 1999, a Command Paper titled Modernising Government (Cm. 4310) was presented by the Blair Cabinet to Parliament. The approach to government was clearly expressed in the introduction made by the Minister of the Cabinet Office, Jack Cunningham, who wrote, "It is a clear statement by the Government of what government is for. Not government for those who work in government, but government for people—people as government, people as citizens" (Cm. 4310, 1999: 5). The influence of managerial doctrines in the organisation of public administration was clear; the idea of efficiency, central in the previous Conservative Governments, was not arrested by the Labour Government, but it was combined with a plan to improve coordination at governmental level, focusing in particular on public services delivery.

To ensure that the government had become more inclusive and integrated, the paper found three aims in the process of modernisation: ensuring that policy-making was more joined up and strategic, making sure that public service users, not providers, were the focus by matching services more closely to people's lives, delivering public services that were high quality and efficient.

The paper focused on five key attainments in the Blair Government's quest for modernisation of government services. First of all, policy-making was centralised in the new Centre for Management and Policy Studies, then joint training for ministers and public servants was introduced together with a peer review system for departments. Second, the "joined-up government system" was enforced with local partnerships and one-stop shops as well as with the involvement of the needs of all different groups in society. Third, to improve the quality of public services the government established a review of all central and local government department services and activities to identify the best supplier in each case, new targets were introduced for all public bodies in order to improve effectiveness in public services, and monitoring of performance was applied to all suppliers of public services. Fourth, a new IT strategy was settled and new targets for electronic service were established. Last of all, modernisation of the Civil Service, revision of performance management arrangements, and tackling of under-representation of women and ethnic minorities were undertaken.

The addition of the New Labour Government was based on two main concepts: coordination and inclusion. As far as concerned the first, the paper argued "in general too little effort has gone into making sure that policies are devised and delivered in a consistent and effective way across institutional boundaries. [...] An increasing separation between policy and delivery has acted as a barrier to involving in policy making those people who are responsible for delivering results in the front line" (ibidem: 15). In the list made by Modernising Government of new policies, the Government wrote about inclusion—"We will devise policies that are fair and take full account of the needs and experience of all those—individual or groups, families, and business—likely to be affected by them"—because this meant developing new relationships between Whitehall, the devolved administrations, local government and the voluntary and private sectors and consulting outside experts, those who implemented policy and those affected by it, early in the policy-making process so the government could develop policies that were deliverable from the start (ibidem: 16).

The Command Paper set up the Social Exclusion Unit to tackle inequalities, the Women's Unit to represent the needs of women, the Performance and Innovation Unit to focus on coordination and delivery of public services, the UK anti-drugs coordinator to tackle the drugs problems, the Small Business Unit to improve support for small business, and the crime reduction programme to coordinate the efforts of central and local government in fighting crime. The Customs and Excise/ Inland Revenue agreed cross-representation on each other's boards and appointed a joint programme director to improve coordination of their tax policies.

Hundreds of civil servants in central government were involved in this new system of functions. The aim of the Prime Minister and his Cabinet was "developing, in the newly formed Civil Service Management Committee of Permanent Secretaries, a more corporate approach to achieving cross-cutting goals and providing the leadership needed to drive cultural change in the Civil Service. One of its tasks will be to ensure that the principles of better policy making are translated into staff selection, appraisal, promotion, posting, and pay systems ... and joint training to Ministers and officials which will allow them to discuss the way policy is, and should be, made to address particular areas of policy" (ibidem: 18). Furthermore, a peer review system was introduced to ensure departments implemented the principles of Modernising Government (ibidem: 20).

Another crucial aspect of Blair's modernisation programme was "listening to people." The Modernising Government launched the People's Panel initiative, "a 5,000-strong nationally representative group—a world first—to tell us what people really think about their public services and our attempts to make them better." The initiative was carried on by individual parts of government, including local organisations such as citizens' juries, community forums and focus groups. This action taken by government was the continuation and the update of the Citizen's Charter launched and promoted by Major's government in 1991. Consumeristic rhetoric continued in the paper: "Government Departments and agencies must be sensitive to their customers. This is true even of organisations whose work does not bring them into daily contact with the public" (ibidem: 25).

The policies were also divided into three typologies: national, citizen-focused programmes managed by central government, such as employment policy; group-focused programmes, such as Service Families Task Force, based at national or local level; and area-based programmes focused on a particular geographic area, mostly managed by local governments.

Another innovation introduced by the Government with the 1999 Modernising Government were one-stop shops. What were they? The paper explained that "they can take the form of places people visit to get advice and information about different services, such as the Public Record Office's Family Records Centre and the Lewisham and Camden one-stop shops for benefits." They could be real (a desk) or virtual (such as via telephone or Internet). One-stop shops were introduced to "reduce the number of separate visits people have to make to get services. They also lead to a more efficient use of resources by service providers" (ibidem: 30).

As far as concerned the public services, the Cabinet adopted a very managerial approach, based on pragmatism more than ideology. First of all a problem of correlation between public expenditure and services was highlighted: "Governments have not always looked closely enough at the link between spending and what the public is really getting in the way of results. Sometimes they have to cut resources in one area without being fully aware of what the consequences across the system will be. At other times, resources have been increased with no real certainty that this is leading to improvements in services as experienced by users" (ibidem: 35). Despite this pragmatism, neoliberal and conservative echoes were still present; indeed, the paper argued that it was not to be assumed that "everything the government does has to be delivered by the public sector." In the vision of Blair's government, competition was a tool to deliver improvements but not a holy creed as it was for Major's Cabinet. In the end, "this means looking hard—but not dogmatically—at what services government can best provide itself, what should be contracted to the private sector, and what should be done in partnership" (ibidem: 35). These aims were achieved through a set of policies: CSR, PSAs, public expenditure planning and control, introducing targets and measures for all public bodies and services.

A new Cabinet Committee called PSX was set up to monitor progress on a regular basis, a Public Service Productivity Panel was established, bringing together public and private experiences to help departments to achieve the improvements necessary, and an annual report was institutionalised for presenting progress to Parliament and to the public. A new system of inspections was elaborated to ensure effectiveness and evaluate value for money for both national and local public services, and this policy was pursued with the help of the Public Audit Forum, which represented all the national audit agencies. Auditors were used to obtain value for money and to support innovation and risk-taking in public services. Deregulation was carried on with the proposal "to extend the Deregulation and Contracting Out Act 1994 to make it easier to remove burdens from public sector organisations" (ibidem: 38). The Public Sector Benchmarking Programme was launched "to spread use of the Business Excellence Model across the public sector. The Model is widely used by leading private sector companies, but for the public sector this project is the world leader in scale and ambition. It is helping to spread best practice across boundaries, not just within the public sector, but between public and private users of the Model and internationally. Uptake of the Model has already reached 65% of central government agencies and 30% of local authorities" (ibidem: 39).

At the heart of the strategy to modernise government, there was the identification of the best supplier; in any case, it didn't matter if this was private, public, or public–private partnership. As the paper established, "Winning suppliers will need to offer improved quality, as well as better productivity and lower costs. [...] We will mount a co-ordinated programme across the public sector based on common principles, embracing the Better Quality Services initiative for central departments and agencies, and Best Value in local government" (ibidem: 41). New standards were set by the paper in order to deliver real improvements such as the Charter Mark for customer service, Investors in People for skills and motivations of staff, ISO 9000 for services and processes, and the Business Excellence Model to achieve better organisation.

The idea of modernisation was developed by the government even through the use of information technology. The concept of "Information age government" was coherent to the Third Way ideas sustained by Blair in order to face the issues raised by globalisation and 24/7 media development at the end of the twentieth century. Managing information through new technologies at the heart of government became central. As the paper argued, technology "can give us access to services 24 hours a day, seven days a week. It will make our lives easier" (ibidem: 45). The programme was to expand the use of IT from central government to services like schools and healthcare, to foster the development of e-commerce and to decentralise IT spread in a way that departments and agencies could provide for their own needs of modernisation.

Once again a managerial rhetoric was adopted with the catchphrase "a corporate IT strategy for government." The paper set five objectives: elaborate key guidelines for managing, authenticating, and identifying data, use commercial open standards wherever possible, establish frameworks for specific technologies where stronger coordination is needed, ensure that government acts as a champion of electronic commerce, use the Government Secure Internet to boost cross-departmental working and to make the public-sector work more coherently, and strengthen the protection of privacy and human rights while providing a clear basis for sharing data between departments. A set of new frameworks across government was established to cover data standards, digital signatures, call centres, smartcard access to some governmental functions, digital TV and websites, government gateways to a wide range of services and information provided by the government through Internet, online services for business (ibidem: 51).

The last part of the paper was focused on public servants. On this topic, the government set out an approach based on three assumptions. First, there was the necessity of restoring the pride of public servants after a long period of administrative reforms led by Conservative Governments: "Public service has for too long been neglected, undervalued, and denigrated. It has suffered from a perception that the private sector was always best and the public sector was always inefficient. The Government rejects these prejudices." Second, continuity with the past would not be withdrawn, yet neither would progresses achieved by Conservatives be denied, the government argued in the paper: "The reforms of the last two decades in the Civil Service, for example, have done much to develop a more managerial culture. The quality of management has improved: There is a better focus on developing people to deliver improved performance and there is greater professionalism." Third, a new spin in public services and bureaucracies for the twenty-first century had to be built because "we must not jeopardise the public service values of impartiality, objectivity, and integrity. But we need greater creativity, radical thinking, and collaborative working. We must all, both the politicians elected by people and the officials appointed to serve, move away from the risk-averse culture inherent in government.

We need to reward results and to encourage the necessary skills" (ibidem: 55). Flexibility and opening up became two central concepts, as the paper argued: "We want the Civil Service to reinforce its effort to be more open and to recruit more experience, skills, and ideas from outside. This must happen at all levels. We must be more flexible in bringing people in for short periods to provide specific skills for a particular policy area or project" (ibidem: 56).

This was an aim that, as we will see further, was to be achieved with a massive increase of appointments of special advisers, introducing de facto a very limited and singular spoils system as the paper outlined. Several challenges were established for the Civil Service, such as implementing constitutional reform in a way that preserves a unified Civil Service and ensures close working between the UK government and the devolved administrations, getting staff in all departments to integrate the EU dimension into policy thinking, focusing work on public services so as to improve their quality, make them more innovative and responsive to users, and ensure that they are delivered in an efficient and joined-up way, creating a more innovative and less risk-averse culture in the Civil Service, and improving collaborative working across organisational boundaries.

To meet these points, a learning organisation for training and development was necessary, and Modernising Government introduced a series of reforms. A Centre for Management and Policy Studies was created. It incorporated the Civil Service College with the mission of: be responsible for corporate Civil Service training and development, ensure that current and future leaders of the Civil Service are exposed to the latest ideas and thinking on management and leadership, keep abreast of the latest developments in public governance and management, act as a repository for best practice, and work closely with research and evaluation units in departments to develop and strengthen policy evaluation capacity and coordinate evaluations of cross-cutting policies (ibidem: 57).

In the meantime, the Department for Education and Employment set up the new National College for School Leadership, and the Armed Forces had a new Joint Services Command and Staff College. As far as concerned pay the government commitment was to revise pay scales and introduce new grades based on skills for all public servants, making best use of non-pay incentives such as better training and development opportunities, good career prospects, improved working environments, flexible working, family-friendly working practices, national awards and honours. Then, the government focused on rewarding results and performance; the best results of individuals and teams had to be best rewarded. The paper argued, in very broad terms, that in the Civil Service, performance management was not always clear and that pay performance had to be used in a more creative way to sustain high-quality performance.

An equality policy was launched to reduce the difference between men and women, ethnic minorities and disabled people in the Civil Service. A five-year plan was started in order to achieve targets established by the government, such as 35% of women in the SCS and 25% at top posts by 2005. Other targets were established for ethnic minorities and disabled people. The same principle was applied for public appointments. Furthermore, the paper argued, "The Government will improve access to public appointments. We are committed to ensuring that public appointments are open to a wide field of candidates so we can draw on the widest possible range of expertise and backgrounds" (ibidem: 60). Every year a departmental action programme would devise plans about improved accessibility to and equal representation in public posts.

In the conclusions, the White Paper highlighted a vast programme of a "change in the way government makes policy, in the way services are delivered, in the way government use technology, and in the way public services are valued. It will involve everyone working in the public services, and everyone who uses public services." To check results, "the Government will set milestones to chart our course and success criteria so that the users of public services can judge whether the modernisation programme is working. We will report annually on progress." As with a company, an annual report by the Government was introduced to give updates on reform progress.

The pillar for Blair's government Civil Service reform action was built with a greater continuity with the past, shuffling managerialism, tradition, and a new attention towards delivery, inclusion and social issues.

THE IMPLEMENTATION OF PERFORMANCE EVALUATION: GOOD PRACTICE IN PERFORMANCE REPORTING

On 7 March 2000, the House of Commons issued a report called *Good Practice in Performance Reporting in Executive Agencies and Non-Departmental Public Bodies* (HC 272, 2000) to ensure improvements in performance evaluation of public bodies. The report was realised under the direction of the National Audit Office and the Comptroller and Auditor General in consultation with the Cabinet Office, the Treasury and executive agencies. Its purpose was "to assist agencies to improve further their performance reporting by setting out guidance based on their own good practice in collecting and reporting performance information" (HC 272, 2000: 5) This was the first report on this issue, and it was a consequence of Modernising Government and the PSAs practice. Once again managerialist influence was consistent: "Performance measurement and reporting are intrinsic to the whole process of public management, including planning, monitoring, evaluation, and public accountability" (ibidem: 6). The advice on performance measurement was based on data collection, specialist advice and clear measure definitions, designating who was accountable for performance data, developing and implementing methods for collecting data and establishing clear guidelines for the validation of performance data. The paper listed a checklist to collect, evaluate and present data focused on costs, value for money, establishing routines, controlling the use of information, considering methodology and quality.

The executive agencies were required to report performance against key targets set by ministers in their annual reports and accounts, to provide a complete picture of performance by including information on achievements against internal managerial targets and other performance measures.

In July 2000, the spending review focused on a better delivery of public services through the use of PSAs, which became a central issue in governmental action. The spending review "continues that process by setting out, for every major government department, its aims, objectives, and the targets against which success will be measured, including targets on improving value for money and efficiency" (Cm. 4808, 2000: 1). Coordination was another aim to achieve, and the paper set out actions taken by the government in this area: "To improve coordination further, 15 cross-departmental reviews were undertaken as part of the 2000 Spending Review, focusing on key issues from crime reduction and intervention in deprived areas to science research and the knowledge economy" (ibidem: 2) and "there are around 160 of these performance targets in total, some jointly held by more than one department, focused on the key strategic goals for departments and the Government as a whole" (ibidem: 3).

The foundations for another managerialist propulsion in the public sector, establishing a new form of performance measurement and political control of bureaucracy's outcomes, had been set up.

THE NEW CENTRE OF GOVERNMENT

After the Labour Party won the general election of 7 June 2001, a new phase started for Blair's government. Some new arrangements were introduced in the autumn of 2001 to support the Prime Minister's leadership and to achieve aims set by the Cabinet. A new strategy based on four key principles for the Cabinet Office was outlined (HC 262-I, 2001): a national framework on standards and accountability; within this framework, devolution of power to front-line professionals, enabling local leaders to innovate and develop new services; better and more flexible rewards and conditions of service for front-line staff; more choice for the consumers of public services and the ability, if provision falls below acceptable standards, to have an alternative provider.

Following the recommendation of Modernising Government, the Cabinet Office was strengthened by the creation of the Office of the Deputy Prime Minister, which worked closely with the Prime Minister's own office in playing a central role in ensuring that the government's strategic objectives were met. The Deputy Prime Minister had responsibility for supporting the Prime Minister in the delivery of key government priorities and programmes, and he took on specific tasks at the request of the Prime Minister. He was responsible for some issues directly through units such as: social exclusion, regional coordination, regional governance, international matters and climate change, devolution, and the British Irish Council (HC 262-I, 2001: 2). The minister for the Cabinet Office and Chancellor of the Duchy of Lancaster, in the person of Lord Macdonald, assumed the day-to-day responsibility for the work of the Prime Minister's Delivery Unit, for which he reported to the Prime Minister. Lord Macdonald focused particularly on policy implementation in the fields of education, health, crime and transport. These changes had resulted in a strengthening and deepening of the relationship between the Cabinet Office and Number 10. The strategic leadership of the Cabinet Office was empowered, creating a stronger steering from the centre, which benefited the Prime Minister. This framework left Tony Blair to play a key role in delivering the government's objectives and improving the delivery of public services.

In summer 2001, another innovation was established in Whitehall—the Prime Minister's Delivery Unit—which helped government to achieve key objectives. The new unit reported to the Prime Minister and was under the day-to-day supervision of the Minister of the Cabinet Office. It was headed by the Prime Minister's Chief Advisor on Delivery, Sir Michael Barber, who was based in Number 10 Downing Street. The role of the Unit was to ensure that the government achieved its delivery priorities during this Parliament across the key areas of public service: health, education, crime, asylum and transport.

The Unit's work was carried out by a team of staff with practical experience of delivery, drawn from the public and private sectors. The Delivery Unit reported regularly to the Prime Minister on progress towards achievement of these priorities and established the agenda for regular meetings with the ministers concerned; it helped in holding the public service departments to account through the established PSX monitoring process to make sure that they met their agreed PSA targets; ensured problems of delivery were solved as rapidly as possible undertaking specific processes; sustained government's focus on the key objectives over time.

Furthermore, the Office of Public Services Reform, also in the Cabinet Office, was created to advise the Prime Minister about the reforms of the Civil Service and public services. It considered competence and capacity in the public service, checked the respect of national standards and local innovation, and ensured intervention from the centre only when justified. It provided for alternatives for service users where provision was below minimum standard set in the PSA, and it promoted better conditions of service and more flexible rewards for front-line staff (ibidem: 4).

Using these two tools, Blair's government tried to enforce the role of the central government and the policy-making process, promoting a shift from the traditional policy-advisory role of civil servants to a policy-implementation role for the most of them.

The Delivery Unit: Creation and Aims

As we have already seen, after June 2001 the government restructured parts of the core executive and it created the Prime Minister's Delivery Unit. The mission of the Unit was to "ensure the delivery of the Prime Minister's top public service priority outcomes" (PMDU 2005).

The timing of the creation of the PMDU was an answer to some failures in policy implementation of Blair's first term. A PMDU official observed: "I think there was a general frustration from Number 10 and 11 about how tricky it was just to get stuff transferred through the machine," and Geoff Mulgan (Head of Policy Directorate 2001–2005) argued, "I always thought it was very dangerous for policy makers just to sit at the top of the hierarchy and push things down, expecting that if you pull a lever something predictable will happen at the other end" (Richards and Smith 2006: 334).

The view from the centre was that two key problems had emerged in the course of Labour's first term concerning effective policy delivery. The first problem was that there had been too much emphasis on imposing national standards in a top-down, hierarchical structure. Frameworks of national standards had been established across different public services—health, education, policing, etc.—but even clearly defined standards imposed from the centre did not necessarily translate further down the policy chain to the street level. The second problem was that departments were still not responding to the briefs of the centre. This partly reflected the nature of the British system of government and the power and resources available to departments compared to the relatively weak structural resources available to Number 10.

There was an attempt to change the focus, moving from process, which has always been one of the traditional Civil Service characteristics, to outcomes, where the Civil Service has been weak.

Originally located in the Cabinet Office, the PMDU was moved to the Treasury in 2002, although it still continued to report directly to the Prime Minister. This move was predominantly the choice of its director, Michael Barber, who believed that success would be dependent on establishing a close working relationship with the Treasury, and in particular the Public Services Directorate. Michael Barber was an academic who became an adviser in the Department of Education before being appointed as the Head of PMDU. He was appointed for his analytical approach, and he was very keen to appoint people from outside Whitehall to work with him.

The unit also drew on what it referred to as "the expertise of a wider group of Associates with experience of successful delivery in the public, private, and voluntary sectors" (PMDU 2005). After 2005, the unit was part of the wider building capacity section within the Cabinet Office which included other units responsible for delivery, such as the

E-Government Unit, the Office of Public Sector Reform and the Better Regulation Unit (Richards and Smith 2006). This allocation again exalted the explicit importance of central capacity building to the Blair Government. However, the PMDU was the lead body which had direct and frequent access to the Prime Minister.

Measurement became a key concept for the mission of the unit. As the Cabinet Secretary Andrew Turnbull argued: "We are not saying we have gone through an era in which we set targets very tightly from the centre and now all of that is being let go. We are trying to move on, not go back, to a world in which certain things we set very tightly, certain national standards and minimum standards, while encouraging greater freedom to tailor how that service is delivered and how that target is achieved and also to vary in local areas so that you match more closely what people want" (Richards and Smith 2006).

The Delivery Unit had created a direct relationship between the centre and policy delivery actors such as agencies. There was an important shift in resources going on, with executive power shifting from departments to the Prime Minister's Office. The Delivery Unit established a direct line of responsibility between those on the ground and Number 10 in a way that had not existed (Richards and Smith 2006). However, the right to increased autonomy was not being given to front-line professionals completely. Instead, it was given on a "carrot and stick" basis: "Better services should get more freedom and flexibility—earned autonomy for schools, hospitals, local government, and other public services. Failing services should be given the incentives to improve, and receive intervention in proportion to the risk of damaging under-performance" (Office of Public Service Reform 2002: 17).

A key element in this process was the targets developed under the guidance of PSAs, developed in cooperation with the Treasury. This pointed out another important relationship of the PMDU: while it was accountable to the Prime Minister, the Treasury also had an important influence on its work. Thus, although the Prime Minister's Delivery Unit was, as the name suggests, responsible to the Prime Minister, the role of the Treasury was also important because the Treasury established the targets that departments had to meet. However, to underline the point about personalism, the PSAs could be considered as targets set by the Prime Minister.

Another key role of the Delivery Unit was to check that progress was made in achieving departmental policy goals as specified in the

PSAs. PSAs were established after the 1998 CSR by the Modernising Government paper (1999), and they contained the aims, objectives and performance targets for each main government department. They included value-for-money targets and a statement of which office was responsible for delivering these targets. PSAs were decided on by the individual department following discussions with the Treasury and the Prime Minister's Delivery Unit.

Where organisations failed to achieve the prescribed targets set up by government, they were penalised in different ways ranging from a simple cut in government funding to the outright closure of an organisation, such as had occurred, for example, with a number of "failed" secondary schools. The practice of target setting had become the key tool of control exerted by government, as a report by the comptroller and auditor general, focusing specifically on Next Steps Agencies, argued: "Performance measurement and reporting are intrinsic to the whole process of public management, including planning, monitoring, evaluation, and public accountability" (Report by the Comptroller and Auditor General 2000: 2). The bulk of the unit was to ensure that policy priorities identified by the Prime Minister were attended to, such as health, education, crime and transport.

Michael Barber, the Prime Minister's chief adviser on delivery and the first head of the Delivery Unit (2001–2005) believed that for PMDU to be successful it needed to concentrate on key targets and indicators, rather than trying to address a whole range of targets across every policy field (Seldon 2004). Focusing on a relatively small proportion of PSAs allowed the PMDU to maintain a clear, strategic focus over key policy areas. As Geoff Mulgan, the head of the Cabinet Office strategy unit, pointed out an aim of the PMDU "was to help the system focus better on a few really compelling targets and to use those targets really to fix problems rather than just to become compliance exercises or to divert attention from other important priorities" (Richards and Smith 2006: 339). In organisational terms, the use of PSAs and the PMDU had led to a major change in the relationship between the centre (the Prime Minister's Office, the Cabinet Office and the Treasury) and departments. Before, only departments had had responsibility for the delivery of services, but the PMDU institutionalised Number 10's and the Treasury's role in monitoring what traditionally had been a relatively autonomous area of departmental activity. The PMDU, in discussion with the relevant departments, planned the process of delivery and how results were to be measured. From a constitutional side, ministers remained responsible to Parliament for the delivery of services, but the PSAs created a new line of responsibility directly to the centre. This created a strong connection between the PMDU and those responsible for delivering policy. Once the targets were established, there was a planning process which followed up the implementation of the targets. This included "the prime ministerial 'stock-take,' the Delivery Report, and the Delivery Planning Process." The delivery planning process involved examining the data flows and operationalised the targets by relating them to deliverables. Then, through the delivery report, the PMDU analysed the processes of delivery in order to assess whether targets were realisable.

A Joint Action Programme was developed to coordinate concerned departments and to find the most appropriate indicators. One such official observed: "And they can be projects that sort of—should I say, not made up—but are designed specifically for a particular problem or we've got some standard tools. The PMDU may also use what is called the priority review, which is a very rapid analysis down the delivery system, looking at what's going on, what's going wrong with it, you know, what's kind of blocking delivery" (Richards and Smith 2006). These tools constituted new ways for the centre to intervene in the policy process: public-sector reform fragmented the delivery process and new instruments had been re-established at the centre to re-impose central control. The Prime Minister no longer oversaw the direction of government but became involved in the process of policy delivery.

THE RISING IMPORTANCE OF POLICY-MAKING PROCESS ORGANISATION

On 1 November 2001, the Comptroller and Auditor General published the report *Modern Policy Making: Ensuring Policies Deliver Value for Money* (HC 289, 2001–2002), which was a manual for civil servants and politicians to build effective policy-making and to achieve better value for money between taxation and public services. The paper was a technical guide to introduce the fundamentals of policy-making within Whitehall, and it was the last one of a series of papers produced from the beginning of the Blair era. It was a very practical paper based on case studies, solutions and empirical principles to improve the chain of command in decision-making and to deliver better services.

The series of papers based on this issue started in 1999 with the Modernising Government White Paper, which stated that the government would improve the way in which policies were designed and managed around user needs and make use of the best available evidence. It also emphasised the need to assess, manage and communicate risks, part of the policy-making process. In June 1999, the Centre for Management and Policy Studies was established, incorporating the Civil Service College, to work with partners from the Civil Service, the wider public sector, private sector and academia to ensure that the Civil Service was cultivating the right skills, culture and approach to perform the task, to ensure that policy-makers across government had access to the best research, evidence and international experience, and to help government to learn better from existing policies.

In summer 1999, the Cabinet Office published the paper *Policy Makers' Rapid Checklist*, which was a source of advice and guidance on impact assessment and appraisal systems in policy-making, providing questions on whether and what needs to be done to take account of areas such as regulatory impact assessment, sustainable development, environmental appraisal, policy appraisal for equal treatment, health impact assessment, and health and safety and scientific advice. In September 1999, the Strategic Policy Making Team in the Cabinet Office published the paper Professional Policy Making for the Twenty-First Century. The report aimed to examine what professional modernised policy-making should look like; provide a snapshot of current good practice; suggest possible levers for change; and promote a vision for policy-making.

In January 2000, the Innovation Unit issued *Adding it Up— Improving Analysis and Modelling in Central Government*, which examined ways to ensure that analysis and modelling are given due weight in policy advice to ministers and senior managers, and that analysis, like policy itself, is properly joined up. The report concluded that there needs to be fundamental change in culture to place good analysis at the heart of policy-making, thereby developing leadership from ministers and senior officials, openness from analysts and policy-makers, better planning to match policy needs and analytical provision, best practice across departments and professions, and innovative solutions to recruit and retain the best people.

To tackle the problems of coordination, the Innovation Unit published *Wiring it Up* in the same month in order to deal better with cross-cutting issues, and to remove some of the barriers to joining up to improve public service delivery. In July 2000, the Office of Science and Technology published *Guidelines 2000: Scientific Advice and Policy-Making*, which set out key principles that should apply to the development and presentation of scientific advice for policy-making. The key messages were that departments should think ahead and identify early the issues on which they need scientific advice, get a wide range of advice from the best sources, particularly when there is scientific uncertainty, and publish the scientific advice and all relevant papers. In August 2000, *Good Policy Making: A Guide to Regulatory Impact Assessment* set out the importance of integrating regulatory impact assessments as a tool into the policy process for assessing the impact in terms of costs, benefits and risks of any proposed regulation which could affect business, charities and voluntary bodies. In March 2001, *Better Policy Delivery and Design* drew on case studies of policy delivery to identify the factors for success in successful policy delivery, to encourage more rigorous thinking about delivery issues and to focus attention on what can be done to achieve better results.

Another interesting report, written by the PASC and titled *On target? Government by Measurement*, was published on 10 July 2003 (HC 62-I, 2001–2). The report outlined two cultures of public service reform: the first approach "emphasises capacity-building in organisations, with attention to leadership and management issues," and the second approach "is typified by targets, its time frame is shorter, and its techniques are more mechanistic." The paper argued "both have their place, but it is important that the former is not crowded out by the latter" (HC 62-I, 2002: 7).

The paper highlighted the importance of targets because they "provide a clear statement of what the Government is trying to achieve. They set out the Government's aims and priorities for improving public services and the specific results Government is aiming to deliver. Targets can also be used to set out standards to achieve greater equity" (ibidem: 10). Delivery by the early 2000s had become central in the public service reform: "Targets provide a focus on delivering results. By starting from the outcome Government is trying to achieve, the targets encourage departments to think creatively about how their activities and policies contribute to delivering those results. They also encourage departments to look across boundaries to build partnerships with those they need to work with to be successful" (ibidem: 11).

In the second chapter, problems of the measurement culture were exemplified and the Committee found five main failings: failure to produce equity that meant lack of clarity about what government was trying to achieve; failure to communicate a clear message to staff; failure to focus on delivering results; failures in reporting and monitoring; confused accountability and the problems with league tables. In the last chapter, the Committee concluded with some recommendations, such as decentralisation of performance measurement in the main public services, increasing local government involvement in target setting, to enforce the use of targets among providers, the moving from absolute targets to measure progress in performance, better information for civil servants about service delivery and front-line experience, strengthening of reporting by executive agencies, local government and providers to the Cabinet.

As it can be noticed, the commitment of government to improve policy-making, implementation and delivery was strong and it included many governmental bodies employed periodically on research about management techniques. This period marked the passage from the exclusive interest in reducing public expenditure and promoting efficiency in public services of the 1980s and the 1990s to the development of a more comprehensive administrative science and management practices focused on quality, value for money, results' control and delivery process in decision and policy-making. During the Blair's period at Downing Street, a "new managerial" lexicon and practices began to permeate all the branches of British political system. From the analysis of these papers, it is clear that the aim of the Blair Government was, in continuity with administrative reforms developed from Fulton Report (1968) onwards, to strengthen professionalisation of civil servants and to develop new technicalities which would have enabled public servants to deal with societal changes, emerging markets and technological development.

The Rise of Leadership in the Civil Service

On 25 April 2003, the Cabinet Secretary and Head of the Civil Service Sir Andrew Turnbull sent a letter to all the members of the SCS titled "Improving Leadership in the Senior Civil Service" (Cabinet Office 2003) asking his colleagues to work on leadership in the Civil Service. He created a Civil Service Management Board Sub-Group to: establish a clear picture of what successful leadership looks like; examine investment in the development of leaders; change the approach to performance management to support high-performance culture; challenge assumptions about a lifelong career in the Service; and examine how to refresh talent at senior levels by both bringing in and bringing on talent.

Sir Turnbull wanted to achieve more active organisational and personal performance management that meant measurement and outcomes, more active career management that meant flexibility and more investment in development that meant education and training. In the last letter of 22 September 2003, the Cabinet Secretary outlined the vision and the programme of the Civil Service Management Board, stressing these points: offer more and better-quality training and development opportunities to staff at or approaching SCS level; introduce a new high-potential development scheme to equip the best for top posts; improve the approach to performance management, by simplifying the process, using better evidence and adopting a more systematic approach to improving the lowest performers; improve the reward and incentives package; introduce time-limited postings; develop more flexible employment patterns in the SCS by encouraging new career options; and develop more active exit strategies.

The letters showed the big shift that had occurred in the Civil Service in the previous 20 years. Until the 1980s a programme and a vision on leadership were inconceivable. Civil servants were considered in the traditional role of "servants of the Crown," anonymous players at the heart of central government. In the twenty-first century, their speeches had become based on leadership, reform commitment and a self-reformist approach to the Civil Service issues. The changes that had occurred in the media, society and politics showed their impact on the institution, which was adapting itself to play a new role in government.

This vision was then elaborated by the Performance and Innovation Unit in the review *Strengthening Leadership in the Public Sector* (Cabinet Office 2000). The research opened with a very reformist approach, arguing, "Britain's public services face unprecedented challenges at the start of the 21st century. They include: demands to modernise public services and orient them more closely to the needs and wishes of customers; higher expectations on the part of the general public, who expect public services to keep up with private ones; increased opportunities, and requirements, for partnerships both across the public sector and with private and voluntary organisations; pressures to harness new technology and deliver government services electronically."

The Performance and Innovation Unit suggested that "the public services are not attracting or keeping the best leaders, and do not have sufficiently robust strategies for recruiting them to the posts that matter most; jobs and careers in the public services are undervalued, and top leadership jobs are, arguably, underpaid" (PIU 2001: 1).

The report continued considering that "government must offer a better deal for public service leaders to make the public sector more attractive. This should build on attractive careers, conditions of work, and valuing expertise, but with a new emphasis on public sector values, on pay, and valuing outstanding leadership."

The PIU concluded with the recommendation that "public service leaders require appropriate challenge from those to whom they are accountable (politicians, non-executives, and inspectorates). But they also need to be given the space in which to lead from politicians and central government. Policy-makers should more systematically take account of the effects of policies, guidance, and legislation in either encouraging or constraining leadership. Departments should ensure that relations between politicians and chief executives are clarified and promote initiatives in joint training of political and administrative leaders. Inspection bodies should collectively look at leadership performance. Non-executives should be trained in best recruitment practice and in the effective holding of leaders to account for performance. The PIU should undertake scoping work on a project to examine in more detail the options for encouraging greater entrepreneurship and risk within the public sector" (ibidem: 6).

A leadership-centred approach spread from politics and Cabinet to the Civil Service in order to satisfy the pressures and the expectations of the public. A new role for the senior civil servants was designed, considering individual responsibility, skills and competence as guidelines to set a new public management.

After these transformations an assessment by government was considered proper, and in November 2004, the Minister for Cabinet Office presented to Parliament a draft of a Civil Service Bill in order to give a legislative shell to the developments of that institution. The Bill aimed to regulate the Civil Service Commission, which is responsible for appointments and recruiting, shape the roles and responsibilities of special advisers, protect core values of the Civil Service such as loyalty and impartiality, and enforce managerial issues, in particular budgetary delegation as set out by the Civil Service Management Act of 1992. Despite this moderate and gradualist approach embedded in the British administration tradition, expressed by the balance between managerialism, leadership and traditions, this consultative Bill never became an Act of Parliament.

THREE REVIEWS FOR EFFICIENCY IN THE PUBLIC SECTOR IN THE TWENTY-FIRST CENTURY: GERSHON, LYONS AND HAMPTON REVIEWS

In August 2003, Prime Minister Tony Blair and the Chancellor of the Exchequer appointed Sir Peter Gershon for an Independent Review of Public Sector Efficiency that was completed in July 2004 with the publication of the report. The role of the Treasury, which officially commissioned the research, was enforced in the intergovernmental interplay with Downing Street, and it gave major power in managing economic resources to the Chancellor of the Exchequer, a sign that Blair's second term was becoming much more a diarchy than a "presidential" government of the Prime Minister (Rhodes 2011). The objectives of the review were: reduced numbers of inputs (people and assets), while maintaining the same level of service provision, lower prices for the resources needed to provide public services or additional outputs for the same level of inputs, or improved ratios of output per unit cost of input; or changing the balance between different output aimed at delivering a similar overall objective in a way which achieves a greater overall output for the same inputs (Gershon 2004: 6). Considering the previous spending review, some changes were introduced by Gershon, such as a move to multi-year (three-year) plans for public spending at the departmental level and full end-year flexibility, allowing departments to carry over unspent resources and any efficiency savings into later years within the settlement period.

Furthermore, the PSA, including value for money PSA targets focused on the efficiency with which public services are delivered, introduced resource accounting and budgeting, plus Departmental Investment Strategies, which placed an emphasis on asset management and estate rationalisation in departments, and the replacement of previous running cost controls by administration cost limits for government departments (ibidem: 7). The review focused on back-office activities, introducing simplification and standardisation of policies and processes, adoption of best practices within each function and sharing of transactional support services to achieve economies of scale through clustering with other central government bodies. As far as concerned procurement, some best practices were highlighted by Sir Gershon, who found procurement savings in particular through better supply-side management seeking to communicate and manage likely aggregate public-sector demand in a strategic way with the supply sector, thereby enabling the supply side better to anticipate and plan for shifts in public-sector demand and further professionalisation of the procurement function within the public sector through either use of shared procurement models, or the enhancement of procurement skills (ibidem: 14). As far as concerned transactional services, the review recommended the enforcement of the IT investments in managing practices and data and a rationalisation of functions to stop duplications.

Delivery chain and policy-making structure had to be reformed as recommended by Gershon's review. In particular, the institution of policy, funding, and regulation (PFR) monitoring for the public sector was highly recommended in order to achieve a better value-for-money control, performance measurement and quality control. The same scheme had to be applied in relation to the private sector.

The estimated savings were between £15 billion and £20 billion within the 2007/2008 budget, and it set a reduction of 84,000 posts by April 2008 in the Civil Service, of which 13,500 had to be relocated to front-line activities, giving continuity to the governmental policy of enhancing delivery of public services. An Efficiency Team led by John Oughton, chief executive of the OGC (Office of Government Commerce), was set up to supervise the project of spending review, working closely with the Treasury and reporting directly to the Prime Minister and the Chancellor. The Team cooperated with the Prime Minister Delivery Unit, directed by Michael Barber, in order to exploit the experience of this unit about PSA framework. Moreover, the departments had to produce *Efficiency Technical Notes*, setting out the measures and methodologies that they would use to assess efficiency savings. These Notes were scrutinised by the Audit Commission and the National Audit Office in order to check the reliability and credibility of these measures. In the end, cooperation of civil servants and ministers was fundamental to achieving the objectives of Gershon's plan.

The spending review undertaken by the Blair Government went further by 15 March 2004 with the publication of the Lyons Review.

The Chancellor announced a new review of Civil Service dispersals during his 2003 Budget statement: "Successful relocation out of London by private sector companies suggests that public sector jobs transferred to regions and nations could exceed 20,000, to the benefit of the whole country. Today, therefore, we are asking Departments to submit updated workforce development plans and asking Sir Michael Lyons of Birmingham University to advise with a view to decisions on relocation by the next spending review" (HC Deb 9 April 2003 c. 280).

Some examples of dispersals are listed below. The first two are straightforward dispersals, while the second two involve the location of new agencies outside London and the South East: 1760 staff of the Manpower Services Commission to Sheffield; 850 staff of the Patent Office to Newport; 650 staff of the Contributions Agency in Newcastle; and 2500 staff of the Child Support Agency in Dudley, Falkirk, Birkenhead, Belfast and Plymouth.

Press reports the following day indicated that the report itself had been delayed: "The Treasury admitted the delay was to allow 'close engagement' with Government departments that needed a 'better understanding of the opportunities' of moving out of the capital" (HC Deb 10 December 2003 c. 1066).

At least three departments are believed to have received a clear letter from Sir Michael Lyons, who was conducting the review. They were told the number of staff they planned to relocate was "disappointing" and ordered to think again. Some were told to double the number to hit their targets. In the end, in 2004 Chancellor Gordon Brown announced a further development by the Lyons Review in the future. In the Spending Review statement, he announced a new target for asset sales: "As a result of this relocation and rationalisation, I can now make a further reform. I will also today set a new objective for the disposal of Government assets for the period from now to 2010. I have asked Sir Michael Lyons to work with each Department to rationalise its use of property and land and, where necessary, to arrange asset sales and disposals. I can tell the House that the objective that I am setting is an overall total of £30 billion of asset sales" (HC Deb 12 July 2004 c. 1132).

The last review of these years was requested by the Treasury which in the Budget 2004 asked businessman Phillip Roy Hampton to conduct a review of the British government regulatory framework considering how to reduce unnecessary administration for businesses; an action which showed continuity with the simplification of administrative forms undertaken by Thatcher's government in the early 1980s.

The Hampton Report was published in March 2005, and it was titled *Reducing Administrative Burdens: Effective Inspection and Enforcement*

(HM Treasury 2005). The review found that the current regulatory system imposed too many forms, duplicate information requests, and multiple inspections on businesses. Hampton recommended that introducing risk assessment could reduce inspections by up to a third, meaning around one million fewer inspections, and cut the number of forms sent by regulators by almost 25%.

The report also stated that risk assessment would help regulators target non-compliant businesses more effectively, and reduce the burden on those businesses that do comply. Other recommendations made by the report were: reducing inspections where risks are low, but increasing them where necessary, making much more use of advice, applying the principle of risk assessment, and substantially reducing the need for form-filling and other regulatory information requirements; applying tougher and more consistent penalties where necessary; reducing the number of regulators that businesses deal with from 31 to seven, entrenching reform by requiring all new policies and regulations to consider enforcement, using existing structures wherever possible; creating a business-led body at the centre of government to drive implementation of the recommendations and challenge departments on their regulatory performance.

As a result of this final recommendation, the government created the Better Regulation Executive (BRE) to oversee the reduction of regulatory burdens on business, and hold government departments and regulators to account.

These three reports enhanced how the British Civil Service continued to be a poster child institution for the New Public Management techniques and innovations even in the twenty-first century. Even with different tools and promoting a "social story-telling" in the Civil Service and through the public, the three Es (Economy, Efficiency, Effectiveness) celebrated by the Thatcher Government in the 1980s continued to be the driver for British administrative reforms even in the twenty-first century.

Departmental Capability Reviews: Enforcing Delivery in the Core Executive

As we have seen delivery of public services had become a serious issue for the Blair Government, in particular during the second term. However, the Prime Minister's Delivery Unit was very effective in setting and promoting key priorities of the Prime Minister, but it remained a body to serve only Downing Street while departments were not equipped to improve their delivery. For this reason, the Cabinet Secretary Gus O'Donnell proposed in June 2005 to "do for departmental capability what (Blair) had done for delivery," creating a Capability Review programme in a letter to the Prime Minister titled "Transforming Departments' Capability to Deliver" (27 July 2005). Even if the Delivery Unit checked the progress of PSA targets, it had begun to embed a focus on delivery in selected departments and civil servants soon understood that a long-term public service reform could be achieved successfully only if the capability of all departments was enforced. As Michael Barber stated in 2005: "We discovered that the departments were not really up to driving the kind of agenda that we were setting them. So we could help them deliver these outcomes, but for sustainable reform, we needed to strengthen the departments as institutions" (Kemplay 2006).

This idea was promoted through a series of high-profile reports such as *Delivery and Reform* (2003) and *Delivery and Values* (2004). In continuity with these recommendations, the Cabinet Secretary argued that the Capability Reviews would focus on a department's capability to meet its future challenges. He would apply to permanent secretaries the same scheme applied by the PMDU to ministers in delivering key prime ministerial priorities, making them personally accountable for strengthening this capability.

One month after O'Donnell proposed the reviews, a Capability Reviews Team was set up in the PMDU, led by Peter Thomas, who had been director of performance development at the Audit Commission. In the team, there were four directors and ten deputy directors, and as the Cabinet Secretary said, "If we are going to fail, it won't be because we lacked good people" (ibidem). The composition of the team followed that of the PMDU: there was a mix of career civil servants and individuals with experience from the wider public and private sectors.

The team followed a similar path made by similar initiatives: priority reviews for PSAs, developing the best-value inspection methodology for local government, and the later Comprehensive Performance Assessment for local government star ratings. They also developed and tested elements of what became the review methodology during a commissioned review of performance management for the principal's public institutions.

There was a combined approach to performance management that mixed what were seen as the most effective elements of each approach.

With this method, techniques for delivery, leadership and strategy were compounded with other functions such as IT development (Panchamia and Thomas 2014). The model linked the capability issue directly to the quality of leadership in each department, developing a framework that went beyond O'Donnell's initial view, and it was considered completely new in the British Civil Service.

The first series of Capability Reviews started in March 2006. They focused on three broad areas of management capability: leadership, strategy and delivery. A review team was established, and it was composed of five senior people from inside and outside Whitehall, including two directors general from other departments and three external members from the private, public and voluntary sectors (Panchamia and Thomas 2014: 5). A former headhunter, Esther Wallington, recruited high-profile outsiders, such as Richard Baker of Virgin Active, Rob Whiteman, chief executive of the London Borough of Barking and Dagenham, and Amelia Fawcett, chairperson of Pension First. Each team was helped by two members of the Capability Review Team, who drove the development and implementation, facilitating the review team's analysis and conclusions.

The reviews made use of the evidence provided by the department as well as a combination of interviews and workshops held over a two- or three-week period. There was daily feedback to the department and regular conversations with the permanent secretary about the progress of the initiative. Then, the review team produced a report scoring the department against each element of the capability model. An independent moderation panel was set up to ensure coherence between the scores given to each department and to allow for comparison between them (Panchamia and Thomas 2014: 7).

The reviews aimed to provide a shared diagnosis of the situation and a sense of perspective on the challenge. To be precise, it was not a technical review but a "look in and make a judgement" about the capability of a department compared with its peers. This process generated anger and resistance among some permanent secretaries concerning the scores they received and some challenged O'Donnell hard not to publish the findings of the first tranche of reviews.

However, despite these difficulties there was a high level of acceptance of the remarks made by the review team. Many ministers and permanent secretaries who were reluctant and sceptical at the beginning then used the scores to carry on their internal reforms, and some others, such as Alistair Darling and David Miliband, appreciated the value of the reviews. To achieve such commitment, the participation of directors general in the initiative as external reviewers was essential to make supporters and advocates grow. Thanks to these efforts, the programme of reviews became a functional and permanent reform in central government.

THE FREEDOM OF INFORMATION ACT AND THE CIVIL SERVICE

In the period from the 1980s, the Civil Service started its process of open government to slowly adapt the institution to pressure for major openness by citizens. Considering the culture of secrecy was a typical element of the Civil Service; this new openness has been a major challenge for officials and politicians. Indeed, the dominant culture of secrecy in the British government imposed severe constraints on civil servants and contributed to a crisis of conscience in situations where officials believed they should be able to serve the public interest by disclosing sensitive information. These difficulties were best exemplified by the cases of Sarah Tisdall and Clive Ponting.

The dynamics of these cases included prosecution of the officials concerned, with mixed results (Tisdall convicted, Ponting acquitted), a severe restatement of the limited nature of institutional accountability in the form of the Armstrong Memorandum, an issue that was faced a year later with the Westland affair. While this reduced the restrictions on certain types of government information, it failed to meet the desire of reformers for a "whistleblower's Charter." The trend began to change with the Major Government, which published its White Paper on *Open Government* in 1993 (Cm. 2290), and the subsequent 1994 Code of Practice on Access to Government Information put increased amounts of information automatically into the public domain. When the Labour Party won the election in 1997, it had a clear programmatic commitment to legislate for open government and freedom of information, but the policy became very delicate for disagreement between ministers on the Bill and for the lobbying of civil servants on the draft bill and the White Paper. The Freedom of Information Act was approved by Parliament in 2000, but with a long delay by central government in providing for full implementation. From November 2002, government departments were required to produce publication schemes, setting out the information they would publish proactively, and how this information could be accessed (Burnham and Pyper 2008). It was a long and difficult process for the Civil Service, and the public right of access was completely enforced only in January 2005 and some exemptions were maintained by the law in these cases: information related to national security, ongoing investigations, material whose release is prohibited by another law, or where the information can "reasonably" be obtained elsewhere. In the case of a refusal for information, a citizen could appeal to the Information Commissioners. The Freedom of Information Act represented a new form of scrutiny of the Civil Service introduced by Parliament, even if the last decision on information disclosure remained in the hands of ministers. The flow of certain types of information from within government departments to the public domain has become fairly routine, and for new civil servants, there has been the acknowledgement that in the future FoI requests could be made by citizens about the documents they have drafted and created.

Recommendations by the Public Administration Committee (2002) persuaded the Blair Government to establish the Phillips Review to reform its system for communicating government information. The Phillips Review (2004) found that a culture of secrecy and insufficient disclosure of information was at the heart of the breakdown in trust between government and politicians, the media and the citizens. This situation prompted the government to enforce the implementation of the Act in order to create a "powerful tool to help rebuild public trust," by announcing that ministers would not use their veto and by assuming disclosure as a default position. In 2006, departments and the largest executive agencies and regulatory agencies (all staffed by civil servants) were together receiving about 1200 requests a month at that time. For around 60% of requests, the information was provided in full; and for 20%, it was refused entirely (Burnham and Pyper 2008: 188–189).

The most common reasons to deny access to information are that the request involves personal information or information provided in confidence or may prejudice a criminal investigation; "formulation of government policy" and "prejudice to the effective conduct of public affairs" are more controversial reasons to deny access to information, and they have been applied in 13% of cases. Moreover, Richard Thomas, the Information Commissioner for England, tried to resolve disputes over non-disclosure amicably and he issued 187 formal decision notices in 2005–2006, some ordering disclosure, some agreeing that the information need not be disclosed. The former group included a notice to the DES that it must provide minutes of some meetings (Information Commissioner's Office 2006: 14).

The Freedom of Information Act and its implementation completed a long walk of 20 years towards a more transparent state and more open Civil Service. It moved the UK closer to the norms and practices of other Western democracies. However, these formal procedures did not prevent scandals and affairs in later years that became the unintended consequences of transparency and freedom of information. Indeed, in his autobiography (2010), Tony Blair expressed regret about the FoI's effects: "The truth is that the FOI Act isn't used, for the most part, by 'the people'. It's used by journalists. For political leaders, it's like saying to someone who is hitting you over the head with a stick, 'Hey, try this instead,' and handing them a mallet. The information is neither sought because the journalist is curious to know, nor given to bestow knowledge on 'people'. It's used as a weapon." He concluded, "It didn't impact much in 2005. It was only later, far too late in the day, when the full folly of the legislation had become apparent, that I realised we had crossed a series of what should have been red lines, and strayed far beyond what it was sensible to disclose" (Blair 2010: 517).

CONCLUSIONS: DELIVERY, POLITICISATION, COORDINATION IN BLAIR'S ERA

To conclude, there is much evidence of continuities between the Blair and the Conservative Governments regarding in particular spending reviews, efficiency strategies, development of public management techniques following ideas of New Public Management and restrictive manpower policy. There were also some differences: the Blair Government supported the Prime Minister's office more strongly, creating a number of units focused on objectives established by Downing Street, coordination among units and departments became a driver to achieve objectives, the use of special advisers was increased by Prime Minister and ministers, the government aimed to shape a Civil Service more focused on delivery than on policy-making, the Cabinet coped more with social issues than in the past when the Conservatives were in Downing Street.

With the Freedom of Information Act and quango reform, the government aimed to introduce more transparency and openness in statecraft, even if with fluctuating political results. There was also a deeper politicisation effect of bureaucracy, which does not mean a spoils system was introduced or civil servants were politicised, but that the political control on public bureaucracy outcomes was strengthened through tools like the Delivery Unit, performance measurement and management. As far as concerned the institutional position of the Civil Service, continuity was not damaged, the project of a Civil Service Bill failed in the parliamentary debate and the "constitutional conservatism" continued to be preserved even in Blair's era, with the graft of a new codification process to preserve traditional values and practices of the Civil Service. So this period was aligned to the previous two decades, arresting any substantial change in constitutional principles and institutional conformance of the Civil Service and fostering, in the meantime, managerialist policies.

References

Books, Journals, and Articles

Barber, M. (2007). *Instruction to deliver. Tony Blair, public services, and challenge of achieving targets.* London: Politico's.

Barber, M. (2015). *How to run a government? So that citizens benefit and taxpayers don't go crazy.* London: Penguin.

Blair, T. (2010). *A journey.* London: Hutchinson.

Burnham, J., & Pyper, R. (2008). *Britain's modernized civil service.* Basingstoke: Palgrave Macmillan.

Gershon, P. (2004). *Releasing resources to the front line: Independent review of public sector efficiency.* London: Stationery Office.

Giddens, A. (1998). *The third way: The renewal of social democracy.* Cambridge: Polity Press.

Giddens, A. (2000). *The third way and its critics.* Cambridge: Polity Press.

Giddens, A. (2002). *Where now for new labour?* Cambridge: Polity Press.

Hampton, P. (2005). *Reducing administrative burdens.* London: HM Treasury.

Horton, S., & Farnham, D. (1999). *Public management in Britain.* London: Macmillan Press.

Kemplay, M. 2006. *Tony Blair delivery unit: Why did Tony Blair form the Prime Minister's delivery unit and was it successful in the years 2001–2005?* BA undergraduate thesis.

Macleavy, J., & Gay, O. (2005). *The quango debate* (Research Paper 05/30). House of Commons Library.

Massey, A., & Pyper, R. (2005). *Public management and modernisation in Britain.* Basingstoke: Palgrave Macmillan.

Newman, J. (2001). *Modernising governance: New Labour, policy and society.* London: Sage.

Painter, C. (1999). Public service reform from Thatcher to Blair: A third way. *Parliamentary Affairs, 52*(1), 94–112.

Panchamia, N., & Thomas, P. (2014). *Capability reviews.* London: Institute for Government.

Parliament and Constitution Centre. (2005). *Freedom of information implementation* (Research Paper 04/84).

Rhodes, R. A. W. (2011). *Everyday life in British government.* Oxford: Oxford University Press.

Richards, D., & Smith, M. (2006). Central control and policy implementation in the UK: A case study of the Prime Minister's delivery unit. *Journal of Comparative Policy Analysis, 8*(4), 325–345.

Seldon, A. (2004). *Blair.* London: Free Press.

Skelcher, C., Weir, S., & Wilson, L. (2001). *Advance of the quango state: A report for the LGIU.* London: Local Government Information Unit.

Archive Sources, Parliamentary Papers, and Official Publications

Cabinet Office. (2000). *Good policy making: A regulatory impact assessment.* London: Stationery Office.

Cabinet Office. (2003). *Improving leadership in the senior civil service. Letter by the head of the home civil service, Sir Andrew Turnbull, 25 April 2003.* London: Cabinet Office.

Cm. 2290. (2003). *Open government.* London: HMSO.

Cmnd 3638. (1968). *Report of the committee of the civil service* (Fulton Report). London: HMSO.

Cm. 4011. (1998). *Modern public services for Britain: Investing in reform.* London: Stationery Office.

Cm. 4808. (2000). *2000 Spending review: Public service agreements July 2000.* London: Stationery Office.

Cm. 4310. (1999). *Modernising government.* London: Stationery Office.

Commissioners for Revenue and Customs Act. (2005). London: Stationery Office.

HC 62-I. (2001–2). *House of commons. Public administration select committee. On target? Government by measurement.* London: Stationery Office.

HC Deb 9 April 2003 c. 280.

HC Deb 10 December 2003 c. 1066.

HC Deb 12 July 2004 c. 1132.

HC Deb 17 March 2004 c. 331.

HC 165-1. (2002–3). *Government by appointment: Opening up the Quango state, Fourth report*. Public administration select committee. London: Stationery Office.

HC 209-I. (1998–9). *Quangos public administration select committee*. London: HMSO.

HC 262-I. (2001–2). *Public administration select committee. The new centre. Minutes of evidence*. London: Stationery Office.

HC 272. (1999–00). *Report by the comptroller and auditor general. Good practice in performance reporting in executive agencies and non-departmental public bodies*. London: Stationery Office.

HC 289. (2001–2). *Modern policy-making: Ensuring policies deliver value for money. Report by the comptroller and auditor general*. London: Stationery Office.

HC 346. (2000). Deb. c115WH. London: Stationery Office.

HM Treasury. (2003). *Press notice 78/03*. London: HM Treasury.

Information Commissioner's Office. (2006). *Freedom of information act awareness guidance*. London: Stationery Office.

Office of Public Service Reform. (2002). *Reforming public services: Principles into practice*. London: Stationery Office.

Performance and Innovation Unit. (2001). *Better policy delivery and design: A discussion paper*. London: Cabinet Office.

Phillips Review. (2004). *Review of honours system*. London: Stationery Office.

Prime Minister's Delivery Unit. (2005). Available at http://webarchive. nationalarchives.gov.uk/20060213213351/cabinetoffice.gov.uk/ pmdu/ and http://siteresources.worldbank.org/EXTGOVANTICORR/ Resources/3035863-1285601351606/NovemberGetNote.pdf.

CHAPTER 5

Management and Tradition in the British Civil Service: Assessing Institutional Development—Issues and Conclusions

This journey through the contemporary history of the Civil Service and administrative reforms has reached its conclusion.

The process of Civil Service reform has been long and complex. It is of course simply a means to an end, which involves deliberate changes to the structures and processes of public-sector organisations with the purpose of getting them to run better (Pollitt and Bouckaert 2011). Analysis of public management reforms by the influential public administration scholars Christopher Pollitt and Geert Bouckaert has identified the following effects: making savings in public expenditure; improving service quality; making government operations more efficient; increasing the likelihood that the chosen policies will be effective (ibidem: 8).

The two scholars also identified some intermediate ends: strengthening the control of politicians over bureaucracy; freeing public officials from bureaucratic restraints that inhibit their opportunities to manage; and enhancing the Government's accountability to the legislature and citizenry for its policies and programmes (ibidem: 8).

Symbolic and legitimacy benefits of reform for leaders (politicians, officials, consultants) include: showing actions and creating storytelling while announcing reforms; criticising bureaucracy and praising new management techniques; restructuring ministries and agencies; and making a reputation or career from modernising and streamlining activities.

Over the three decades of reform, these ends and benefits have been recognisable. Most prime ministers, Cabinet secretaries, senior civil servants, occasional commissions and select Committee inquiries have argued

© The Author(s) 2018
L. Castellani, *The Rise of Managerial Bureaucracy*,
https://doi.org/10.1007/978-3-319-90032-2_5

for Civil Service reform at some point or another. The logic has been remarkably consistent over the years, and appetite for reforms remained unchanged.

However, some other issues more related to historical roots, traditions and institutional development of the Civil Service need to be considered to finish the picture and to present a more complete overview of this institution.

THE NEW LEGAL FRAMEWORK OF THE CIVIL SERVICE: PRESERVING THE TRADITION

In 1985, following the Clive Ponting affair, in which a civil servant was accused of breaking Section 2 of the Official Secrets Act 1911 by leaking information on the Belgrano affair, Sir Robert Armstrong, then Head of the Home Civil Service, issued a note titled "The Duties and Responsibilities of Civil Servants in relation to Ministers," best known as the Armstrong Memorandum (see Chapter 2). It stated, "Civil Servants are servants of the Crown—for all practical purposes the Crown in this context means and is represented by the Government of the day" (para. 2). Civil servants who felt that a fundamental issue of conscience was involved were told to consult a superior officer or the Permanent Secretary, who could consult the Head of the Home Civil Service (para. 11). The memorandum was based on an unpublished paper written in the 1950s by Sir Edward Bridges and a memorandum prepared by Sir Warren Fisher, Head of the Home Civil Service from 1919–1939, for a Parliamentary Committee. The trade union for senior civil servants, the FDA, argued for a Code of Ethics for Civil Servants and produced a draft discussed at its 1986 Conference. Following Ponting, the Treasury and Civil Service Committee (TCSC) conducted an inquiry into the duties and responsibilities of civil servants.

Interest was further increased by the Westland affair of 1986, where there was controversy over publicity given to the actions of individual civil servants. The TCSC Report commented, "Those whose prime loyalty is to the government of the day look to the Crown as a more enduring expression of their position within the constitution" (HC 92 Session 1985/1986). The appeal to the Head of the Home Civil Service was introduced into a revised version of the memorandum issued in 1987 following the drafting of a recommendation on this point in the Treasury and Civil Service Committee Report (para. 4.16 HC 92 1985/1986). The FDA had argued for an independent body for appeals. The revised memorandum was issued following comments from the TCSC, the Defence Select Committee, and the Civil Service unions (HC Deb 2/12/87 c.572-575 W). Following a further recommendation by the TCSC (HC 260 1989/1990), the Armstrong Memorandum was embedded into the Civil Service Management Code. The TCSC Report in November 1994 (HC 27 Session 1993/1994) summarised contemporary thinking on the status of the Armstrong Memorandum and argued for its replacement: it recommended the establishment of a Civil Service Code of ethics (paras. 103–107) and an independent appeals procedure based on a strengthened Civil Service Commissioner body (para. 108–112). Moreover, it called for a Civil Service Act to provide statutory backing to maintain the essential values of the Civil Service (para. 116). The government response, published in *The Civil Service: Taking Forward Continuity and Change* (Cmnd 2748), accepted the proposal for a new Civil Service Code and provided a revised version of the Committee's draft as an Annex.

Then, the Nolan Committee (Committee on Standards in Public Life) was set up by the then Prime Minister John Major in October 1994 to act as an "ethical workshop" for the public service in the UK. Its first report, published in May 1995, also considered the text of the proposed code and the planned independent appeal mechanism. Nolan was concerned with ensuring that the Code covered circumstances that might loosely be described as "whistle-blowing." Moreover, it recommended that departments nominate an official to investigate staff concerns raised confidentially and that the Civil Service Code be introduced without waiting for legislation (Chapter 3, paras. 53–54, Cmnd 2850).

The government response accepted the whistle-blowing recommendations (Cm. 2931, 1995) while renominating the terms to reflect a duty to report evidence of criminal or unlawful activity (Response to Recommendation 23). Civil servants would not be required to use the confidential channel proposed, but officials would be nominated, and guidance incorporated into the Civil Service Management Code (Response to Recommendation 24). It refused to implement recommendations from Nolan for the Civil Service Commissioner to give detailed information about appeals made before them, leaving the nature and extent of reporting up to the Commissioners to decide.

The new code came into force legally from 1 January 1996 (Cabinet Office News Release 28/12/95; the text of the 1996 Code may be found in Library Research Paper 97/5). The Armstrong Memorandum was overruled by the Code, which had been incorporated into the Civil Service Management Code that was redrafted in April 1996 (Paragraph 11 of the Armstrong Memorandum, which deals with an instruction which would give rise to a clear breach of the law, has been preserved in paragraph 7.7.6 of the Management Code). However, in evidence to the Public Service Committee, the Cabinet Office advised "the Memorandum remains a valuable statement of constitutional principles, and the Chancellor of the Duchy of Lancaster indicated his intention to issue a revision in due course" (Extract from a letter to the Clerk of the Committee 17/7/96 HC 313 II: 198). Such a revision was never issued.

Thereafter, the text of the Code wasn't the subject of debate. It was revised on 13 May 1999 following devolution to Scotland and Wales to make clear that civil servants in devolved areas owed their loyalty to the devolved government for which they worked. The Committee on Standards in Public Life called again for a Civil Service Act, which would affect the status of the Code. Further details are contained in Library Standard Note no. 2863 The Civil Service Bill 2003–2004. In the 2004–2005 session, the government issued a draft Civil Service Bill for consultation. However, no plans have been announced to bring forward legislation.

Sir Gus O'Donnell was appointed Cabinet Secretary in August 2005, and he launched a consultation on a new draft of the Code in January 2006, together with the First Civil Service Commissioner. The consultation closed on 21 April 2006. An innovation in the new Code was that it allowed appeals directly to the Civil Service Commissioners for some cases outlined in the new paragraph 18. In addition, civil servants would have also been able to report actions by others, as recommended by the Civil Service Commissioners. However, there was no new power for the Commissioners to initiate inquiries without a complaint.

The new text covered much of the same ground as the old version in more accessible language, but omitted any reference to the fact that civil servants are servants of the Crown, which formed part of paragraph 2 of the 1996 Code. It didn't reproduce the commentary of paragraph 3 which noted that the Code should be seen in the context of the duties and responsibilities of ministers as set out in the Ministerial Code. Finally, in the last paragraph, the draft code reminded civil servants that the Code is "part of the contractual relationship between you and your employer." This contractual relationship had not previously been set up, and this "contractualisation" can be considered as a result of the affirmation of managerial ideas within the Civil Service.

To conclude, it can be argued that the historical period considered was an "age of codification" (Blick 2016), and it was a reaction to a managerialisation and contractualisation process undertaken by the British Civil Service; it was the attempt to crystallise a changing relationship with ministers, to establish a clearer legal framework during a season of administrative reforms and, at the same time, to answer a need to reaffirm the traditional principles of the Civil Service. Once again, the coexistence between managerialism and tradition showed its double face even in the (self) regulation of the central government's bureaucracy.

The Rise of Special Advisers and Their Process of Institutionalisation

The British Civil Service has never had a complete monopoly on giving policy advice. Throughout the history of central government, the Prime Minister and the Cabinet have used other sources to design policies and to make decisions. Party research departments, academic experts, and think tanks have played an influential role in governmental policy-making (Campbell and Wilson 1995).

For example, the Thatcher Governments had developed a close working relationship with a number of independent research bodies such as the Centre for Policy Studies, the Adam Smith Institute and the Institute of Economic Affairs that elaborated the bulk of ideas for "the new Right" of Mrs. Thatcher. Blair's New Labour was influenced particularly by a number of think tanks that offered research mainly focused on public policies, such as Demos and the Institute for Public Policy Research. By the 1980s, civil servants understood that their policy papers were considered within a broader comparative context and that the work of external bodies would be taken seriously by ministers.

As Andrew Blick (2004) pointed out particularly by 1964, with Harold Wilson's government, civil servants had begun to cooperate with political advisers co-opted directly by the Prime Minister and ministers, who revived the practice of appointing advisers which had started during the Second World War in order to face technical difficulties presented by the war.

However, the British administrative system has never developed the practice of appointing ministerial Cabinets, a small team of policy advisers made up of civil servants and outsiders recruited mainly from the party or with a direct relationship with the minister, which are common across continental Europe. In the UK, special advisers are temporary civil servants whose destiny is related to the minister or Prime Minister who appointed them. They are paid by the government, and they finish their term once the minister or the government has ended their time in office (Yong and Hazell 2014).

Individual special advisers have been appointed by increasing numbers of ministers since the first experience in the mid-sixties. After a decade, the total number of special advisers had risen to 38. In this period, a debate took place on the relationship between these political appointees and the Civil Service (Blackstone 1979), stimulated by some tensions that had arisen between Tony Benn's special advisers and officials in the Department for Trade and Industry. Thatcher's centralised and polarised Cabinet maintained fairly tight control over the numbers and types of special advisers appointed by her ministers, but her successor, John Major, expanded the political appointments, and, in 1997, when he finished his term, there were 35 special advisers in Whitehall. The view in the Civil Service at this time was that special policy advisers offered ministers tailored, expert advice and support which were not achievable within the conventional Civil Service institutional framework. They insulated the Civil Service from political matters by providing ministers with politically oriented advice and providing additional channels of communication to ministers which the Civil Service could use in a positive way to help persuade ministers of a course to follow (Burnham and Pyper 2008).

When in May 1997 New Labour won the general elections and came to office, there was an immediate increase in the appointments of special advisers. By the end of 1999, there were 74 special advisers (Richards 2000), and in 2001, there were 81 (Jones and Weir 2002). In 2007, after ten years in government, Blair and his Cabinet had appointed 297 special advisers (UCL Constitution Unit 2014), a massive growth compared to the 181 appointed in the Conservative era by Thatcher and Major. The reaction to this wave of appointments by the Cabinet Secretary (1998–2002) Richard Wilson was pragmatic and moderate: "I do not think the senior Civil Service of 3700 people is in danger of being swamped by 70 special advisers" (Richards 2000: 91–117).

His successor, Andrew Turnbull, argued that numbers were not a real problem, as he stated on 4 March 2004 in front of the Public Administration Committee of the Commons (2004). He used statistics to contextualise: "Is the Civil Service being politicised? I do not think you can judge this by simply looking at the number of special advisers ... There has been roughly a doubling of the numbers of special advisers from 36/7 to 70-something. Most of that increase has been in Numbers 10 and 11, the Treasury and particularly Number 10. Out in the world of departments, the two-per rule, two special advisers per secretary of state, pretty much rules ... by and large ... the number of special advisers is not significantly different from what it was, say, 15 years ago."

In this dynamic, the social changes and Blair's leadership style played a major role. Indeed, special advisers were broadly of two kinds: the policy advisers who mainly worked in the departments advising ministers and secretaries of state on policy agenda and policy design and helping to coordinate them with the different policy units, and the media experts and the spin doctors who worked in the communication roles. The "media obsession" became evident with New Labour Governments, especially in Number 10, where news management and spin-doctoring became one of the main activities of the prime ministerial staff (Yong and Hazell 2014).

Appointing special advisers was a way to achieve better media management and react to the pressure of 24/7 information and new media as the Internet. Some advisers such as Alastair Campbell and Jonathan Powell in Number 10 became very influential, and the Prime Minister reserved for them a special regulation through an order in council that allowed them to give orders to civil servants (Civil Service Order in Council 1997 on 3 May 1997).

During these years of increasing appointments of special advisers, there had been some disciplinary problems particularly as far as concerned the relation between them and civil servants. There had been a series of public allegations of misconduct concerning special advisers, and the two best-known cases are those of Jo Moore and Damian McBride.

Briefly, Damian McBride was an official turned special adviser who was accused of planning to smear opposition politicians by diffusing rumours about their private lives (Yong and Hazell 2014), but it is the case of Jo Moore that illustrates the importance of personal relationships and of the subtle bond between civil servants and special advisers and the ambiguities of the special adviser's role.

Jo Moore was one of two special advisers to Stephen Byers, the Secretary of State for Transport, Local Government, and the Regions in 2001. Before, she had been special adviser in the Department for Trade and Industry. As a special adviser, she primarily focused on media relations. There were bad relations between her and the department's press officers, who were all civil servants; she was accused of trying to push the press officers to compromise their political impartiality. On 11 September 2001, Moore sent an email suggesting that it was "a very good day" to "get out anything we want to bury." Department officials leaked her mail, and by October, it had become news. As a temporary civil servant, Moore was subject to disciplinary action by Sir Richard Mottram, her Permanent Secretary, who was responsible for the conduct of all civil servants in the department. Moore was issued with an official disciplinary warning and a personal reprimand from minister Byers. In October 2001, it was further reported by the media that Moore had asked her department press officers to brief the media against Bob Kiley, then Transport Commissioner for London. This action breached the then Code of Conduct for Special Advisers, which established that special advisers could not ask officials to violate Civil Service impartiality. The press officers refused to complete her request. At this point, Mottram, who wanted to preserve his good relationship with Secretary of State Byers, decided to manage Moore himself rather than directly confront him.

On 14 February 2002, there were press reports that Moore had suggested that inconvenient news on rail statistics could be announced on the day of Princess Margaret's funeral. Martin Sixsmith, who was appointed in November 2001 as new Director of Communications of the department, sent around an interdepartmental email blocking this initiative. This later email was then leaked and led to the resignation of Moore on 15 February. In May 2002, Byers resigned as Secretary of State, having been curbed by various political troubles. The case was investigated with an inquiry by the Public Administration Select Committee (PASC) in 2002 (PASC 2002). The PASC Report highlighted a very serious breach of Civil Service principles in the Moore case and recommended that the government should review the system by which disputes were handled between ministers, special advisers and career civil servants. A later recommendation of 2003 by the Committee on Standards in Public Life led to the Ministerial Code being amended to state that ministers were personally accountable for the management and discipline of their special advisers (Cm 5775, 2003). However, special advisers remain subject to disciplinary action by their department's Permanent Secretary.

These problems had emerged mainly during the Blair era because of the massive use of special advisers in central government to manage news and media. The Cabinet recognised, in particular during Blair's second term, the need to regulate the role of special advisers. In 2001, the Code of Conduct for Special Advisers, which regulated the work of those temporary and partisan civil servants, was issued under the supervision of Sir Richard Wilson. Indeed, from the early days of the Blair Government, there was tension between some elements of the Civil Service and the special advisers, particularly the spin doctors focused on media and news management. Just a few weeks after the general elections of 1997, seven civil servants, including the Treasury's senior information officer, had left their posts; by the summer of 1998, a total of 25 Heads or Deputy Heads of Information had been substituted, and by August 1999, only two Directors of Communications who had been in position when Labour came to office were still in post (Oborne 1999).

During these years, there was an intensive intra-governmental debate about the impact of special advisers on the Civil Service. The Prime Minister was asked by the Civil Service First Commissioner, who had supervised the system of appointments, to limit their number in Whitehall. An internal review in 1997 led by Robin Mountfield concluded that special advisers did not do any damage and that the Civil Service should be prepared to learn lessons from the efficiency of the new Labour approach to media relations (Oborne 1999). For this reason, permanent civil servants and appointed civil servants were put to work together in the new Strategic Communication Unit based in Downing Street.

In 1998, the Select Committee on Public Administration of the House of Commons launched an investigation into the role and the responsibilities of the PM's official spokesman, Alastair Campbell, who benefited from a special regulation under the Order in Council Amendment of 1997. During this investigation, the strong influence of Number 10 Special Advisers on the executive became evident; for example, it emerged that Campbell had ordered social security ministers to seek advance clearance of their process communication with him (Oborne 1999: 156–157). In 2001, the Committee faced the issue again with an inquiry focused on the politicisation of the Civil Service.

The evidence submitted to the Committee during the inquiry showed different ideological positions about the impact of the special advisers on the Civil Service, from those worried about the politicisation of the Civil Service to those who defended special advisers as a tool to insulate officials from political matters, which were managed directly by special advisers sheltering civil servants from political responsibility. As a consequence of this debate, the Code of Conduct for Special Advisers was drafted shortly afterwards.

The Code offered a better perspective on the role of the special advisers in the UK government. It stated that the employment of Special Advisers adds a political dimension to the advice and support available to ministers while reinforcing the political impartiality of the permanent Civil Service by distinguishing the source of political advice and support. Then, the Code established that special advisers were "exempt from the requirement that civil servants should be appointed on merit and behave with political impartiality and objectivity. They are otherwise required to conduct themselves in accordance with the Civil Service Code." It limited the functions of special advisers, specifying that "Special Advisers must not: ask civil servants to do anything inconsistent with the Civil Service Code; behave towards civil servants in a way inconsistent with the standards set by the employing department; have responsibility for budgets or external contracts; suppress or supplant the advice prepared for ministers by permanent civil servants (although they may comment on such advice); be involved in issues affecting a permanent civil servant's career such as recruitment, promotion, reward or discipline (with the exception of up to three posts in the Prime Minister's office)" (Cabinet Office 2001).

To conclude, the rise and the process of institutionalisation of special advisers were a consequence of the development of 24/7 media and the new leadership style interpreted by Tony Blair. They had been an addition to the eroded advisory function of the Civil Service, a process that began in the 1980s with the managerialisation of the British public administration. They expressed the will of the Blair Government to set objectives and achieve them in controlling the Civil Service's work and using it as a tool more than as the "Prince's adviser." However, the traditional framework of the Civil Service was preserved with the intervention of regulations such as the Code of Conduct for Special Advisers and the Civil Service Code. Indeed, special advisers were temporary civil servants, and they were involved only as policy consultants and not as real decision-makers. Consequently, the founding principles of the institution remained untouched by managerial transformation and the massive use of special advisers.

MINISTERIAL RESPONSIBILITY: IMPLICATIONS PRODUCED BY THREE DECADES OF ADMINISTRATIVE REFORMS

This work would be incomplete without an overview of the impact of administrative reforms in the 1980s and the 1990s on the constitutional convention of ministerial responsibility. A fundamental principle of the British political system and constitution is that the government is accountable through its ministers to Parliament. The constitutional requirement and the political need for accountability are most obvious when mistakes have been made and the government is under pressure, but there is also the expectation of routine accountability of ministers for the actions of their departments. Such accountability is central to the concept of responsible government, and it is considered essential in a system with a dominant executive and a lack of a written constitution that establishes legal checks and balances ensured by a constitutional court (Marshall 1989). Traditionally, accountability is seen as operating through conventions of both collective and individual responsibility. Collective responsibility provides Parliament with the means of holding the government as an accountable body, and individual ministerial responsibility enables the House of Commons to dwell on a single minister and his responsibilities without the need to censure the whole government (Woodhouse 1994).

The Next Steps agencies reform (1988) had the potential for making accountability stronger in the areas in which they operated. The rigidity of the Policy and Resources Documents, which established responsibilities and procedures, suggested a realistic definition of responsibilities for decision-making. The concerns of the Next Steps Programme were with internal or managerial accountability, and there had been little commitment to explore a method of making this compatible with the public accountability that was required by constitutional conventions. Internally, there was a structure of accountability which equated power with responsibility, but externally the dominant constitutional theory prevented officials being held personally accountable. At managerial level, the executive agencies required chief executives to be personally accountable for their responsibility as detailed within the Policy and Resource Document, while at the constitutional level ministers retained the entire responsibility for the agencies within their departments, and the personal accountability of civil servants was denied (Woodhouse 1994).

Furthermore, although the names of chief executives were public knowledge and they gave evidence about their responsibilities to select Committees, in theory they acted only on behalf of their minister, with all the attendant protections and limitations that implied. Despite the apparent continuity in the application of the constitutional convention, these internal changes affected the practical application of external or public accountability. This had already been demonstrated by the redirection by ministers of questions from Parliament to chief executives. The answers of the CEO were daily published, as we have seen before, in the Official Report of the Hansard.

Thus, ministers were less exposed and they provided less information to Parliament than before the Next Steps programme. Indeed, even the Accounting Officials became accountable in front of the Public Administration Committee as far as concerned the financial facts of the agency they worked for. The success of the Next Steps Programme was based on a further delegation of powers to civil servants in delivering public services with a managerial approach, and these powers were technically exercised only on behalf of the minister; this fact determined a less pronounced difference between internal and external accountability. chief executives were often outsiders recruited from the private sector, and they used to account personally to select Committees in the same way as they did with the minister, thereby suggesting a greater openness or transparency of government and improved public accountability. However, the ministers could limit benefits in accountability originated by Next Steps reforms imposing limitations of ministerial responsibility through the application of the Osmotherly Rules, which are guidance for civil servants on giving evidence to Parliamentary select Committees (Marshall 1989).

One of the most significant developments during the 1980s and 1990s in relation to accountability was the erosion of the anonymity of officials regarding Civil Service accountability. The scrutiny by select Committees has determined a diminution as civil servants appear in public and addressed by name. The creation of Next Steps agencies extended the process, with chief executives having personal responsibility for the operation of the agency as detailed within the framework document. Indeed, the Next Steps development suggested a fundamental change in accountability: a passage from the ministerial accountability towards a division of accountability between minister and civil servants. Despite the government's defended tradition and the immutability of the constitutional convention of individual ministerial responsibility, the responsibility of civil servants was clearly enforced and a stronger accountability was developed towards officials. Considering that ministers and civil servants worked together in the department, in some cases there was a lack of clear division of responsibility. This new shape of ministerial responsibility raised some questions about constitutional arrangements. The identification of civil servants with specific policy decisions created a problem if the civil servants had to be or did not have to be responsible and accountable for policy formulation. Indeed, the function of officials is to advise ministers on policy options. It is the minister who makes the decision, and any reduction in his responsibility for policy choice reduces his role to that of a policy presenter. This is the extension of the principle expressed by Kenneth Baker, then Home Secretary, after the Brixton escape, when he implied that he was merely doing as he had been advised and that responsibility lay with those who had advised him (Woodhouse 1994: 291).

With Next Steps agencies and managerialism, ministers tended to push responsibility downwards to officials, because budget and functions decentralisations obtained with the creation of executive agencies gave more responsibility to civil servants in policy implementation and services delivery. With the setting up of the Next Steps agencies, on one side civil servants were more free to manage their bureaucratic organisation, but on the other side they became more responsible for policy results. However, the dilemma over who was and who should have been responsible remained uncertain. At the end of the nineties, after two decades of administrative reforms and a long historical reconstruction, we can argue that the constitutional convention of ministerial responsibility was not suppressed or substantially changed but that it was "pluralised." Next to the traditional principle of ministerial responsibility that the minister is personally accountable to Parliament for all the policies and activities of his department, there was an expansion of senior civil servants' and administrative chief executives' responsibility owing to their more prominent role, Committees' power of scrutiny and pervasiveness of media. As civil servants became more visible and responsible for policy implementation and delivery, more cases that implicated their responsibility increased. We might argue that individual ministerial responsibility had been eroded by administrative reforms, but it seems fair as well to state that ministerial responsibility was expanded to senior and top-management civil servants.

PERFORMANCE MANAGEMENT: A PERMANENT EVOLUTION TOWARDS A GOVERNMENT BY MEASUREMENT

In the twenty-first century, performance measurement is at the heart of public-sector management, and it shapes administrative organisation. Many aspects of public management such as contracts, regulations and organisational framework depend upon a comprehensive performance measurement system being in place for all public-sector organisations that was developed during the historical period examined. As Christopher Hood (1991) underlined, New Public Management's principles were transmitted, such as "hands-on professional management" in the public sector, explicit standards and measure of performance, greater emphasis on output control, shift to disaggregation of unit in the public sector, greater competition, private-sector style of management practice, discipline and parsimony in the use of resources.

Prior to the establishment of a comprehensive performance measurement regime, the public sector frequently operated just using the traditional accounting methodology. There was a deep ignorance within government regarding costs and outputs prior to the 1980s. It was not until the late 1970s that any effort was made to assert the kind of financial and accounting regimes common to the private sector. In 1982, Sir Derek Rayner was shocked to discover, working on public sector scrutinies, that not only were the costs of individual services unknown, but until the 1980s no one had thought it important enough to investigate how much it costs to run departments of state (Massey 1993; Carter et al. 1992). The true costs of government were not known, and there was no existing methodology to calculate them accurately. The incremental approach to budgeting had progressed slowly since the days of Gladstone (Massey and Pyper 2005).

During these years of administrative reforms, new tools, techniques and organisations were developed, tested and applied. A new regime of performance management was implemented as an answer to the pressure of 24/7 media, public expectations and global economic competition.

As we assessed, the story started under the leadership of Sir Derek Rayner during the first term of the Thatcher Government when in May

1982 the Financial Management Initiative was published. It was the first document that introduced performance indicators. The Initiative introduced the monitoring of objectives and performance indicators covering efficiency and productivity for all government departments.

In 1988, the Next Steps Initiative established that executive agencies were required to report their performance against targets set by their departments covering the volume and the quality of services, financial performance and efficiency, and in 1991, the Citizen's Charter, introduced by John Major, set indicators for quantifiable standards of service that had to be monitored and reported by the public bodies that delivered public services. In 1998, the White Paper *Modern Public Services—Investing in Reform* (Cm. 4011, 1998) was published, and this reported the results of the Comprehensive Spending Review and contained a restatement of departmental objectives in line with governmental priorities. In the same year, another White Paper on *Public Services* (Cmnd 4181) established a public service agreement for each department and cross-cutting areas, showing their aims and objectives and the progress they were expected to make. Furthermore, the Charter Programme was renamed Service First and given a new emphasis to promote quality, effectiveness and responsiveness and the need for service providers to adapt in order to deliver services across sectors and different tiers of government. In 1999, the *Modernising Government* White Paper (Cmnd 4310) was published, and it enforced the role of public service agreements (PSAs). It emphasised the shift to outcome measures, and it reinforced the linkages between organisational and individual objectives.

In 2000, *Wiring it Up*, drafted by the Cabinet Office, recommended an extended use of performance to defeat the weaknesses in the handling of issues that crossed departmental boundaries. In the same year, the spending review document enforced the use of PSAs, making performance indicators (PIs) inherent to them, and the Statistics Commission was established as an independent body, and part of its new job was to measure progress against PSAs targets. The Lyons Review of 2003 introduced some criteria of rationalisation in order to help achieve better value for money and measuring outcomes. In 2005, the Departmental Capability Reviews were started under the leadership of the Cabinet Secretary Sir Gus O'Donnell, and the aim was to apply to departments the same indicators, developed in the PSAs, established for agencies and administrative bodies that provided public service. A comparative approach was used to look into any department and to align each department to best performance and practices. The method met with good success, mostly because of the decision to give scores to every department, to compare them and to improve organisation on the basis of these results.

The impact of the FMI's announcement of "a general and co-ordinated drive to improve financial management in government departments" has been likened by some commentators to the storming of the Bastille (Carter et al. 1992: 5). The FMI's authors announced that they would seek to achieve its results for each departments through "a clear view of their objectives and assess, and wherever possible measure, outputs or performance in relation to these objectives" (Carter et al. 1992: 5). With this statement, a new season in government was launched, a new regime that has annually gathered momentum, generating an abundant series of initiatives, projects and methods. Carter, Klein and Day noted that: "Following the Financial Management Initiative, performance indicators did indeed multiply. In 1985 the annual Public Expenditure White Paper contained 500 output and performance measures. In the two succeeding years, the figure rose first to 1200 and then to 1800. And by the time that the 1998 White Paper was published, the PI explosion had been such that no one was counting any more" (ibidem: 20). The first experiments of performance indicators had been deemed a success by the Treasury, and by 1987, their own expansion and progress were ensured (Durham 1987). Performance measurement implementation was a complex process for government officials. There were problems of quantifying qualitative data such as that pertaining to quality issues and public satisfaction. There were other problems in attempting to compare dissimilar services, and outputs, to compare inputs with outputs, efficiency with effectiveness, etc. (Carter et al. 1992). For example, early performance indicators were just Treasury tools to improve efficiency in the public sector. Later performance indicators, especially those developed under the Labour Governments that had been elected after 1997, have switched emphasis emphatically towards populist indicators, such as league tables of schools, universities and hospitals, that are aimed at the public in their role as citizens/customers (Massey and Pyper 2005). They were used to measure and report on the delivery of public services and their quality. As we have pointed out, there was a seamless transfer from the Conservative Government to Labour as far as New Public Management was concerned. As soon as they came to office, Labour understood that performance measurement was the most effective tool to control the machinery of government and its outcomes. In part, this also reflected the conversion of the highest echelons of the Civil Service to an acceptance of the NPM principles to exercise control over the agencification process; it especially reflected the efficacy and adaptability of performance measurement as a managerial tool of control (Durham 1987).

In this process, the National Audit Office (NAO) took a leading position as far as concerned the elaboration of performance indicators within each department and agency. PSAs were the mechanism for achieving this. Introduced by Gordon Brown, Chancellor of the Exchequer, in the Comprehensive Spending Review of 1998, PSAs were a "clearly stated commitment to the public (and specific stakeholders) on what they can expect, and each agreement sets out explicitly which Minister is accountable for delivery of targets underpinning that commitment" (Massey 2002: 37).

The aim of the targets was to optimise the link between administrative activity and outcomes in order to improve organisation and methods in providing public services. The performance indicators and benchmarking activities imposed upon the public sector have sometimes resulted not in improved performance, necessarily, but in an improved ability of civil servants to play the game. For this reason, performance indicators increased rapidly; there were many hundreds of PSAs and SDAs, which raised the number of individual PIs to well over a thousand. At the end of the Blair era, each major area of government found itself constrained to operate within the performance regime.

The NAO's view was that "the format of targets can be varied so that they closely address the policy objective" (2001: 4). However, mistakes in the indicators formulation could happen; indeed, "targets may unintentionally create incentives for [...] unwanted activity, or they may create so tight a focus on targeted areas that no attention is paid to important but untargeted areas" (NAO 2001: 4).

To conclude, documents such as *Measuring the Performance of Government Departments* were useful papers not only because they provided a guide to "how performance measurement works," but also because they provided a clear indication of the perspectives underpinning the rising performance measurement regime.

This framework was a natural development of the New Public Management-oriented reforms, and it was a manifestation of the new approach promoted by political leaders and ministers on civil servants and special advisers in policy-making, which enforced the oversight on the public-sector organisation and results of this organisation in providing public services through a managerialist regime. This process represented two faces of the same coin: a tool of command and control for the political executive, it was designed to inspect and report upon the performance of the bureaucracy and, at the same time, to check the quality of the public sector.

Finally, performance measurement of government and public services represents the historical product of the "managerialist siege" on the public sector developed from the late 1960s to the dawn of the new century. It is the more tangible effect of the penetration managerial techniques, imported from the private sector, in governmental institutions. As we have written, it has been an incremental process begun with de-unionisation, manpower and waste reduction, continued with new pay arrangements, budgeting devolution, new information process for ministers and senior civil servants, new administrative structure through executive agencies and consolidated with customisation, contracting out, privatisation that increased the distance between politics (and policy-making) and bureaucracy (and policy implementation) and, finally, culminating in public service delivery techniques, results monitoring and performance measurement.

This is how performance measurement became institutionalised, and it moved from being a "fashionable" policy tool yielded by managerialism to a permanent reform in central government, embedded within Civil Service practices.

EVERYTHING CHANGES BUT CONSTITUTIONAL CONVENTIONS: ADMINISTRATIVE REFORMS AND CONSTITUTIONAL CONSERVATISM

As this research reveals, there was a continuous change in the British Civil Service by the end of the seventies as far as concerned organisation, pay schemes, performance measurement, functions distribution, recruiting and manpower policies. The evolution, in terms of administrative reforms, became accelerated in the nearly 30 years examined. However, traditional constitutional principles that regulated the institutional life of the Civil Service remained unchanged.

The central argument is that while there have been a number of periods in the last 200 years in which the British Civil Service has undergone a process of reform (particularly the 1850s, the 1940s and from the 1980s onwards), the nature of change has been evolutionary rather than revolutionary. To explain this argument, the chapter concentrates on the reverence that both major political parties, Conservative and Labour, have always maintained towards the British constitution (see Greenleaf 1987; Heady 1979; Hojnacki 1996; Marsh et al. 2001). Even on the rare occasions when either of these parties has been elected on a radical platform, particularly in the case of the Thatcher Government of 1979, their period in office has been characterised by an unwillingness to provide a new constitutional settlement that would fundamentally transform the foundations on which both the Civil Service and the state were legitimised.

As we have seen, real changes were introduced in the British administrative state by Mrs. Thatcher. The political will to initiate and persevere with management reforms derived from Mrs. Thatcher's style of "conviction politics." Conviction politics refers to a basic set of attitudes which underpinned Margaret Thatcher's approach to policy-making and governing. Conviction politics stood in contrast to consensus politics, which Mrs. Thatcher fought and which were characterised by indecision, drift and muddling through, leading to waste of taxpayers' money, inefficiency, administrative confusion and duplication. Conviction politics defined better management as the means to put the government's house in order, control public expenditure and reduce Civil Service numbers, by targeting resources more narrowly (Metcalfe 1993).

The most important changes of the Conservative era were: decentralisation of operational management responsibilities to individual units; creation of a business management ethos, cost consciousness, management by objectives, financial accountability within organisations; competition between providers in health and education; the public as customers rather than clients in a purchaser–provider contracting system; centralised financial control over local management discretion; centrally established policy parameters.

Despite all these real transformations, any reform of the British Civil Service has always been contained within the existing constitutional framework, and this has limited the scope for overhauling the institutional arrangements at organisational level. The political cost to the Thatcher Government of reforming the constitution was too high, so the reform of the Civil Service in the 1980s was both constrained and evolutionary. A similar argument can be used for the Blair Labour government, elected in 1997 on a progressive modernising agenda that aimed to join up public services, implement managerialist reforms of the previous period and develop a more open and delivery-oriented Civil Service. It is therefore argued here that, although in the last 30 years the British Civil Service has undergone structural, cultural and personnel reforms similar to those experienced by other liberal–democratic states, the reform process itself has always been constrained by continued maintenance of the constitutional conventions that define Britain's institutional arrangements (Halligan 2003). The Westminster model of government continues to condition the way both ministers and civil servants operate within the British political system (Marsh et al. 2001).

Indeed, the impact of administrative reform on the Civil Service, both under the Conservatives from 1979 and under Labour from 1997, led a number of authors to conclude that Britain is moving towards a federal Civil Service (see Pilkington 1999; Gray 2000; Pyper and Robins 2000). This analysis came from the observation that the vast bulk of the Civil Service was deployed outside Whitehall, in either agencies or the newly devolved assemblies, evidence that the old hierarchical and centralised model of an integrated Civil Service had disintegrated and had been replaced by a structure that was much more federal in nature.

Indeed, in many ways, these arguments were repetition of the mid-1990s thesis proclaiming the death of the Whitehall paradigm (see Campbell and Wilson 1995; Foster and Plowden 1996).

Whereas in the mid-1990s the "end of the Whitehall paradigm" thesis may have been overstated, by the end of the Labour Government's era the structure of a "federalised" Civil Service was emerging more clearly. Structurally, much had changed. But other elements of the Westminster model have persisted. For example, Theakston (2000: 58) observed that senior civil servants continue to play a vital role at the fulcrum between politics and administration by virtue of their expertise in making the system work. Ministers seem to look for and to value the traditional mandarin skills of managing the political interface, political nous and a thorough knowledge of the governmental and parliamentary process.

The point here was that while some elements of the Westminster model had clearly been eroded others were still safe and firmly in place. Furthermore, confirmation of the collapse of the Westminster model would require explicit recognition of such a state of affairs by both the incumbent government and the Senior Civil Service (Halligan 2003). This did not happen; Britain has tended to avoid facing up to constitutional problems for as long as possible (see Campbell and Wilson 1995: 314).

For sure, the most important regulations of the Civil Service in the period considered reaffirmed the traditional principles of the British Civil Service such as non-partisanship, impartiality, access by competition and promotion with merit, neutrality, bureaucratic professionalism immune to politicisation, self-government. From the Armstrong Memorandum (1985) to the Civil Service Code (1995), the Code of Conduct for Special Advisers (2001) and the last never approved by Parliament Civil Service Bill proposal (2004), traditional values were never underestimated and they were present in all the Major Governmental papers of the period examined as this research shows. The tension between managerial reforms and tradition was a constant characteristic of this historical phase of British government. The government answered this problem by issuing new codes to secure traditional Civil Service principles while managerialist reforms were ongoing. However, some principles, such as the power of advising in policy-making, may have been eroded or reduced by administrative reforms, but the bulk of the Civil Service values and the Whitehall model, meaning professional bureaucracy, hierarchical, non-political, meritocratic, were respected and untouched by the managerial storm in practices and organisation. Frameworks, methods and organisations changed; political and constitutional architecture resisted. As Martin Painter and B. G. Peters (2010) argue, any contemporary administrative systems now appear to have a number of layers within them, so that some more contemporary elements exist along with the traditional elements (see Streeck and Thelen 2005; Tolbert and Zucker 1983). These layers may coexist, with some aspects of governing displaying the more modern traits and others the more traditional.

Conclusions: The Rise of Managerial Bureaucracy

As we have pointed out in this research, the history of the British Civil Service from 1979 to 2007 was based on the interplay between the development of managerialist policies and the resistance of administrative traditions. The process of reform was continuous but without revolutionary fractures, and it is to argue that it was an evolutionary institutional transformation, because the boost of new managerialism, market openness and competition were compensated by the resistance of traditional principles of the Civil Service as hierarchical, self-governed, neutral, professional bureaucracy.

Managerialism was a set of inherited beliefs about how private-sector management techniques would increase the economy, efficiency and effectiveness, the 3Es, of the public sector. Initially, the beliefs focused on costs and manpower cuts; explicit standards and measures of performance; managing by results; and value for money. Subsequently, it also embraced marketisation, promotion of competition and openness to new markets. It introduced ideas about restructuring the incentive structures of public service provision through contracting out, quasi-markets and consumer choice. Margaret Thatcher introduced both managerial and neoliberal ideas, and both were adopted by New Labour, with a twist.

Managerialism has had a long history which cannot be retold here (see Pollitt 1993; Ferlie et al. 2005, Chapter 1) that became central by the end of the seventies, and it still persisted in Blair's reforms. The core concern for decades has been better performance management, whether called accountable management or management by objectives, which the Fulton Report sought to introduce in 1968. Only the labelling has changed: "Effective performance assessment within government helps to identify how well public organisations are meeting their objectives, as well as highlighting where improvements could be made, so that government is better able to work towards its desired outcome" (PASC 2009: 3).

Over the last decade of this historical research (1997–2007), several innovations have come and gone, including total quality management, performance management, Capability Reviews and the myth of the development of leadership at all levels.

The principles of delivery and choice were embedded in neoliberalism, and the free marketer approach to government developed by Margaret Thatcher, as the Next Steps programme witnessed, but they greatly expanded in the nineties, providing major theoretical elaboration, institutional transformations and administrative techniques in Blair's period at Downing Street.

Indeed, even today, ministers and civil servants act as if the nineteenth-century liberal constitution sets the rules of the political game. The British constitution reminds one of "geological strata," a metaphor which captures the longevity of the beliefs and practices (Rhodes 2011). Obviously much has changed, but much has remained. Managerialism and network governance produced by privatisation, hiving off functions and marketisation had not replaced earlier beliefs and practices; rather, they coexisted with the inherited Westminster tradition. Ministers and civil servants were fluent in all these practices, yet they continue to act as if earlier constitutional beliefs and practices are reliable guides for present-day behaviour (Halligan 2003). The UK government continuously dealt with its incommensurable traditions and heritage.

Administrative history remained an important guide to interpret recent administrative reforms. The history of the Civil Service's "managerialisation," in its various forms, and the new institutional arrangement that arose in the period considered have not replaced the Westminster system central operating code. Rather they have been grafted on, and managerialism and Civil Service traditions developed side by side.

During these three decades of reforms, the concepts of "management" and "bureaucracy" had been fused together, without losing their own significance and balancing innovation and tradition, and this dynamic originated a new phase of the UK's history of government.

References

Books, Journals, and Articles

Blackstone, T. (1979, July 19). Helping ministers do a better job. *New Society*.

Blick, A. (2004). *People who live in the dark: The history of the special advisers in British politics*. Cambridge: Politico's.

Blick, A. (2016). *The codes of the constitution*. London: Bloomsbury.

Burnham, J., & Pyper, R. (2008). *Britain's modernized civil service*. Basingstoke: Palgrave Macmillan.

Campbell, C., & Wilson, G. (1995). *The end of Whitehall: Death of a paradigm*. Oxford: Basil Blackwell.

Carter, N., Klein, R., & Day, P. (1992). *How organizations measure success: The use of performance indicators in government*. Abingdon: Routledge.

Durham, P. (1987). *Output and performance measurement in central government: Some practical achievements*. London: HM Treasury.

Ferlie, E., Lynn, L. E., & Pollitt, C. (Eds.). (2005). *The Oxford handbook of public management*. Oxford: Oxford University Press.

Foster, C., & Plowden, F. (1996). *The state under stress*. Buckingham: Open University Press.

Gray, J. (2000). A hollow state. In R. Pyper & L. Robins (Eds.), *United Kingdom governance*. Basingstoke: Macmillan.

Greenleaf, W. H. (1987). *The British political tradition, vol. 3. A much governed nation*. London: Methuen.

Halligan, J. (2003). *Civil service systems in Anglo-American countries.* Cheltenham: Edward Elgar.

Heady, F. (1979). *Public administration: A comparative perspective* (2nd ed.). New York: Marcel Dekker.

Hojnacki, W. (1996). Politicization as a civil service dilemma. *Civil service systems in comparative perspective* (pp. 137–164).

Hood, C. (1991). A public management for all seasons? *Public Administration, 69*(1), 3–19.

Jones, N., & Weir, S. (2002, February 25). The master of misinformation: Behind Jo Moore affair lies a spin machine that has corrupted the senior civil service itself. *New Statesman.*

Marsh, D., Richards, D., & Smith, M. J. (2001). *Changing patterns of governance: Reinventing Whitehall?* Basingstoke: Palgrave.

Marshall, G. (1989). *Ministerial responsibility.* Oxford: Oxford University Press.

Massey, A. (1993). *Managing the public sector: A comparative analysis of the United Kingdom and the United States.* Aldershot: Edward Elgar.

Massey, A. (2002). *The state of Britain: A guide to the UK public sector.* London: Public Management and Policy Association.

Massey, A., & Pyper, R. (2005). *Public management and modernisation in Britain.* Basingstoke: Palgrave Macmillan.

Metcalfe, L. (1993). Conviction politics and dynamic conservatism. *International Political Science Review, 14*(4), 351–371.

Oborne, P. (1999). *Alastair Campbell: New labour and the rise of the media class.* London: Aurum Press.

Painter, M., & Peters, B. G. (Eds.). (2010). *Tradition and public administration.* Basingstoke: Palgrave Macmillan.

Pilkington, C. (1999). *The civil service in Britain today.* Manchester: Manchester University Press.

Pollitt, C. (1993). *Managerialism and the public services* (2nd ed.). Oxford: Blackwell.

Pollitt, C., & Bouckaert, G. (2011). *Public management reform: A comparative analysis—New public management, governance, and the neo-Weberian state.* Oxford: Oxford University Press.

Pyper, R., & Robins, L. (2000). *United Kingdom governance.* Basingstoke: Macmillan.

Rhodes, R. A. W. (2011). *Everyday life in British government.* Oxford: Oxford University Press.

Richards, D. (2000). The Conservatives, New Labour and Whitehall: A biographical examination of the political flexibility of the mandarin cadre. In K. Theakston (Ed.), *Bureaucrats and leadership.* Basingstoke: Palgrave Macmillan.

Streeck, W., & Thelen, K. A. (Eds). (2005). *Beyond continuity: Institutional change in advanced political economies.* Oxford: Oxford University Press.

Theakston, K. (2000). Permanent secretaries: Comparative biography and leadership in Whitehall. In *Transforming British government* (pp. 125–145). Basingstoke: Palgrave Macmillan.

Tolbert, P. S., & Zucker, L. G. (1983). Institutional sources of change in the formal structure of organizations: The diffusion of civil service reform, 1880–1935. *Administrative Science Quarterly, 28,* 22–39.

Woodhouse, D. (1994). *Ministers and parliament: Accountability in theory and practice.* Oxford: Clarendon Press.

Yong, B., & Hazell, R. (2014). *Special advisers: Who they are, what they do, why they matter.* Oxford: Hart Publishing.

Archive Sources, Parliamentary Papers, and Official Publications

Cabinet Office. (2001). *Code of conduct for special advisers.* London: Cabinet Office.

Cm. 2931. (1995). *The government's response to the first report from the committee on standards in public life.* London: HMSO.

Cm. 4011. (1998). *Modern public services for Britain: Investing in reform.* London: Stationery Office.

Cm. 5775. (2003). *Defining the boundaries within the executive: Ministers, special advisers and the permanent civil service.* London: Stationery Office.

HC 27. (1993–4). Treasury and civil service committee. *Fifth report. The role of the civil service,* Vol. I. London: HMSO.

HC 92. (1985–6). *Seventh report from the treasury and civil service committee: Civil servants and ministers, duties and responsibilities. Vol. I Report. Vol. II Annexes, Minutes of evidence and Appendices.* London: HMSO.

National Audit Office. (2001). *Managing the performance of government departments.* London: National Audit Office.

Public Administration Select Committee. (2002). *"These unfortunate events": Lessons of recent events at the former DTLR, HC 303, 2001–2002.* London: Stationery Office.

Public Administration Select Committee. (2009). *Good government: Eighth report of session 2008–09,* Vol. 1. London: Stationery Office.

The Constitution Unit. (2014). Research on special advisers. London: UCL. Available at http://www.ucl.ac.uk/constitution-unit/research/government/special-advisers.

BIBLIOGRAPHY

Books, Journals, and Articles

Abel-Smith, B. (1964). *Freedom in the welfare state* (No. 353). London: Fabian Society.

Allen, F. H. (1981). The basis and the organization of recruitment. *Management Services in Government, 36*, 21–28.

Balogh, T. (1959). The apotheosis of the dilettante. In H. Thomas (Ed.), *The Establishment* (pp. 83–128). London: New English Library.

Barber, M. (2007). *Instruction to deliver. Tony Blair, public services, and challenge of achieving targets.* London: Politico's.

Barber, M. (2015). *How to run a government? So that citizens benefit and taxpayers don't go crazy.* London: Penguin.

Barberis, P. (Ed.). (1996). *The Whitehall reader.* Milton Keynes: Open University Press.

Barron, A., & Scott, C. (1992). The Citizen's Charter Programme. *Modern Law Review, 55*(4), 526–546.

Bekke, H., Perry, J. L., & Toonen, T. A. J. (Eds.). (1996). *Civil service systems in comparative perspective.* Bloomington: Indiana University Press.

Blackstone, T. (1979, July 19). Helping ministers do a better job. *New Society.*

Blackstone, T., & Plowden, W. (1988). *Inside the think tank: Advising the cabinet 1971–83.* London: Heinemann.

Blair, T. (2010). *A journey.* London: Hutchinson.

Blau, P. (1956). *Bureaucracy in modern society.* New York: Random House.

Blick, A. (2004). *People who live in the dark: The history of the special advisers in British politics.* Cambridge: Politico's.

Blick, A. (2016). *The codes of the constitution*. Bloomsbury.

British Gas pulls out of charter mark award. (1995, November). *The Independent*.

Buchanan, J. M. (1960). *Fiscal theory and political economy*. Chapel Hill: University of North Carolina Press.

Buchanan, J. M. (1975). *The limits of liberty: Between Anarchy and Leviathan*. Chicago: University Press of Chicago.

Buchanan, J. M., & Tullock, G. (1962). *The calculus of consent*. Ann Arbor: University of Michigan Press.

Buchanan, J. M., & Wagner, R. E. (1977). *Democracy in deficit: The political legacy of Lord Keynes*. New York: Academic Press.

Burnham, J., & Pyper, R. (2008). *Britain's modernized civil service*. Basingstoke: Palgrave Macmillan.

Butler, Robin. (1993). The evolution of the civil service—A progress report. *Public Administration, 71*(3), 395–406.

Campbell, J. (1993). *Heath: A biography*. London: Jonathan Cape.

Campbell, C., & Wilson, G. (1995). *The end of Whitehall: Death of a paradigm*. Oxford: Basil Blackwell.

Carter, N., Klein, R., & Day, P. (1992). *How organizations measure success: The use of performance indicators in government*. Abingdon: Routledge.

Cassels, J. S. (1983). *Review of personnel work in the civil service: Report to the Prime Minister*. London: HMSO.

Chapman, L. (1978). *Your disobedient servant*. London: Chatto and Windus.

Chapman, R. A., & Greenaway, J. R. (1980). *The dynamics of administrative reform*. London: Croom Helm.

Chipperfield, G. H. (1983). *RIPA management information and control in Whitehall* (p. 2). London: RIPA.

Cooper, J. P. (1963). A revolution in Tudor history. *Past and Present, 26*, 110–112.

Cosgrave, P. (1985). *Thatcher: The first term*. London: The Bodley Head.

Council of Civil Service Unions. (1988/89/90). *Bulletin*. London.

Council of Civil Service Unions. (1992). *Competing for quality: Jobs for sale*. London: CCSU.

Council of Civil Service Unions. (1993). *CCSU comments on the government's guide to market testing*. London: CCSU.

Craig, S. J. (1955). *A history of red tape: An account of the origin and development of the civil service*. London: Macdonald & Evans.

Dale, H. E. (1941). *The higher civil service of Great Britain*. London: Oxford University Press.

Deakin, N. (1994). Accentuating the apostrophe: The Citizen's Charter. *Policy Studies, 15*(3), 48–58.

Donoughue, B. (1987). *Prime minister: The conduct of policy under Harold Wilson and James Callaghan*. London: Jonathan Cape.

Drewry, G. (1994). The civil service: From the 1940s to "next steps" and beyond. *Parliamentary Affairs, 47*(4), 583–596.

Drewry, G., & Butcher, T. (1991). *The civil service today.* Oxford: Blackwell.

Drucker, P. (1977). *Management.* London: Pan Books.

Dunleavy, P. (1986). Topics in British politics. In H. Drucker, P. Dunleavy, A. Gamble, & G. Peele (Eds.), *Development in British politics* (pp. 329–372). Melbourne: Macmillan.

Dunnill, F. (1956). *The civil service: Some human aspects.* London: Allen & Unwin.

Durham, P. (1987). *Output and performance measurement in central government: Some practical achievements.* London: HM Treasury.

Elton, G. (1953). *The Tudor revolution in government: Administrative changes in the reign of Henry VII.* Cambridge: Cambridge University Press.

Evans, M. (1994). The true cost of government. *Parliamentary Brief, 3*(1), 31–32.

Ferlie, E., Lynn, L. E., & Pollitt, C. (Eds.). (2005). *The Oxford handbook of public management.* Oxford: Oxford University Press.

First Division Association. (1984–1989). *News.* London: FDA.

Flynn, A., et al. (1988). Accountable management in British central government: Some reflections on the official record. *Financial Accountability and Management, 4,* 169–189.

Foster, C., & Plowden, F. (1996). *The state under stress.* Buckingham: Open University Press.

Friedman, M. (1962). *Capitalism and freedom.* Chicago, IL: University of Chicago Press.

Fry, G. K. (1985). *The changing civil service.* London: Allen & Unwin.

Fry, G. K. (1993). *Reforming the civil service: The Fulton committee on the British home civil service.* Edinburgh: Edinburgh University Press.

Fry, G. K. (1995). *Policy and management in the British civil service.* Hemel Hempstead: Prentice Hall.

Gamble, A. (1986). The political economy of freedom. In R. Levitas (Ed.), *The ideology of the New Right* (pp. 25–44). Cambridge: Polity Press.

Gamble, A. (1994). *The free economy and the strong state.* Basingstoke: Palgrave Macmillan.

Garrett, J. (1980). *Managing the civil service.* London: William Heinemann.

Gershon, P. (2004). *Releasing resources to the front line: Independent review of public sector efficiency.* London: Stationery Office.

Gibbon, S. G. (1943). The civil servant: His place and training. *Public Administration, 21,* 85–90.

Giddens, A. (1998). *The third way: The renewal of social democracy.* Cambridge: Polity Press.

Giddens, A. (2000). *The third way and its critics.* Cambridge: Polity Press.

Giddens, A. (2002). *Where now for new labour?* Cambridge: Polity Press.

Glaister, S., Burnham, J., Stevens, H., & Travers, T. (1998). *Transport policy in Britain*. London: Palgrave Macmillan.

Goldsworthy, D. (1991a). *Setting up next steps*. London: HMSO.

Goldsworthy, D. (1991b). *Setting up next steps: A short account of the origins, launch, and implementation of the next steps project in the British civil service*. London: HMSO.

Goldsworthy, D. (1993). The Citizen's Charter in the United Kingdom [Edited text of address to the University of New South Wales Symposium' Australia's uncertainty: What should the public sector be doing in the 1990s?'(1993)]. *Canberra Bulletin of Public Administration, 75,* 89.

Gosling, R., & Nutley, S. (1990). *Bridging the gap: Secondments between government and business*. London: Royal Institute of Public Administration.

Gray, J. (2000). A hollow state. In R. Pyper & L. Robins (Eds.), *United Kingdom governance*. Basingstoke: Macmillan.

Gray, J., & Jenkins, K. (1982). Policy analysis in British central government: The experience of PAR. *Public Administration, 60,* 429–450.

Greenleaf, W. H. (1987). *The British political tradition, vol. 3. A much governed nation*. London: Methuen.

Greenwood, J., et al. (2002). *New public administration in Britain*. Abingdon: Routledge.

Haddon, C. (2012). *Reforming the civil service. The efficiency unit in the early 1980s and the 1987 next steps report*. London: Institute for Government.

Halligan, J. (2003). *Civil service systems in Anglo-American countries*. Cheltenham: Edward Elgar.

Hampton, P. (2005). *Reducing administrative burdens*. London: HM Treasury.

Hancock, C. J. (1974). MBO in the government service. *Management Services in Government, 29*(1), 16–26.

Hayek, F. (1944). *The road to serfdom*. Abingdon: Routledge.

Hayek, F. (1960). *Constitution of liberty*. Abingdon: Routledge.

Heady, F. (1979). *Public administration: A comparative perspective* (2nd ed.). New York: Marcel Dekker.

Heclo, H., & Wildavsky, H. (1981). *The private government of public money*. Melbourne: Macmillan.

Hennessy, P. (1990). *Whitehall*. London: Fontana Press.

Heseltine, M. (1987). *Where there's a will*. London: Bloomsbury Reader.

Hewart, Lord B. G. H. (1929). *The new despotism*. London: Ernest Benn.

Hojnacki, W. P. (1986). Politicisation as a civil service dilemma. In H. Bekke, J. L. Perry, & T. A. Hunt (Eds.), *Managing people at work*. Maidenhead: McGraw Hill.

Hojnacki, W. (1996). Politicization as a civil service dilemma. *Civil service systems in comparative perspective* (pp. 137–164).

Hood, C. (1991). A public management for all seasons? *Public Administration,* *69*(1), 3–19.

Hood, C. (1995). The "New Public Management" in the 1980s: Variations on a theme. *Accounting, Organizations and Society, 20*(2/3), 93–109.

Hood, C., & Peters, G. (2004). The middle aging of new public management: Into the age of paradox? *Journal of Public Administration Research and Theory, 14*(3), 267–282.

Horton, S., & Farnham, D. (1999). *Public management in Britain.* London: Macmillan Press.

Hoskyns, J. (1983). Whitehall and Westminster. An outsider's view. *Parliamentary Affairs, 36,* 137–147.

Hoskyns, J., et al. (1984). Conservatism is not enough. *Political Quarterly, 55,* 3–16.

Hoskyns, J., et al. (1986). *Re-skilling government: Proposals for the experimental introduction of ministerial cabinets.* London: Institute of Directors.

Hunt, J. (1986). *Managing people at work.* Maidenhead, Berkshire: McGraw Hill.

Hurd, D. (1979). *An end to promises: A sketch of government.* London: Collins.

Institute for Professional Civil Servants. (1988/89/90). *Bulletin.* London: IPCS.

James, O., Moseley, A., Petrovsky, N., & Boyne, G. (2011). Agencification in the UK. In K. Verhoest, S. van Thiel, G. Bouckaert, & P. Laegreid (Eds.), *Government agencies in Europe and beyond: Practices and lessons from 30 countries.* Hampshire: Palgrave Macmillan.

Jenkins, K. (2010). *Politicians and public services: Implementing change in a clash of culture.* Northampton: Edward Elgar Publishing.

Johnson, N. (1985). Change in the civil service: Retrospect and prospects. *Public Administration, 63,* 415–433.

Jones, N., & Weir, S. (2002, February 25). The master of misinformation: Behind Jo Moore affair lies a spin machine that has corrupted the senior civil service itself. *New Statesman.*

Judge, D. (1993). *The parliamentary state.* London: Sage.

Kahn H. R. (1962). *Salaries in the public services in England and Wales.* London: Allen & Unwin.

Kandiah, M., & Lowe, R. (Eds.). (2007). *The civil service reforms of the 1980s.* London: CCBH Oral History Programme.

Kellner, P., & Crowther-Hunt, L. (1980). *The civil servants: An inquiry into Britain's ruling class.* London: Macdonald.

Kemp, P. (1993). *Beyond next steps: A civil service guide for the twenty-first century.* London: Social Market Foundation.

Kemp, P. (1994). The mandarins emerge unscathed. *Parliamentary Brief, 2*(10), 49–50.

Kemplay, M. 2006. *Tony Blair delivery unit: Why did Tony Blair form the Prime Minister's delivery unit and was it successful in the years 2001–2005?* BA undergraduate thesis.

King, A. (Ed.) (1976). *Why is Britain becoming harder to govern?* London: BBC.

Lawson, N. (1992). *The view from No. 11: Memoirs of a Tory radical.* London: Bantam Press.

Lee, R., et al. (1998). *At the centre of Whitehall.* London: Macmillan.

Likierman, A. (1982). Management information for ministers: The MINIS system in the department of the environment. *Public Administration, 60*(2), 127–142.

Lowe, R. (2011). *The official history of the British civil service,* Vol. I (1966–1981). Abingdon: Routledge.

Lyons, S. M. (2004). *Well placed to deliver? Shaping the pattern of government service.* Independent review of public sector relocation. London: HMSO.

Mackenzie, W. J. M., & Grove, J. W. (1957). *Central administration in Britain.* London: Longmans.

Macleavy, J., & Gay, O. (2005). *The quango debate* (Research Paper 05/30). House of Commons Library.

Major, J. (1999). *John Major: The autobiography.* London: HarperCollins.

Manning hot lines. (1993, May). *Financial Times.*

Marsh, D., Richards, D., & Smith, M. J. (2001). *Changing patterns of governance: Reinventing Whitehall?* Basingstoke: Palgrave.

Marshall, G. (1984). *Constitutional conventions: The rules and forms of political accountability.* Oxford: Clarendon Press.

Marshall, G. (1989). *Ministerial responsibility.* Oxford: Oxford University Press.

Massey, A. (1993). *Managing the public sector: A comparative analysis of the United Kingdom and the United States.* Aldershot: Edward Elgar.

Massey, A. (2002). *The state of Britain: A guide to the UK public sector.* London: Public Management and Policy Association.

Massey, A., & Pyper, R. (2005). *Public management and modernisation in Britain.* Basingstoke: Palgrave Macmillan.

Metcalfe, L. (1993). Conviction politics and dynamic conservatism. *International Political Science Review, 14*(4), 351–371.

Metcalfe, L. (1993). Public management: From initiation to innovation. In J. Kooiman (Ed.), *Modern governance: New government-society interactions.* London: Sage.

Metcalfe, L., & Richards, S. (1987). *Improving public management.* London: Sage.

Murray, K. A. G. (1990). *Reflections on public service selection.* Privately published.

Newman, J. (2001). *Modernising governance: New Labour, policy and society.* London: Sage.

Nicholson, M. (1967). *The system: The misgovernment of modern Britain.* New York: McGraw-Hills.

Niskanen, W. A. (1971). *Bureaucracy and representative government.* Chicago: Aldine.

Niskanen, W. A., et al. (1973). *Bureaucracy: Servant or master?* London: Institute of Economic Affairs.

Oborne, P. (1999). *Alastair Campbell: New labour and the rise of the media class.* London: Aurum Press.

Oliver, D. (1991). Active citizenship in the 1990s. *Parliamentary Affairs, 140,* 157–171.

Painter, C. (1975, December). The civil service: Post-Fulton malaise. *Public Administration.*

Painter, C. (1999). Public service reform from Thatcher to Blair: A third way. *Parliamentary Affairs, 52*(1), 94–112.

Painter, M., & Peters, B. G. (Eds.). (2010). *Tradition and public administration.* Basingstoke: Palgrave Macmillan.

Panchamia, N., & Thomas, P. (2014a). *The next steps initiative.* London: Institute for Government.

Panchamia, N., & Thomas, P. (2014b). *Civil service reform in the real world. Patterns of success in UK civil service reform.* London: Institute for Government.

Panchamia, N., & Thomas, P. (2014c). *Capability reviews.* London: Institute for Government.

Parliament and Constitution Centre. (2005). *Freedom of information implementation* (Research Paper 04/84).

Parris, H. (1969). *Constitutional bureaucracy. The development of British central administration since the eighteenth century.* London: Allen & Unwin.

Peters, B. G. (1999). *Institutional theory in political science: The new institutionalism.* London: Pinter.

Pierson, P. (2004). *Politics in time: History, institutions and social analysis.* Princeton: Princeton University Press.

Pilkington, C. (1999). *The civil service in Britain today.* Manchester: Manchester University Press.

Pliatzky, L. (1982). *Getting and spending: Public expenditure, employment and inflation.* Oxford: Basil Blackwell.

Pollitt, C. (1990). *Managerialism and the public services: The Anglo-American experience.* Oxford: Blackwell.

Pollitt, C. (1993). *Managerialism and the public services* (2nd ed.). Oxford: Blackwell.

Pollitt, C., & Bouckaert, G. (2011). *Public management reform: A comparative analysis—New public management, governance, and the neo-Weberian state.* Oxford: Oxford University Press.

Ponting, C. (1986). *Whitehall: Tragedy and farce*. London: Hamish Hamilton.

Prior, D. (1995). Citizen's Charter. In J. Stewart & G. Stocker (Eds.), *Local government in the 1990s* (pp. 86–103). London: Palgrave Macmillan.

Pyper, R. (1985). Sarah Tisdall, Ian Wilmore and the Civil servants' right to leak. *Political Quarterly, 56,* 72–81.

Pyper, R. (1995). *The British civil service*. Hemel Hempstead: Prentice Hall.

Pyper, R., & Robins, L. (2000). *United Kingdom governance*. Basingstoke: Macmillan.

Raadschelders, J. C. N. (2000). *The handbook of administrative history*. London: Transaction Publisher.

Raadschelders, J. C. N., & Vigoda-Gadot, E. (2015). *Global dimensions of public administration and governance*. Hoboken, NJ: Wiley.

Radcliffe, J. (1991). *The reorganisation of British central government*. London: Dartmouth Publishing.

Ramsden, J. (1980). *The making of conservative party policy: The conservative research department since 1929*. London: Longman.

Rayner, D. (1984). *The unfinished agenda*. London: University of London.

Rhodes, R. A. W. (2011). *Everyday life in British government*. Oxford: Oxford University Press.

Richards, S. (1987). The Financial Management initiative. In J. Gretton & A. Harrison (Eds.), *Reshaping central government* (pp. 22–41). Oxford: Policy Journals.

Richards, D. (1993). *Appointments in the higher civil service*. Strathclyde papers in government and politics, no. 93. University of Strathclyde, Glasgow.

Richards, D. (1997). *The civil service under the conservatives, 1979–1997*. Brighton: Sussex University Press.

Richards, D. (2000a). The Conservatives, New Labour and Whitehall: A biographical examination of the political flexibility of the mandarin cadre. In K. Theakston (Ed.), *Bureaucrats and leadership*. Basingstoke: Palgrave Macmillan.

Richards, S. (2000b, January). The special advisers are here to stay. *New Statesman*.

Richards, D. (2003). The civil service in Britain: A case study in path dependency. In J. Halligan (Ed.), *The civil service systems in Anglo-American countries*. Cheltenham: Edward Elgar.

Richards, D., & Martin, S. (2006, December). Central control and policy implementation in the UK: A case study of the Prime Minister's delivery unit. *Journal of Comparative Policy Analysis, 8*(4), 325–345.

Richards, D., & Smith, M. J. (2000). New labour, the constitution and reforming the state. In S. Ludlum & M. J. Smith (Eds.), *New labour in government*. Basingstoke: Macmillan.

Richards, D., & Smith, M. (2006). Central control and policy implementation in the UK: A case study of the Prime Minister's delivery unit. *Journal of Comparative Policy Analysis, 8*(4), 325–345.

Rose, R., & Karran, T. (1994). *Governing by inertia*. Abingdon: Routledge.

Rothschild, N. M. V. R. B. (1977). *Meditations of a broomstick*. New York: HarperCollins.

Saltman, L. M., & Lund, M. S. (Eds.). (1981). *The Reagan presidency and the governing of America*. Washington, DC: Urban Institute Press.

Seely, A., & Jenkins, P. (1995). *The Citizen's Charter* (Research Paper 95/66). House of Commons Library.

Seldon A. (2004). *Blair*. London: Free Press.

Skelcher, C., Weir, S., & Wilson, L. (2001). *Advance of the quango state: A report for the LGIU*. London: Local Government Information Unit.

Stewart, J., & Walsh, K. (1992). Change in the management of public services. *Public Administration, 70*, 499–518.

Streeck, W., & Thelen, K. A. (Eds.). (2005). *Beyond continuity: Institutional change in advanced political economies*. Oxford: Oxford University Press.

Thatcher, M. (1993). *The downing street years*. London: HarperCollins.

Theakston, K. (1995a). *The civil service since 1945*. Oxford: Blackwell.

Theakston, K. (1995b). Continuity, change and crisis: The civil service since 1945. *Public Policy and Administration, 10*(3), 45–59.

Theakston, K. (2000). Permanent secretaries: Comparative biography and leadership in Whitehall. In *Transforming British Government* (pp. 125–145). Basingstoke: Palgrave Macmillan.

Thelen, K. A., Longstreth, F., & Steinmo, S. (Eds.). (1992). *Structuring politics: Historical institutionalism in comparative analysis*. Cambridge: Cambridge University Press.

Thompson, J. W. (1984). Fast-stream training at the civil service college. *Management Services in Government, 39*, 48–54.

Tolbert, P. S., & Zucker, L. G. (1983). Institutional sources of change in the formal structure of organizations: The diffusion of civil service reform, 1880–1935. *Administrative Science Quarterly, 28*, 22–39.

Tullock, G. (1965). *The politics of bureaucracy*. Washington, DC: Public Affairs Press.

Tullock, G. (1976). *The vote motive: An essay in the economics of politics. With applications to the British economy*. London: The Institute of Economic Affairs.

Vinen, R. (2009). *Thatcher's Britain*. London: Simon & Schuster.

Wade, E. C. S., & Phillips, G. G. (1977). *Constitutional and administrative law* (9th ed.). London: Longman.

Waldegrave, W. (1993). *Public services and the future: Reforming Britain's bureaucracies*. London: Conservative Political Centre.

Wass, D., & Kegan P. (1984). *Government and the governed*. Abingdon: Routledge.

Wildavsky, A. (1979). *The politics of budgetary process*. Boston: Brown.

Wilding, R. W. (1983). *The need for change and the financial management initiative* (pp. 39–51). London: HM Treasury, Peat Marwick/RIPA.

Wilson, R. (1999). *The civil service in the new millennium*. London: Cabinet Office.

Woodhouse, D. (1994). *Ministers and parliament: Accountability in theory and practice*. Oxford: Clarendon Press.

Wootton, B. (1955). *The social foundations of wage policy*. London: Allen & Unwin.

Yong, B., & Hazell, R. (2014). *Special advisers: Who they are, what they do, why they matter*. Oxford: Hart Publishing.

Zifcak, S. (1994). *New managerialism. Administrative reform in Whitehall and Canberra*. Philadelphia: Open University Press.

Archive Sources, Parliamentary Papers, and Official Publications

Atkinson Report. (1983). *Selection of fast stream graduate entrants to the home civil service, the diplomatic service, and the tax inspectorate; and of candidates from within the service*. London: Civil Service Commission.

Cabinet Office. (1979). *Standing order No. 152*. London: HMSO.

Cabinet Office. (1994). *Press notice*. "Better access to public services information." London: HMSO.

Cabinet Office, Office for Public Service. (1998). *Quangos: Opening the doors*. London: Stationery Office.

Cabinet Office, Office for Public Service. (1998). *Quangos: Opening up appointments*. London: Stationery Office.

Cabinet Office. (2000). *Good policy making: A regulatory impact assessment*. London: Stationery Office.

Cabinet Office. (2001). *Code of conduct for special advisers*. London: Cabinet Office.

Cabinet Office. (2003). *Improving leadership in the senior civil service. Letter by the head of the home civil service, Sir Andrew Turnbull, 25 April 2003*. London: Cabinet Office.

Cabinet Office. (2005). *Model of contract for special advisers*. London: Cabinet Office.

Cabinet Office. (2006a). *Civil service management code*. London: Cabinet Office.

Cabinet Office. (2006b). *Civil service code*. London: Cabinet Office.

Citizen's Charter Unit. (1992). *The Charterline Service*. London: Research International.

Civil Service Commission. (1986). *119th Annual report*. London: HMSO.

Civil Service Commission. (1987). *120th Annual report*. London: HMSO.

Civil Service Department. (1972). *Civil service statistics*. London: CSD.

Civil Service Department. (1976). *Civil service statistics*. London: CSD.

Clements Bedford Report. (1992). *Fast stream cohort research: Ten to twenty year follow up. Analysis of the relationship between CSSB procedures and subsequent job performance*. London: Recruitment and Assessment Service.

Cmnd 78. (1986–7). *Accountability of ministers and civil servants: Government response to the first report from the treasury and civil service committee and to the first report from the Liaison committee, session 1986–87.* London: HMSO.

Cm. 585 (1988–9). *Ministry of defence business appointments: Government response to the second and the ninth reports from the defence committee.* London: HMSO.

Cm. 841 (1988–9), *Developments in the next steps programme: The government reply to the fifth report from the treasury and civil service committee.* London: HMSO.

Cm. 914. (1993). *The financing and accountability of next steps agencies.* London: HMSO.

Cm. 1261. (1990). *Improving management in government: The next steps agencies review 1990.* London: HMSO.

Cmnd 1432. (1961). *Control of the public expenditure.* London: HMSO.

Cm. 1599. (1991). *The Citizen's Charter: Raising the standard.* London: HMSO.

Cmnd 1713. (1854). *Report on the organization of the permanent civil service.* London: HMSO.

Cm. 1730. (1991). *Competing for quality: Buying better public services.* London: HMSO.

Cm. 1760. (1991). *Improving management in government: The next steps agencies. Review 1991.* London: HMSO.

Cm. 1761. (1991). *The next steps initiative: The government's reply to the seventh report from the treasury and civil service committee, session 1990–1.* London: HMSO.

Cm. 2101. (1992). *The Citizen's Charter: First report.* London: HMSO.

Cm. 2111. (1992). *The next steps agencies: Review 1992.* London: HMSO.

Cm. 2290. (1993). *Open government.* London: HMSO.

Cm. 2430. (1993). *Next steps agencies in government: Review 1993.* London: HMSO.

Cm. 2540. (1994). *The Citizen's Charter: Second report.* London: HMSO.

Cm. 2627. (1994). *The civil service: Continuity and change.* London: HMSO.

Cm. 2748. (1995). *The civil service: Taking forward continuity and change.* London: HMSO.

Cm. 2931. (1995). *The government's response to the first report from the committee on standards in public life.* London: HMSO.

Cmnd 3638. (1968). *Report of the committee of the civil service* (Fulton Report). London: HMSO.

Cm. 3880. (1998). *Next steps report 1997.* London: Stationery Office.

Cmnd 3909. (1931). *Report on the royal commission of the civil service.* London: HMSO.

Cm. 3920. (1998). *The government expenditure plans 1998–1999.* London: Stationery Office.

Cm. 4011. (1998). *Modern public services for Britain: Investing in reform.* London: Stationery Office.

Cmnd 4156. (1969). *Report of the (Davies) committee of inquiry. The method II system of selection for the administrative class of the home civil service.* London: HMSO.

Cm. 4157. (1998). *Executive non-departmental public bodies 1998 report.* London: Stationery Office.

Cm. 4181. (1999). *Public services for the future: Modernisation, reform, accountability comprehensive spending review: Public service agreements 1999–2002.* London: Stationery Office.

Cm. 4310. (1999). *Modernising government.* London: Stationery Office.

Cm. 4311. (1999). *Modernising government.* London: Stationery Office.

Cmnd 4506. (1970). *The reorganization of central government.* London: HMSO.

Cm. 4808. (2000). *2000 Spending review: Public service agreements July 2000.* London: Stationery Office.

Cm. 5456. (2001–2). *Audit and accountability in central government. The government's response to Lord Sharman's report "Holding 'Holding to account' to account."* London: Stationery Office.

Cm. 6243. (2004). *Transforming public services: Complaints, redress and tribunals.* London: Stationery Office.

Cm. 6373. (2004). *A draft civil service bill. A consultation document.* London: Stationery Office.

Cmnd 7797. (1979). *Report on non-departmental public bodies.* London: HMSO.

Cmnd 8590. (1982). *Report of the (Megaw) inquiry into civil service pay.* London: HMSO.

Cmnd 8616. (1982). *Efficiency and effectiveness in the civil service: Government observation on the third report from the treasury and the civil service committee,* session 1981–2, HC 236. London: HMSO.

Cmnd 9058. (1983). *Financial management in government departments.* London: HMSO.

Cmnd 9297. (1984). *Progress in financial management in government departments.* London: HMSO.

Cmnd 9465. (1983–4). *Acceptance of outside appointments by crown servants: Government observations on the eighth report from the treasury and civil service committee.* London: HMSO.

Cmnd 9613. (1955). *Report of the royal commission on the civil service 1953–55.* London: HMSO.

Cmnd 9841. (1986). *Civil servants and ministers: Duties and responsibilities. Government response to the seventh report from the treasury and civil service committee, session 1986–87.* London: HMSO.

Cmnd 9916. (1985–6). *Westland plc: The defence implications of the future of Westland plc. The Government's decision-making: government response to the third and the fourth reports from the defence committee, Session 1985–6.* London: HMSO.

Cm. 5775. (2003). *Defining the boundaries within the executive: Ministers, special advisers and the permanent civil service.* London: Committee on Standards in Public Life, HMSO.

Commissioners for Revenue and Customs Act. (2005). London: Stationery Office.

Conservative Party, Conservative General Election Manifesto. (1979, April). *Margaret Thatcher Foundation Archive.*

Coster, P. R. (1987, June). The civil service senior management programme. *Employment Gazette,* 291–300.

Coster Report. (1984). *Training for senior management study: Outline proposals for a senior management development programme.* London: Management and Personnel Office.

Deregulation and contracting out act. (1994). London: Stationery Office.

Efficiency Unit. (1988). *Improving management in government: The next steps.* London: HMSO.

Efficiency Unit. (1991). *Making the most of next steps: The management of ministers' departments and their executive agencies. Report to the Prime Minister* (Fraser Report). London: HMSO.

Efficiency Unit. (1993a). *Career management and succession planning study* (Oughton Report). London: HMSO.

Efficiency Unit. (1993b). *The government's guide to market testing.* London: HMSO.

Efficiency Unit. (1994). *Multi-disciplinary scrutiny of public sector research establishment.* London: HMSO.

Eland Report. (1985). *Scrutiny of the means of identifying and developing internal talent. Central report and action plan.* London: MPO.

Expenditure Committee of the House of Commons. (1977). *The civil service,* HC 535, q. 1510. London: HMSO.

Financial Management Unit. (1983). *Report by MPO/Treasury financial management unit.* London: MPO/HM Treasury.

Financial Management Unit. (1984a). *Budgetary control system.* London: MPO, HM Treasury.

Financial Management Unit. (1984b). *Top management system.* London: MPO/HM Treasury.

Financial Management Unit. (1985a). *Resource allocation in departments: The role of the principal finance officer.* London: MPO, HM Treasury.

Financial Management Unit. (1985b). *Top management systems.* London: MPO, HM Treasury.

Financial Management Unit. (1985c). *Policy work and the FMI.* London: MPO/HM Treasury.

Freedom of Information Act. (2000). London: Stationery Office.

Gershon P. (2004). *Releasing resources to the front line. Independent review of public sector efficiency.* London: HMSO.

HC Deb 2 December 1987 c. 572–575W.

HC Deb 17 March 2004 c. 331.

HC Deb 9 April 2003 c. 280.

HC Deb 10 December 2003 c. 1066.

HC Deb 12 July 2004 c. 1132.

HC 27 (1993–4). Treasury and civil service committee. *Fifth report. The role of the civil service*, Vol. I. London: HMSO.

HC 38. (1982). Debate 6 s.c. 918. London: HMSO.

HC 54. (1980–1). *First report from the treasury and civil service committee: The future of the civil service department.* London: HMSO.

HC 61. (1986–7). *The financial management initiative. Thirteenth report from the committee of public accounts.* London: HMSO.

HC 62-I. (2001–2). *House of commons. Public administration select committee. On target? Government by measurement.* London: Stationery Office.

HC 92. (1985–6). *Seventh report from the treasury and civil service committee: Civil servants and ministers, duties and responsibilities. Vol. I Report. Vol. II Annexes, Minutes of evidence and Appendices.* London: HMSO.

HC 94. (2000–1). *Public administration select committee. Seventh report. Making government work: The emerging issues. Report and proceedings of the committee.* London: Stationery Office.

HC 100. (1986–7). *First report from the Liaison committee: Accountability of ministers and civil servants to select committees of the House of Commons.* London: HMSO.

HC 112. (1994). *First report select committee on the parliamentary commissioner for administration.* London: HMSO.

HC 114. (1987). Deb. 6s. Written answers, c. 656. London: HMSO.

HC 122-I. (2006–7). *Politics and administration: Ministers and civil servants. Public administration select committee third report, in two volumes, with proceedings, evidence and appendices.* London: Stationery Office.

HC 122-II. (2006–7). *Politics and administration: Ministers and civil servants. Public administration select committee third report, in two volumes, with proceedings, evidence and appendices.* London: Stationery Office.

HC 127. (1987–8). Deb.6s. c. 1155. London: HMSO.

HC 156-II. (2006–7). *The efficiency programme: A second view of progress, with opinion pieces on improving government efficiency*, Vol. II. London: Stationery Office.

HC 165-1. (2002–3). *Government by appointment: Opening up the Quango state, Fourth report*, public administration select committee. London: Stationery Office.

HC 170. (1988–9). Deb. 6s. Written answers, c. 386. London: HMSO.

HC 173. (1989–90). Deb 6s. Written answers, c. 192. London: HMSO.

HC 178. (1991). *Third report from the select committee on procedure: Parliamentary questions.* London: HMSO.

HC 195. (1992–3). Deb. 6s. Written answers, c. 604-5. London: HMSO.

HC 209-I. (1998–9). *Quangos public administration select committee.* London: HMSO.

HC 213. (1992–3). Deb. 6s. c. 451-458-996. London: HMSO.

HC 216. (1980–1). *Fourth report from the treasury and civil service committee: Acceptance of outside appointments by civil servants.* London: HMSO.

HC 217. (1988–9). *Sixth report from the treasury and civil service committee: Presentation of information on public expenditure.* London: HMSO.

HC 236. (1981–2). *Third report from the treasury and civil service committee: Efficiency and effectiveness in the civil service. Vol. I, Report; Vol. II, Minutes of evidence; Vol. III, Appendices.* London: HMSO.

HC 238-I. (1999–00). *Public administration committee making government work minutes of evidence.* London: Stationery Office.

HC 260. (1988–9). *Fifth report from the treasury and civil service committee: The civil service pay and conditions code.* London: HMSO.

HC 262-I. (2001–2). *Public administration select committee. The new centre. Minutes of evidence.* London: Stationery Office.

HC 272. (1999–00). *Report by the comptroller and auditor general. Good practice in performance reporting in executive agencies and non-departmental public bodies.* London: Stationery Office.

HC 285. (1997–8). *Select committee on public administration. Role and responsibilities of the head of the home civil service. Minutes of evidence.* London: HMSO.

HC 289. (2001–2). *Modern policy-making: Ensuring policies deliver value for money. Report by the comptroller and auditor general.* London: Stationery Office.

HC 293. (2000–1). *Select committee on public administration. Fourth report. Special advisers: Boon or bane? Report together with the proceedings of the committee and appendices.* London: Stationery Office.

HC 301. (2000–1). *Measuring the performance of government departments. Report by the comptroller and auditor general.* London: Stationery Office.

HC 302. (1983–4). *Eighth Report from the treasury and civil service committee: Acceptance of outside appointments by crown servants.* London: HMSO.

HC 307. (2004–5). *Public administration select committee: Civil service effectiveness. Appendices to the minutes of evidence taken before the committee.* London: Stationery Office.

HC 313. (1996–7). *Public service committee's inquiry on ministerial accountability.* London: Stationery Office.

HC 316. (1995). *Government response to the first report from the select committee on the parliamentary commissioner for administration.* London: HMSO.

HC 346. (2000). Deb. c115WH. London: Stationery Office.

HC 348. (1988–9). *Fifth report from the treasury and civil service committee: Developments in the next steps programme.* London: HMSO.

HC 420. (1988–9). *Thirty-eighth report from the committee of public accounts: The next steps initiative.* London: HMSO.

HC 423-I. (2003–4). *House of commons. Public administration select committee. Civil service issues. Minutes of evidence Thursday 4 March 2004.* London: Stationery Office.

HC 481. (1989–90). *Eighth report from the treasury and civil service committee: Progress in the next steps initiative.* London: HMSO.

HC 494. (1987–8). *Eighth report from the treasury and civil service committee: Civil service management reform: The next steps.* Vol. I, *Report.* Vol. II, *Annexe, Minutes of evidence and Appendices.* London: HMSO.

HC 496. (1990–1). *Seventh report from the treasury and civil service committee: The next steps initiative.* London: HMSO.

HC 519. (1985–6). *Fourth report from the defence committee: Westland plc: The government's decision-making.* London: HMSO.

HC 588. (1986–7). *The financial management initiative: Report by Comptroller and Auditor–General/National audit office.* London: HMSO.

HC 672. (2006–7). *Machinery of government changes. Public administration select committee seventh report with proceedings, evidence and appendices.* London: Stationery Office.

HC 924. (2006–7). *National school of government report and resource accounts for 2006–07.* London: Stationery Office.

HC 958-I. (2006–7). *The centre of government. Minutes of evidence 19 July 2007.* London: Stationery Office.

Heaton–Williams Report. (1974). *Civil service training: Report by R.N. Heaton and Sir L. Williams.* London: Civil Service Department.

HM Treasury. (1984). *Civil service statistics 1984.* London: HMSO.

HM Treasury. (1986). *Multi departmental review of budgeting: Executive summary.* London: HM Treasury.

HM Treasury. (1992). *Civil service statistics 1992.* London: HM Treasury.

HM Treasury. (1993). *Breaking new ground: the private finance initiative.* London: HM Treasury.

HM Treasury. (1994a). *Fundamental review of running costs.* London: HM Treasury.

HM Treasury. (1994b). *Private finance: overview of progress,* News release 118/94. London: HM Treasury.

HM Treasury. (1995). *Financial statement and budget report,* referred to HC 30 1995/96. London: HM Treasury.

HM Treasury. (2003). *Press notice 78/03.* London: HM Treasury.

Information Commissioner's Office. (2006). *Freedom of information act aware-ness guidance*. London: Stationery Office.

Mueller Report. (1987). *Working patterns: A study document by the cabinet office (management and personnel office)*. London: HM Treasury.

National Audit Office. (1989). *The next steps initiative*, HC 410 (1988–9). London: HMSO.

National Audit Office. (2001). *Managing the performance of government depart-ments*. London: National Audit Office.

New Labour Party. (1997). *New labour because Britain deserves better*. London. Available at: http://www.labour-party.org.uk/manifestos/1997/1997-la-bour-manifesto.shtml.

Office for National Statistics. (1997). *Civil service statistics*. London: HMSO.

Office of Public Service Reform. (2002). *Reforming public services: Principles into practice*. London: Stationery Office.

Office of Public Service and Science. (1994). *Review of fast stream recruit-ment*. London: OPSS.

Performance and Innovation Unit. (2000a). *Adding it up. Improving analysis and modeling in central government*. London: Cabinet Office.

Performance and Innovation Unit. (2000b). *Wiring it up*. London: Cabinet Office.

Performance and Innovation Unit. (2001a). *Better policy delivery and design: A discussion paper*. London: Cabinet Office.

Performance and Innovation Unit. (2001b). *Strengthening leadership in the pub-lic sector*. London: Cabinet Office.

Phillips Review. (2004). *Review of honours system*. London: Stationery Office.

Prime Minister's Delivery Unit. (2005). Available at http://webarchive.nationalarchives.gov.uk/20060213213351/cabinetoffice.gov.uk/pmdu/ and http://siteresources.worldbank.org/EXTGOVANTICORR/Resources/3035863-1285601351606/NovemberGetNote.pdf.

Public Administration Select Committee. (2001). *Special advisers: boon or bane?* HC 293. London: Stationery Office.

Public Administration Select Committee. (2002). *"These unfortunate events": Lessons of recent events at the former DTLR, HC 303, 2001–2002*. London: Stationery Office.

Public Administration Select Committee. (2009). *Good government: Eighth report of session 2008–09*, Vol. 1. London: Stationery Office.

RIPA Working Group. (1987). *Top jobs in Whitehall: Appointments and promo-tions in the senior civil service*. London: RIPA.

The Constitution Unit. (2014). *Research on special advisers*. London: UCL. Available at http://www.ucl.ac.uk/constitution-unit/research/government/special-advisers.

Treasury. (1990). *Made to measure: Patterns of work in the civil service.* London: HM Treasury.

Treasury. (1992a). *New pay arrangements for grades 5, 6 and 7: Text of the agreement between HM treasury and the association of first division civil servants, the institution of professionals, managers and specialists and the national union of civil and public servants.* London: HM Treasury.

Treasury. (1992b). *Agreement on the pay, pay system, organization and personnel management arrangement for grades and groups represented by the institution of professionals, managers and specialists.* London: HM Treasury.

Treasury and OPPS. (1993). *A picture of flexible working in government departments and agencies.* London: HM Treasury.

The National Archives (TNA), Kew, UK

TNA, CAB 128/66.

TNA, CAB 128/70.

TNA, CAB 128/76.

TNA, CAB 164/1587.

TNA, CAB 164/1588.

TNA, CAB 164/1628.

TNA, CAB 164/1629.

TNA, CAB 164/1709.

TNA, CAB 164/1740.

TNA, Civil Service College, Fifteenth Report, 1984–5.

TNA, JY/13, Civil Service College Annual Report and Accounts, 13th Report, 1982–3.

TNA, PREM 19/5.

TNA, PREM 19/6.

TNA, PREM 19/48.

TNA, PREM 19/60.

TNA, PREM 19/62.

TNA, PREM 19/147.

TNA, PREM 19/148.

TNA, PREM 19/152.

TNA, PREM 19/242.

TNA, PREM 19/243.

TNA, PREM 19/244.

TNA, PREM 19/245.

TNA, PREM 19/250.

TNA, PREM 19/679.

TNA, PREM 19/680.

TNA, PREM 19/780.

TNA, PREM 19/968.

TNA, PREM 19/1175.

TNA, PREM 19/Civil Service long-term manpower policy.

TNA, PREM 19/Civil Service, Annual Scrutiny of Departmental Running Costs.

TNA, PREM 19/Government Machinery.

Treasury. (1987). *Agreement on the pay, pay system, organization and personnel management agreements for grades and groups represented by the institute of professional civil servants.* London: HM Treasury.

Treasury. (1989a). *New pay agreements for clerical and secretarial grades: Text of the agreement between HM treasury and the civil and public services association.* London: HM Treasury.

Treasury. (1989b). *New pay arrangements for executive, office support and related grades: Text of the agreement between HM treasury and the national union of civil and public servants.* London: HM Treasury.

Trosa Report. (1994). *Next steps: Moving on.* London: Office of Public Service and Science.

Wardale Report. (1981). *Chain of command review: The open structure.* London: HMSO.

Index

© The Editor(s) (if applicable) and The Author(s) 2018
L. Castellani, *The Rise of Managerial Bureaucracy*,
https://doi.org/10.1007/978-3-319-90032-2

253